Praise for

DEMOCRACY [IN]ACTION

"A political scientist surveys the threat of apathy to democracy in this nonfiction work . . . The author writes in an accessible style and supports his argument with a wealth of academic and quantitative data. A well-researched, timely reminder of the centrality of civic engagement to the preservation of democracy."

Kirkus Reviews

"This book is a timely reminder that civic duties remain vital—even when they feel inconvenient or undervalued. Blending research, history, and inspiring stories, it motivates readers to roll up their sleeves and get involved. If you're looking for both encouragement and practical guidance to make a difference in American democracy, this book delivers."

Hon. Mark R. Kennedy, former US representative, president emeritus of the University of Colorado, and founding director of the Wahba Institute for Strategic Competition

"'Democracy is a team sport.' Truer words were never spoken! And as a former elected official, I can say with confidence that citizens are not pulling their weight on the team. *Democracy InAction* lays out a logical argument for why civic engagement is important and gives citizens tangible steps they can take to become informed and engaged in improving the quality of their lives and maximizing the blessings we enjoy as citizens of the greatest country in the world."

Hon. Sharon W. Hewitt, former Louisiana state senator

"*Democracy InAction* is a home-run, common-sense analysis of how government 'of the people, by the people, [and] for the people' has drifted away from these guiding principles. Regardless of the reader's political viewpoint, there are pearls of wisdom to be harvested from Dr. Taylor's writing."

Rep. Tony Bacala, Louisiana state representative

"Having been in the trenches of picking over 500 juries over forty years, I have seen firsthand the increased apathy Americans have toward their government and their own role in making sure it is fully functional, serving the people. Dr. Taylor's analyses and recommendations are spot on. I hope the reader will heed the doctor's advice and find their path to get engaged."

J. Lee Meihls, Ph.D., trial consultant and author of *Handicapping the Handicapped: Decision Making in Students' Educational Careers*

"*Democracy InAction* sheds light on the power of civic participation and how apathy threatens us all. It's practical, motivational, and easy to read, with ideas anyone can implement today. Everyone concerned about America's future should pick up this book and discover how even small actions can have a big impact."

Hon. Tarren Bragdon, CEO, Foundation for Government Accountability and former Maine state legislator

"*Democracy InAction* highlights something I've seen both in my classroom and in my own family: Civic engagement is something that must be learned and practiced if we wish to continue to create a more perfect union. This book is yet another reminder that none of us are truly passive observers of politics, but rather we can be either more or less capable participants. With clarity and optimism, Dr. Taylor shows how we can all take small, practical steps to move from apathy to agency and why doing so is desperately important for the next generation."

Lindsey Cormack, Ph.D., associate professor of political science, Stevens Institute of Technology and author of *How to Raise a Citizen (And Why It's Up to You to Do It)*

"Democracy thrives on participation, yet we witness millions of Americans sitting on the sidelines—not from lack of caring, but from lack of accessible information. At Ballotpedia, we see this challenge daily: voters who want to engage but struggle to find basic details about the candidates on their ballots, especially for crucial local races that directly impact their communities. *Democracy InAction* tackles this critical issue head-on, exploring how citizen disengagement threatens the very foundation of our democratic system. Taylor's insights align perfectly with what we've observed—that apathy often stems not from indifference but from the overwhelming complexity of navigating our electoral landscape without proper tools and information. As we work to close the ballot information gap nationwide, ensuring every voter can easily access candidate information for all their elections, books like this remind us why that mission matters. An informed electorate isn't just an ideal—it's essential for democracy's survival. The path forward requires engaged, enthusiastic, and equipped voters. This book provides a road map for getting there."

Geoff Pallay, editor in chief, Ballotpedia

"*Democracy InAction* is a reminder and a plea for a more engaged citizenry. By failing to register to vote, cast ballots, participate in campaigns, and remain engaged between elections, we dilute the promise and benefits of democracy. Apathy spirals into a doomscroll where alienation devours personal responsibility and breaks the essential role of self-government. We cannot allow this to happen. Dr. Taylor's book is a step toward understanding the decay and how to rebuild. We must leave our homes and reengage our communities. We must get offline and remember what it was like to be social before it was paired with media platforms."

Michael D. Cohen, Ph.D., founder of Cohen Research Group, publisher of Congress in Your Pocket, adjunct professor at Johns Hopkins University, and author of *Modern Political Campaigns*

"*Democracy InAction* is a vitally important book for today's polarized America. Combining history, social science, and common-sense arguments, this book is a reminder of the power of civic participation and the role of an engaged citizenry. This is a research-based clarion call to save American democracy the only way possible—by inspiring 'we the people' to reclaim our role. Buy this book for your children, yourselves, and your country."

Andrew Guthrie Ferguson, professor of law, The George Washington University and author of *Why Jury Duty Matters: A Citizen's Guide to Constitutional Action*

"Any healthy person develops a distaste for partisan politics over time, but this is no reason for apathy. Taylor calls for a more vigorous and deliberative democracy, but he also finds no shortcut to such reforms. We must first overcome apathy and detachment to wake ourselves up and avoid the catastrophes that await any slothful republic."

John Gastil, Ph.D., distinguished professor of communication arts and sciences, public policy, and political science, The Pennsylvania State University and author of *The Jury and Democracy* and *Hope for Democracy*

"In *Democracy InAction*, Taylor shows that democracy requires not just the consent of the governed but also their participation. From voting booths to jury boxes, campaign offices to opinion polls, the health of the republic depends on citizens who take part. This book warns that democracy is becoming a spectator sport. If we want leaders who serve the public, the public must step onto the field."

John Geraci, president of Crux Research and author of *POLL-ARIZED: Why Americans Don't Trust the Polls And How to Fix Them Before It's Too Late*

"*Democracy InAction* should be required reading for every American. Dr. Taylor provides critical context for how politics really works. This book will restore readers' trust in our democratic system while also providing the tools we all need to understand and question everything about it."

Dr. Adam Probolsky, nonpartisan pollster and senior research fellow for the Drucker School of Management at Claremont Graduate University

"With politics increasingly characterized by partisan polarization, escalating rudeness, and media spectacle, many Americans need to be explicitly invited to step back into their roles as citizens. *Democracy InAction* not only provides them with just such an invitation but also with an array of persuasive reasons why their—and specifically their—participation is essential, along with concrete first steps for doing so. Restoring a robust version of our democracy depends on more Americans hearing and responding to such calls."

J. Cherie Strachan, Ph.D., professor of political science and director of the Ray C. Bliss Institute of Applied Politics, University of Akron and author of *High-Tech Grass Roots: The Professionalization of Local Elections*

DEMOCRACY [IN]ACTION

How Citizen Apathy Threatens America *and* What We Can Do About It

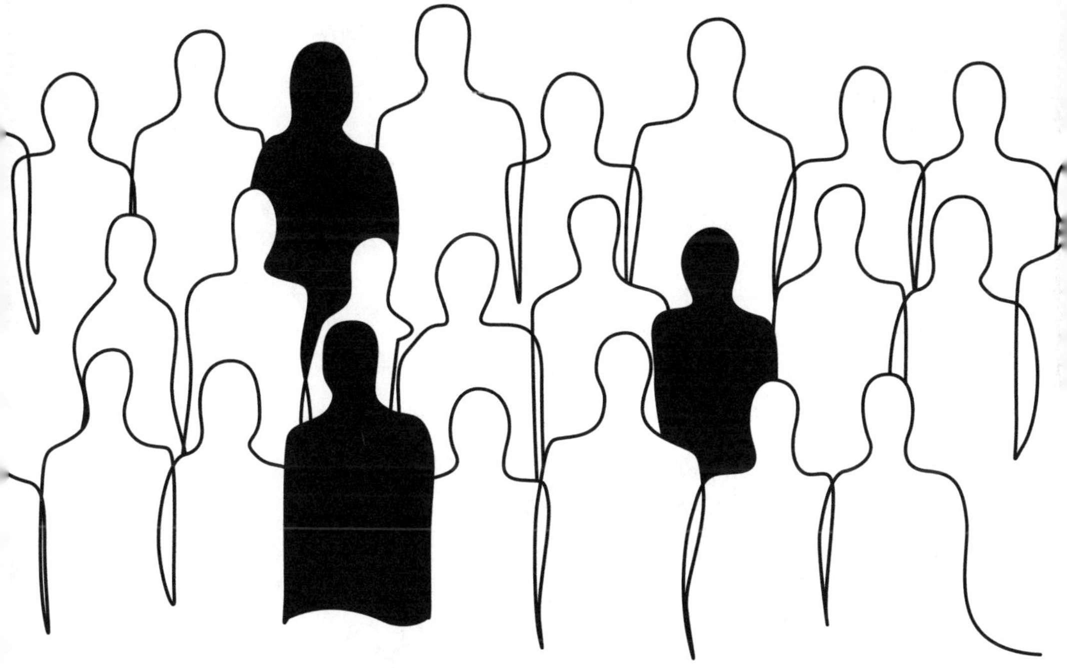

TRAVIS N. TAYLOR, Ph.D.

www.amplifypublishinggroup.com

Democracy InAction: How Citizen Apathy Threatens America and What We Can Do About It

For more information, please contact:
RealClear Publishing, an imprint of Amplify Publishing Group
620 Herndon Parkway, Suite 100
Herndon, VA 20170
info@amplifypublishing.com

Library of Congress Control Number: 2026903625

CPSIA Code: PRV0326A

ISBN-13: 979-8-90026-033-4

Printed in the United States

For Stephanie

CONTENTS

INTRODUCTION

"Those who expect to reap the benefits of freedom, must . . . undergo the fatigue of supporting it."

THOMAS PAINE

Politics in America is nasty. It doesn't have to be, and we can certainly look through the clouds and find some sunshine. But Americans see politics as negative, vitriolic, and just plain dirty. In a 2023 survey by Pew Research Center, 65 percent of respondents told researchers that they are always or often exhausted when thinking about politics, and 55 percent said they are always or often angry.[1] Compare that to the mere 10 percent who said they are always or often hopeful (56 percent say they are rarely or never hopeful) and the 4 percent who say they are always or often excited (78 percent, rarely or never). To some extent, the naysayers of American politics are right in their diagnosis; it is little wonder that Americans are exhausted or angry. To complicate matters, things are not getting any better. Consider the following:

- In 2002, less than one-quarter of political ad spending was spent in opposition to the other candidate; in 2022, it was nearly 70 percent.[2]

- Political rioting in major cities across the US in 2020 caused more than $2 billion worth of damage, which the World Economic Forum called "the first civil disorder catastrophe event to exceed $1 billion in losses."[3]
- In 2024, we witnessed the first attempted assassinations of a president or presidential candidate in a generation when Thomas Matthew Crooks fired multiple rounds from an AR-15 rifle at former president and then-candidate Donald Trump, striking him in the ear and wounding or killing three people attending the rally. A few months later, Ryan W. Routh set up a rifle in an attempt to shoot Trump while the candidate was playing golf in Florida.
- In recent years, other assassination attempts have been carried out on Congressional Republicans practicing for a charity baseball game and on sitting US Supreme Court justices. Successful assassinations have been carried out against state legislators in Michigan and against conservative activist Charlie Kirk during an event at a Utah university.
- Violent political discourse, what legal scholar Jonathan Turley calls "rage rhetoric," is at an all-time high in the US.[4]
- Some of the largest sustained protest movements in American history have faced two of the three most recent presidencies—the Tea Party that stood in opposition to nearly every move made by Barack Obama, while the RESIST movement (for the lack of a unifying brand) challenges Donald Trump's agenda at every turn. There has been no room for common ground between the parties, a phenomenon political scientists call "polarization."
- Even within the parties, things are not great. Within the Republican Party, a strong and vocal Never Trump contingent has existed since his now-famous ride down the golden escalator in 2015. Democrats are in even more disarray.

> Polling from six months into Trump's second term shows Democratic voters express "widespread . . . frustration with congressional leaders and the party's overall direction."[5] Meanwhile, Democrats in New York and beyond held back on endorsing Zohran Mamdani, the socialist candidate for mayor in New York City,[6] despite his persistent lead in the pre-election horserace polling.[7] He went on to win the NYC mayor's race, despite the Democratic infighting.

Given the offensive nature of American politics, perhaps we should be unsurprised that everyday Americans are removing themselves from the political arena. And it's not just in the common ways discussed in popular punditry, some of which are also covered in this book. People are distancing themselves from politics in ways that receive little attention.

According to a 2024 poll from State Policy Network, a majority of Americans, 56 percent, say they have stopped talking about politics because it is too divisive.[8] Think about that: Nearly six in ten Americans are so fed up—and think politics is so far gone—that they have just given up. They don't even bother *talking* about politics, much less consider getting involved.

What's more, parents want their children to avoid politics, too. In a 2013 survey, two-thirds of American parents told Gallup's pollsters they wanted their children to avoid careers in politics.[9] Just seven years later, in 2020, the share of parents who would prefer their kids shun a career in politics increased by nearly one-third to 90 percent.[10] Unless parents recognize the need for more robust civic engagement and spend time educating their children (and themselves) on the issue, the future of American democracy is bleak.[11]

While these facts and figures may not seem to bode well for the future of American democracy, the book you hold in your hands is hopefully one part of the solution—encouraging you to act to preserve democracy for the future.

The Purpose of this Book

With politics crumbling all around us, and the outlook potentially even more tumultuous, we have to turn a corner. To do so, we must encourage Americans—young, old, and everywhere in between—to step up and get involved in our system of government. I hope you agree or are, at the very least, open to agreeing that engagement is the path forward. In the pages that follow, my purpose is to accomplish three things, each of which is motivated by a different part of my background.

First, I am a scholar, but I try to be an accessible scholar, not one of those academics who uses big words when small words will do. But, as a scholar, I like to do research and share that research with the world. In this case, that means exploring and sharing with you the ways apathy shapes our civic attitudes and behaviors. To do that, I discuss five ways in which citizen participation is both vital to democracy and at historically low levels. While there are many indicators of a healthy democracy, I focus on five features that center around citizen participation: 1) registration and voting, 2) campaign activities, 3) responding to public opinion polls, 4) petitioning the government, and 5) jury service. While some of these activities are more conducive to proactive participation than others, all are hallmarks of a functioning democracy. I argue that citizens should do their part, both proactively and reactively, and not begrudgingly.

Second, I am a teacher. No longer in the formal sense, in that I don't stand up in front of a classroom and lecture. (Which also means no more grading papers!) But the reason I pursued my doctoral degree was to teach. So, rather than standing in between four walls and talking to you about political science, this book is our classroom, and the words it contains are my lecture. So, along the way, I will also seek to educate and encourage. The educational component of this book will come through explaining concepts and context. To preview just one example, in the chapter on campaign involvement, I discuss from a campaign manager's perspective why volunteers are important and explain some of the things volunteers do to make a campaign run.

Third, I am what you might call a civics professional and have been for a long time. I have managed and consulted on nearly a hundred political campaigns. I've worked in both state legislative and congressional offices. Now, I am a pollster and jury consultant, and I have conducted (as of this writing) nearly 350 public opinion research projects. In each of these roles, my job is to get people engaged—to vote and volunteer; to respond to polls; to contact their elected officials; and to serve willingly and proudly on a jury. Encouragement is the most important thing this book can do. That's why I don't relegate such motivation to conclusions and footnotes—you'll find encouraging words on nearly every page. Ultimately, this book is about spurring action—my goal is to convince you of the need to participate in our government—so I spend a lot of time offering advice and words of inspiration.

In my first job as a campaign manager, the candidate's slogan was "Be part of the solution." Long-serving Speaker of the House Sam Rayburn is quoted as saying, "Any jackass can kick down a barn, but it takes a good carpenter to build one." Put another way, what is the purpose of identifying a problem if you are unwilling to solve it? The problem I have identified is citizen apathy, so the ultimate purpose of the book is to explore solutions to that problem. Thus, in the book's conclusion, I discuss ways to reengage citizens, reduce apathy, and increase active participation in our democracy and preserve it for posterity.

What is Democracy?

Sir Winston Churchill is often credited with saying that democracy is the worst form of government except all the others that have been tried. Setting aside the Brit's witty turn of phrase for a clearer statement, we might say that democracy is a great way to govern. But why? Why is democracy so great? For one, democracy is great because it's democracy. I don't say that to argue in circles but to say that democracy has what philosopher Robert B. Talisse calls intrinsic value.[12] Democracy is important because of its features—order, stability, the rule of law, and so on. And secondly, as Talisse argues, democracy has instrumental value because it is usually seen in tandem and as a contributor to other social goods, such as better economic conditions, more peaceful societies, and greater protection of human rights.[13] Most of us can agree that democracy is conducive to human flourishing, so let's get into the operation of democracy.

To understand the importance of active participation in a democratic society and why apathy undermines participation, we must first understand democracy and its purpose. Democracy, at its most fundamental, is when the people rule. Indeed, the word "democracy" itself is derived from the Greek words *dēmos*, meaning "people," and *kratos*, meaning "rule" or "power."[14] While the United States is the longest continually surviving democracy on the planet,[15] the invention of democracy in some form predates the US by nearly a millennium—to the sixth century B.C., when the ancient Greek city-state of Athens "allowed all landowners to speak at the legislative assembly, blazing a path" for future democracies.[16]

In the purest form of democracy, every citizen votes on every measure. In some small American communities, pure democracy still exists. For example, journalist Amy Crawford writes that the small Massachusetts town "of Westborough (and hundreds like it across New England) is governed by town meetings, a system in which citizens act as their own legislature, coming together to deliberate and vote on everything from whether to buy the police department a new cruiser to how to zone for medical marijuana dispensaries."[17] However, beyond the enclaves of town-hall governance in New England's hamlets, pure democracy rarely exists.

Two democratic mechanisms, the initiative and referendum, resemble pure democracy and exist in several states. With initiatives and referendums, voters have an individual say in making a collective decision on some issues in what we could call examples of "direct democracy." The initiative and referendum are democratic cousins; they have the same last name but come from different parents. Both end with a vote of the people and are either passed or rejected. Their origins, however, distinguish one from the other.

Initiatives begin with the people. Because they originate from the electorate and are decided directly by the electorate, initiatives are the closest thing many places in the US have to pure democracy. Here's how they work. A group of citizens decides they want a policy passed, but the legislature has refused to pass such a law. The voters, frustrated by the legislative process, then collect signatures from their fellow voters, signifying at least somewhat broad support for the policy proposal; the required number of signatures and the time frame to collect them are usually set by state law. Once the required number of signatures has been collected, they are verified by the state's chief elections officer, usually the secretary of state, and then the proposal is placed on a future ballot for consideration by voters. Much like a candidate for office, groups most often campaign for or against the ballot initiative, encouraging voters to vote one way or another on the issue. Initiatives are a way for voters to exercise democratic control over policy without the involvement of the legislature. Currently, twenty-six states allow citizen-initiated ballot measures for statutes, constitutional amendments, or both.[18]

Then there's the referendum.[19] Like its cousin, the initiative, the referendum concludes with a yes or no vote from the electorate. However, its parent is the legislature. In twenty-four states, legislators can pass a statutory referendum that is then placed on the statewide ballot. The process for a legislative referendum varies from one state to the next. In every state except Delaware, legislators can also refer constitutional amendments to voters.[20]

Most lawmaking in the United States, however, is accomplished through indirect democracy. Rather than allowing citizens to vote on issues, voters select representatives who decide the issues on the citizens' behalf. Nearly all governing in the US, at the federal, state, and local levels, is accomplished through what is commonly called "representative democracy." In a representative democracy, ultimate power still rests with the people (that is, *kratos* is still with the *dēmos*) through the ballot box. But rather than voting on issues, the power of the people is exercised by selecting representatives who, in turn, set the public policy agenda and vote on the issues on behalf of the electorate. Elections are thus an accountability tool for the *dēmos* to exercise their *kratos* over the representatives—keeping them in office when they perform their duties well and calling them home when they step out of line.

Here, it's worth addressing the common argument that "America is a republic, not a democracy." This is true, and it isn't. A republic is a form of democracy in which people elect representatives, and those representatives are constrained by the law. Thus, it is true that America is a republic. But to say that America is not a democracy is false. This is akin to saying that a Honeycrisp is an apple, not a fruit. A republic is a kind of democracy, just like an apple is a kind of fruit. Put another way, America, as a republic, has a democratic form of government in that the people are the ultimate rulers. For the sake of simplicity, in this book, I use the terms "democracy" and "democratic" as shorthand for "America's constitutional democratic-republican form of government." My goal is to convince you of the need to participate in our government, not run up this book's word count.

Because the people possess ultimate authority in a democracy, even a representative one, it is incumbent upon those elected officials to represent the interests of the people who put them in office. But how can elected officials do their job in representing the interests of the people?

One way policy can align with citizen preferences is through elections (see chapter 1 for the importance of participation in elections). In this way, voters take a retrospective accounting of their representatives' behavior in office. By retrospective, I mean that voters look backward in time from Election Day to the official's previous term in office. With that retrospective evaluation completed, voters then either reward their elected officials for representing the public's interests well (by reelecting them) or replace them with a different candidate when they fail to do so. Electoral replacement places the onus on voters to align policy with their preferences by requiring them to (1) be aware of their representatives' legislative record and (2) reward or replace them.

Another way policy can be aligned with mass preferences is through what some scholars call "strategic adaptation."[21] In strategic adaptation, elected policymakers update their preferences (and their own legislative voting behavior) to decide policy based on the (updated) preferences of citizens. Strategic adaptation aligns policy with the preferences of citizens through the actions of the elected official. The burden, then, is on the representatives to align with the represented rather than on the voter to keep the representative in line.

A perennial question, then, is whether elected leaders should respond to public opinion. Democratic norms would say yes: The people's voice should be represented in the halls of power. The majority rules. Democratic norms could also say no: Elected officials have more information on many issues facing their jurisdiction than everyday citizens and are thus equipped to make better decisions. The rights of minorities must be protected. Institutions must endure. Even when the majority thinks otherwise. So, how do we attempt to understand this conflict? Political scientists do so through the trustee versus delegate framework.

Trustees and Delegates

Some people argue that politicians should not respond directly to public opinion. Under this theory, elected officials are selected by the people and then turned loose to do as the official sees best. This is called the "trustee model."[22] In other words, voters *trust* the representative to do the right thing. Doing so releases voters from the cognitive burden of trying to decide what they view as the right policy and the time commitments necessary to track whether the representative does the right thing. The trustee theory of representation does not require politicians, once in office, to place much stock in the preferences of voters.

An example helps illustrate where the trustee model might be a good one. Consider a mayor who forces the local music venue to cancel a Taylor Swift concert. Given the pop star's popularity, the decision to cancel her concert may be held in low regard by a majority of the city's voters. But the mayor might have knowledge of an imminent terror attack on the venue during the show, information that cannot be shared with the public. Should the mayor have yelled, "The show must go on!" despite this knowledge? To carry on with the concert would be the popular choice, but it could also lead to a tragic loss of life. Operating under the trustee model, the mayor made a decision that was out of alignment with public opinion but was the right decision based on information the general public did not have.

Another theory places elected representatives in the role of delegates. As delegates, representatives have been elected to do what the voters would do were they themselves participating in a pure or direct democracy. Put another way, voters have *delegated* power but not ceded their preferences. Thus, representatives in the delegate model of democracy should carry out their duties in a way that would enact public policy that aligns with the preferences of citizens, especially voters.

Why Participation Matters

Democracy, as we have seen, puts everyday citizens at the forefront of America's system of government. Although politicians get all the attention, citizens are the real power brokers in a democracy. It is often said that it is better to be a kingmaker than a king; in democracies, citizens are the kingmakers. Democracy imbues them with the ultimate power to select who represents them and to bring those representatives home when they've outlived their usefulness.

If people are the ultimate authority, it is incumbent upon them to participate in the exercise of that power. Political scientist Lindsey Cormack writes, "A true democracy relies on the active engagement and decision-making of its citizens."[23] James Madison, writing in Federalist

39, put it this way: "It is ESSENTIAL to such a [republican] government that it be derived from the great body of the society, not from an inconsiderable proportion, or a favored class of it" (emphasis original).[24] But, as we will see throughout this book, civic participation in the United States is depressingly low.

It is easy to understand why many don't actively participate. One reason is that people are busy. We live in a day and age when bragging about how busy you are is a sign of importance. Talking about all the activities your kids are involved in is a hallmark of good parenting. That's not the way I see it, but that's a conversation for another book. The point here is that Americans stay busy. They work, shuffle kids to baseball and piano, plan the next vacation, or have a night out with friends. In the hustle and bustle of American life, civic engagement is an afterthought. Or not a thought at all.

This, of course, ignores the fact that people have always been busy. Farmers have always had fields to plow. Shop owners have always had businesses to run. Parents have always had kids to corral and households to manage. Being busy is not unique to modern America. What is unique is its use as a justification to excuse oneself from public life.

Another reason is that politics seems daunting. On the one hand, Americans simply don't have the information they need to participate. Political scientist Arthur Lupia is blunt in his assessment: "When it comes to political information, there are two groups of people. One group understands that they are almost completely ignorant of almost every detail of almost every law and policy under which they live. The other group is delusional about how much they know. There is no third group."[25] In other words, "the mass public appears to know very little about politics, government, and policy."[26] And knowledge is critical to participation. Political scientists Michael X. Delli Carpini and Scott Keeter write, "For citizens to engage in politics in a way that is personally and collectively constructive, however, they must have the resources to do so. A central resource for democratic participation is political information."[27]

A lack of civic knowledge is not entirely your fault. There exists today a crisis of civics education in our public schools. Schools are not teaching students the basics of American government or the importance of civic participation. And parents, many lacking the required knowledge themselves, assume (wrongly) that the schools are providing this education. Ted McConnell, the executive director of the Campaign for the Civic Mission of Schools, points out in a 2019 study that the United States spends five cents per student on civics education, while we spend more than a thousand times that much—fifty-four dollars per student—on science, technology, engineering, and math (STEM) courses.[28] We must do better.

On the other hand, as I said earlier, Americans may just see politics as too far gone to bother with it. Psychologist Phillip McGraw writes, "When a problem becomes so large, there's a tendency to become apathetic. It's almost like we start to say, 'I can't deal with this, so I'm not even going to try.' [Human behavior expert Chase Hughes] calls it 'societally programmed apathy.'"[29] That is evidenced in the polling I cited in which nearly six in ten Americans have given up talking about politics because it is too divisive.

Americans are too busy to think about civic participation. And when they do think about it, civic life is simply too much to handle, so they opt out.

Regardless of the reasons for our collective apathy, participation is important. First, democracy, by definition, requires it. When some subset of "the people" does not participate, the subset that does participate may not be representative of the citizenry as a whole. When participation in government is not representative, the result may not be definitional or functional democracy. If only the wealthiest citizens participate, government becomes an aristocracy, with *aristos*, Greek for "the best," becoming the wielders of *kratos*.[30] When only one religious group participates and enforces their belief system into law, government becomes a theocracy, *theos* being Greek for "god."[31] For a fully functioning democracy to exist and continue, as many of the *dēmos* as possible need to participate.

Second, our fellow citizens depend on us for our participation. Legal scholar Philip K. Howard puts it this way: "Democracy itself [is] sustained on the expectation that others will do their part."[32] Democracy is a team sport. Like every other team sport, each individual on the team must pull his or her weight so the team as a whole can be successful. Without every citizen contributing to our system of government, our democracy's bent will be toward failure.

Each one of the features of democracy covered in this book is a collective action. It is true that each action explored in this book requires individual contribution. However, each individual action contributes meaningfully to a collective whole, the outcome of which is greater than the sum of its parts. A jury decision made collectively by twelve individual jurors is more than just a trial outcome. It is symbolic of a functioning justice system. The outcome of an election is more than just deciding a single contest between competing candidates. It is a powerful indicator that the governed are holding their representatives accountable.

What's more, civically active communities also thrive economically. For instance, locales with higher levels of participation in their civic world have lower unemployment rates, owing to a "social cohesion . . . that keeps people employed."[33] Other research has found, specifically, that volunteerism (covered in chapter 2) and voter registration (see chapter 1) are both strongly correlated with lower unemployment rates.[34] While civic participation alone is not key to creating a community in which more people experience the value of work, these patterns consistently show that there is value for the whole community when more of us pull our civic weight.

A third reason that participation is important may seem self-evident, but it is still a powerful outcome. Civic participation is how change happens. If your child is playing on an unsafe playground at a city park, petitioning your local government (chapter 4) for safety enhancements or repairs is likely to lead to the city taking note and improving the safety of the equipment. If your member of Congress is casting votes that are outside what your community wants, volunteering for an opponent's campaign, getting citizens registered to vote, and everyone voting on Election Day are ways to bring about the change your community desires.

We are fortunate, blessed even, to live in a country where we can be agents of change. We—normal, average, everyday guys and gals—can band together and enact the change we want to see in our communities, our states, and our country. In many places around the world, change is accomplished through violent, often deadly, means. Leaders are not dispatched by voters; they are deposed in a coup d'état. Petitioners and protesters are deemed traitors and gunned down in the streets. In America, we enact change with ballots, not bullets. For that, we should be eternally grateful. Preserving that system of government for our children and their children should spur us to action.

It should not be lost on us that our nation's very existence, which has endured for two and a half centuries, resulted from years of citizen action. From petitioning the government for more representation (and protesting when their petitions went unheard—tea, meet harbor) to the ultimate act of taking up arms in defense of their independence, the colonists who would become American founders were not men and women of apathy. They were men and women of action. And they did not want the outcome of those actions squandered.

In a short fifty-two words, the preamble to the US Constitution lists several reasons for its ratification. The final justification listed is to "secure the Blessings of Liberty for ourselves and our Posterity."[35] The Constitution's framers wanted it known that only through action can we protect and preserve the American way. Ronald Reagan, who would later become the fortieth president, put it this way in his inaugural address after being elected governor of California: "Freedom is a fragile thing and it's never more than one generation away from extinction. It is not ours by way of inheritance; it must be *fought for and defended* constantly by each generation" (emphasis added).[36] It is clear that the preservation of our democracy—our "freedom," our "Blessings of Liberty"—depends on action.

Sadly, many of us have forgotten this or, as an indictment of the sad state of civics education in the US, never learned it at all. As a result, a sizable number of Americans have slipped into a state of civic non-participation. Aside from the Trump-era bumps in turnout, voter registration and participation in America are at historic lows. Campaigns struggle to find volunteers and others to display yard signs or attend rallies. Polling response rates are in the toilet. People no longer contact their representatives in hopes of getting something accomplished or having their opinions heard. And attempting to evade jury service has achieved meme and mockumentary status.[37] We have to turn this around if we want to preserve American democracy "for ourselves and our Posterity."

If you think today's politics is bad, just wait a few years until our national malaise has festered. And then another few years. I believe apathy and alienation lead to worse politics. When politics gets so bad that normal people give up and check out, any sense of normalcy will be missing from our politics. Perhaps American democracy isn't normal right now. But think about this: Will the removal of normal people from American politics make things worse or better?

We are seeing the answer to that question played out in real time. Over the past few years, as apathy has taken root, the fringe elements of American politics have taken hold of things. From the far-left rioters demanding we strip law enforcement agencies of funding and the power to enforce laws and protect citizens (and sometimes getting their way from leftist governments[38]) to those on the far right espousing conspiracy theories like "pizza-gate,"[39] the extremists are making their way into the mainstream. As the so-called silent majority remains silent and apathetic, the loud, obnoxious extremes will get all the attention. And get their way. I know it's probably overdone, but there's truth in the cliché: The squeaky wheel gets the grease. Apathy, in other words, gives way to a tyranny of the fringes, in which government policy is dictated by extreme elements in politics, and insane policy is, in turn, forced upon the rest of us—the normal people who have opted to sit on the sidelines instead of getting involved and protecting our democracy.

How Apathy and Alienation Decrease Participation

In this book, I talk a lot about apathy and alienation as root causes of civic non-participation. But what, exactly, are apathy and alienation? Apathy is a feeling of not caring about civic life, while alienation is a feeling of being pushed out of civic life. Apathy is not caring; alienation is not belonging.

Sami Sage and Emily Amick write about apathy this way: "Civic apathy is not merely an indicator of disinterest in politics; it a symptom of a deeper disconnect with our shared American life."[40] Citizen apathy and alienation will only make the condition of American democracy worse. After all, if I thought the status quo and trajectory of participation were good things, why bother writing this book? Furthermore, I believe apathy and alienation act independently of one another to alter Americans' civic behavior while reinforcing one another.

Inaction, as driven by apathy and alienation, will undo the benefits of participation discussed above. It will reduce our system of government to something other than a functioning, definitional democracy. It will make our communities worse, drive existing wedges even deeper, and embolden the extreme fringes of politics. And it will ensure that nothing changes.

Again, I hope the threat of losing our country—or at least, losing the best parts of it—will spur you and your family, friends, neighbors, colleagues, and congregants to action. And if not, I hope that threat will spur your enemies and opponents to action, in turn lighting a fire under you.

Introduction to the Survey and Statistical Approach in the Book

Many of the factual claims in this book will come from secondary sources, including scholarly articles, nonprofit research, news stories, and governmental reports. Much of the book will be my analysis of the state of the world and the sources just mentioned. I try to keep that analysis fact-based, rarely venturing into my own opinion. Notice I did not say I would never offer my opinion. Sometimes I will.

However, I will bolster my arguments and analysis with results from a survey I conducted specifically for this project—the Democracy InAction Survey.[41]

Each chapter will contain some analysis of the survey data. Many of these analyses will be based on regression models.

I am going to get a bit technical for the next few pages, and I'm sorry. I do this only so that you can approach the figures in this book with confidence. If you want to just read what I write in my analyses, you can skip this part and go to the Plan of the Book heading. If you already know about regression, statistical significance, and how to read regression tables and coefficient plots, you can also skip this part.

One last warning: Here come the technical details. You've been warned!

Regression is a statistical tool that helps get the analyst closer to identifying a causal relationship between a dependent variable—the thing you want to explain—and an independent variable—the thing you think explains the dependent variable. Regression helps approach a causal understanding by "controlling" for other variables that may or may not affect the dependent variable by holding those control variables at their mean, or statistical average.[42] Thus, the analyst can interpret a regression model by saying that a change in the independent variable leads to a change in the dependent variable, holding the control variables at their means. In other words, when everything else is average, the relationship I think exists does indeed exist (if the change is statistically significant) or not (if the change is not statistically significant).

What does "statistically significant" mean? While that phrase may sound fancy or complicated, it really is not. "Statistically significant" means simply that we can say that, to a reasonable degree of certainty—usually that we are 90 to 95 percent certain—that the difference or change we observe is *not zero*, or that it is real.

Let's bring these concepts together with a simple but nonsensical example from the Democracy InAction Survey. I use a nonsensical example because I don't want someone to walk away thinking this is a real finding of this research. It's not. I am using it for illustrative purposes only to show you what each part of the foregoing explanation looks like.

In the details above, I discussed several analytical elements that you can find in the table below. First, the dependent variable. This can be found in the table title; in this model, it is Survey Duration, and the description of the variable can be found in the notes as well. Next is the independent variable, which is Party Affiliation, and a control variable, Age. Next, look for the indicators of statistical significance. In this book, they will be marked by an asterisk or star (*) next to the coefficient. To avoid confusion that might come with identifying multiple levels of statistical significance, as is common in academic research, I will use only one level throughout the book, the .05 level, meaning I am 95 percent confident that the observed relationship or change is real.

So, how do we interpret what we see in this table? It's quite simple. Let's walk through it. The dependent variable, Survey Duration, measures how long it took a respondent to complete the survey. Party Affiliation, our independent variable, is a seven-point scale from strongly Republican to strongly Democratic. Age is a six-point scale that measures the respondent's age in roughly ten-year intervals, and the mean is 3.7, meaning the average respondent is somewhere in their early forties. So, holding Age at its mean of 3.7, every increase in the Party Affiliation scale (one step closer to being a strong Democrat) is associated with a 55.5-second increase in the amount of time it takes a respondent to take the survey, a change that is statistically significant. That means a Democrat takes 55.5 seconds longer than an independent who votes for Democrats, who takes 55.5 seconds longer than a pure independent, and so on.

It also means that, holding Party Affiliation at its mean (4.0—a pure Independent), each step up in the Age scale corresponds to a nearly

118-second increase in the time to complete the survey—someone who is between 45 and 54 (coded 4) takes 118 seconds longer than someone who is between 35 and 44 (coded 3) and 236 seconds longer than someone between 25 and 34 (coded 2). Look at the table and see if you can see what I mean.

TABLE I.1: SURVEY DURATION (DEPENDENT VARIABLE)		
	β	S.E.
Party Affiliation (Independent Variable)	55.51* (Statistically significant)	13.226
Age (Control Variable)	117.79*	18.078
N	1,904	
R2	.093	

Democrats and older respondents take longer to respond to the survey.

However, to keep from filling up the pages of this book with a bunch of tables that take time to look at and interpret, I will present the regression analyses visually. These figures will make it quicker to see (1) whether the effect is positive or negative and (2) whether the change is statistically significant. Here's how.

Look at the figure below. This figure is called a coefficient plot, and it is a visual representation of the regression model we just analyzed above. You can see that the circle (what we call a point estimate or coefficient) for Party Affiliation is to the right of the zero line, meaning the change is positive. We saw that above—it was 55.5 seconds longer for each move in the Party Affiliation scale. Now, look at the horizontal lines sticking out of each side of the circle (what we call confidence intervals). If one of those lines crosses the zero line, the result is *not* statistically significant. If neither line crosses zero, the change is statistically significant.

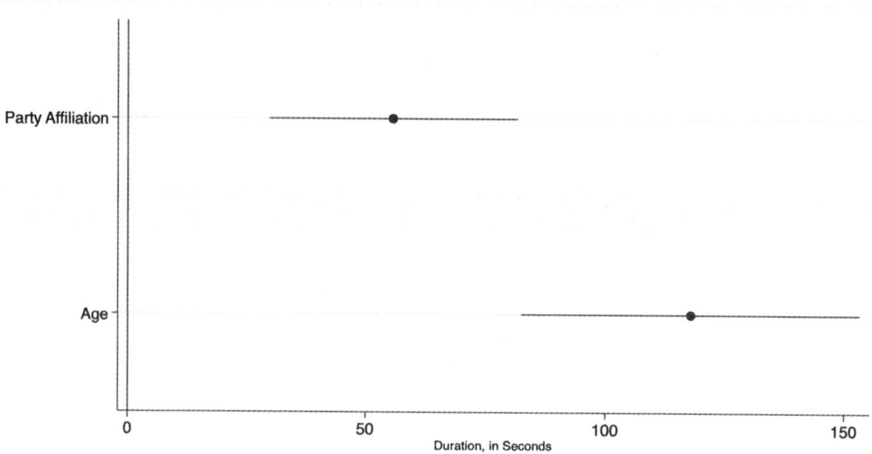

So, now, you'll be able to quickly glance at the figures and see whether the relationships we're talking about are real or not. But don't worry, I'll tell you in my written analyses, too.

Now that you know what these elements are called, let's briefly run through the variables we will use in this book. The table below summarizes them.

Dependent Variables

I will use eleven dependent variables over the course of this book. I summarize them here and explain each one in greater detail in the chapter in which it is used. In chapter 1, Electoral Avoidance is a variable that counts how many undemocratic behaviors related to elections a respondent has engaged in. I also use two variables that measure the extent to which a respondent feels a personal responsibility to (1) register to vote and (2) vote. Chapter 2's dependent variables are Campaign Avoidance, which counts the number of campaign-related undemocratic behaviors, and a campaign-related personal responsibility variable. Chapter 3, the polling chapter, explores a variable that counts avoidance behaviors related to polling and a personal responsibility variable. In chapter 4, I analyze the same two types of variables for contacting elected officials—an avoidance count variable and a personal responsibility one. Finally, in chapter 5, the analyses include Jury Avoidance and personal responsibility for jury service.

Independent Variables

Throughout this book, I will use two independent variables. The first measures Apathy. This variable is constructed through a series of five survey questions designed to measure apathy, and each question has four response options ranging from strongly disagree to strongly agree (coded 1 through 4). You can see the question wording in the appendix. Each question is scored so that larger numbers indicate a more apathetic response. The responses to these five questions are then added together. Thus, the theoretical range on this variable is from 5 (all 1 responses), which represents very little to no apathy, to 20 (all 4 responses), indicating very high levels of apathy.

Alienation is the second independent variable. It is constructed in the same manner as Apathy. The Alienation variable is the addition of eight survey questions, so the theoretical range is from 8 (all 1 responses and very low Alienation) to 32 (all 4 responses and very high Alienation).

Control Variables

For the regression models to allow me to approach a causal claim, I must control for as many variables as possible that do or might impact the outcome of interest (the dependent variables). Since all of the behaviors and attitudes analyzed in this book are related to civic participation, I use the same set of control variables in every chapter. Efficacy, Trust, and Political Knowledge are three additive index variables that are constructed in a manner very much like Apathy and Alienation. Efficacy is the addition of five survey questions that measure how effective one believes they can be in the political system. Trust measures twelve dimensions of institutional and interpersonal trust. Political Knowledge is a battery of five factual questions about American politics, and each one is scored as 1 for the correct answer and 0 for all incorrect answers. I expect higher values on each of these control variables will be associated with more democratic behavior and attitudes.

Demographic control variables are also included in each model. Age is a six-point scale with higher values representing the respondent's placement in an older age bracket. I expect older respondents to engage in more democratic behavior and thinking. Race is an eight-point categorical variable indicating the respondent's race or ethnicity. Since there is no "higher value" of race, the only conclusion that can be drawn if there is a significant result is that race plays a role in shaping the outcome of interest. However, I do not expect any significant findings on Race. I include a variable called Female, which is coded as 1 for female respondents and 0 for males. This allows me to compare the sexes directly. When you see a significant finding for Female, it means women are more (or less) likely to engage in that behavior or thinking. I predict women will have more civic-minded behaviors and mindsets than men.

I also include three socioeconomic control variables. Education is a seven-point variable, with higher values indicating more formal educational attainment, and Income is a six-point variable with higher values indicating greater annual income. I predict that more formal education and higher income will both be associated with more democratic behavior and attitudes. Employment (like Race above) is a categorical variable with no natural numerical ordering, so once again, any significant findings will lack a meaningful explanation.

Finally, I include two political variables that measure a respondent's Party Affiliation on a seven-point scale from strongly Republican to strongly Democratic and Political Ideology on a seven-point scale from very liberal or progressive to very conservative. I do not have a prediction about how these variables will perform in the models, but they do have logical interpretations. An increase in Partisan Affiliation indicates more alignment with the Democratic Party, while an increase in Political Ideology indicates being more politically conservative.

CHAPTER	VARIABLE	VARIABLE TYPE
1	Electoral Avoidance	Dependent Variable
	Personal Responsibility – Register to Vote	Dependent Variable
	Personal Responsibility – Voting	Dependent Variable
2	Campaign Avoidance	Dependent Variable
	Personal Responsibility – Campaign Volunteering	Dependent Variable
3	Polling Avoidance	Dependent Variable
	Personal Responsibility – Respond to Polls	Dependent Variable
4	Elected Official Contact Avoidance	Dependent Variable
	Personal Responsibility – Contact Elected Officials	Dependent Variable
5	Jury Avoidance	Dependent Variable
	Personal Responsibility – Jury Service	Dependent Variable
1–5	Apathy	Independent Variable
	Alienation	Independent Variable
	Efficacy	Control Variable
	Trust	Control Variable
	Political Knowledge	Control Variable
	Age	Control Variable
	Race	Control Variable
	Female	Control Variable
	Education	Control Variable
	Employment	Control Variable
	Income	Control Variable
	Party Affiliation	Control Variable
	Political Ideology	Control Variable

Plan of the Book

Throughout this book, I hope to accomplish three things. First, I document the role of apathy in driving down our civic participation. Second, I want you to learn something new about the topics I discuss. And third, I want to encourage you to get involved. To accomplish these objectives, this book explores five civic activities in which Americans should participate to protect and preserve democracy in the United States. Each chapter is dedicated to one such activity. In my coverage of each activity, I discuss the behavior's importance to democracy, walk through historical evidence and developments, show with original survey research from the Democracy InAction Survey how citizen apathy affects participation and attitudes toward those behaviors, and review results from the survey to explore inaction in further detail.

In chapter 1, I explore the most fundamental activity in a democracy: voting. My discussion of voting in the United States focuses on the act of voting itself and will necessarily dive into the prerequisite activity of registering to vote. I rely on historical registration and turnout data to show that, throughout our history, Americans have not reached full participation in voting. I then show that apathy leads us to avoid voting and diminishes our personal responsibility as it relates to registering and turning out to vote.

Chapter 2 is dedicated to political participation unrelated to voting. In that chapter, I cover the act of campaign volunteerism—everything from the simple act of planting a campaign sign in one's front yard or pasting a bumper sticker on their car to the more labor-intensive (and sweat-producing) act of knocking on doors in the summer heat. I discuss various roles available for volunteers on a campaign and how much modern campaigns rely on volunteer labor. I show that apathy increases our avoidance of campaign activities and has a negative impact on our views of personal responsibility toward campaigning.

While every chapter is important, chapter 3 (and later, chapter 5) are near and dear to me. I'm a pollster and firmly believe polling is critical to our democracy. In chapter 3, I discuss polling by explaining what polling is (and isn't), what goes into constructing a valid poll that accurately (if imperfectly) reflects the will of the people, why it is a vital instrument of democracy, and how readers can become more active and intelligent consumers of polls. I then lean on the survey research to show that citizen apathy toward polls and polling shapes our *views* toward participating in polls but does not directly affect our actual participation in them.

Chapter 4 represents a shift from political activities to policy-centric participation. In it, I explore Americans' lack of direct communication with their elected representatives. Relying on personal experience and what scant data are available, I show that relatively few people contact their elected officials about important issues. Despite constitutional protection to "petition the Government for a redress of grievances," few citizens avail themselves of the opportunity. We look at why that undermines representation, and how apathy drives up avoidance of this vital activity and diminishes our personal responsibility to make the call or send the email.

Chapter 5, like chapter 3, is personal to me because of my profession. In addition to conducting political and policy polling, I am also a trial consultant. In chapter 5, I explore the history of jury service in the United States, dating back to the colonial era and the Declaration of Independence, to explain why jury service is key to a functioning democracy. I then explore citizen apathy toward the jury system and jury service and show that while apathy is unrelated to Americans' avoidance of jury service, it does deplete the feelings of personal responsibility for serving.

At the end of each of these chapters, I include a set of three discussion questions and three actions. The questions should encourage you to think more deeply about the content and topic of that chapter. When we think more critically about a topic and attempt to see both sides of the issue, we tend to understand it better. And when we understand the importance of individual action to democratic stability, we should be more willing to take action. But you may not know where to start.

That's where the three actions come in. They serve as a jumping-off point for you to get involved. I have attempted to offer some low-risk activities and some that are a bit bolder, so you can choose your own adventure. But don't feel like you must stick to that list. If some other opportunity catches your attention, jump on it. It matters less *what* you do to advance democracy and more that you do *something*.

I conclude this book with a chapter that reiterates the problems I identify throughout the book—namely, citizen apathy toward democratic activities—and moves toward a solution. As I said earlier, there is no point in raising an issue if you cannot propose a solution. In the conclusion, I seek to become Rayburn's carpenter rather than a jackass. The solutions I propose put the responsibility for implementation both on the individual and on civic institutions. I also offer solutions for businesses to encourage civic participation among their employees.

With that, let's dive in.

Three Questions

1. What is most important to you in life? In what ways do politics, government, and civic life touch that most important thing?
2. When you think about politics, government, and civics, what three words come to mind? How does thinking about civic life make you feel?
3. What, if anything, has been holding you back from engaging in civic life?

CHAPTER 1

REGISTRATION AND VOTING

"We do not have government by the majority. We have government by the majority who participate."

THOMAS JEFFERSON

"If you don't vote, you can't complain." Such is the common refrain from voters to their fellow citizens who, for whatever reasons, choose not to vote. Perhaps the forcefulness of this statement is because voting is the fundamental act of citizenship in a democracy. Those who vote wear it, quite literally, as a badge of honor. After having cast their vote, they parade to work, the grocery store, and football practice proudly displaying the coveted sticker declaring to the world, "I VOTED!" Those who don't vote are met (by voters) with silent scorn and ridicule.

Voting is the fundamental responsibility of a democratic citizen. As we saw in the introduction, public policy comes into alignment in one of two ways. The first way is through electoral replacement, and that is the subject of this chapter.

Voting as a Process

Voting is not a single act. Yes, traveling to the polls on Election Day and physically voting—or sitting at your kitchen table or in your living room recliner and completing your absentee ballot—is a single activity, but that action is the culmination of a voting process. The voting process consists of four distinct phases: Registering to vote, deciding whether or not to vote in an election, deciding for whom to vote in each race in that election, and finally, the physical act of turning out to the polling place on Election Day.

Figure 1.1: The Voting Process

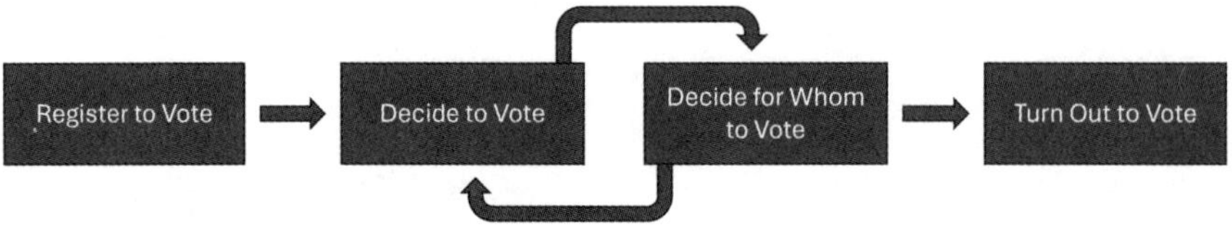

Register to Vote	→	Decide to Vote	⇄	Decide for Whom to Vote	→	Turn Out to Vote

Voting is not a single act; instead, it is a four-step process.

In the United States, citizens must register as voters before being allowed to cast a ballot. However, because the Constitution grants the authority to administer elections to the states,[1] requirements vary from state to state. For example, registration is a necessity in forty-nine of the fifty states, with South Dakota as the exception. Some states allow citizens to register to vote on Election Day, while most have a deadline for registration in advance of Election Day. Regardless of the variations in state registration rules, phase 1 in the voting process for most Americans is to register to vote.

Phases 2 and 3 are decision-making phases rather than action phases. In phase 2, a registered voter must decide whether to vote in an upcoming election. There are myriad factors that impact a voter's decision about whether to participate. Some may be too busy, and others may not know about an upcoming election. Once a voter has decided to vote, he or she must decide for whom they want to vote. Again, voters consider many things when making their candidate choice, but political scientists have long agreed that the leading factor in a voter's choice of candidates is party affiliation—Republicans overwhelmingly vote for Republican candidates and Democrats overwhelmingly vote for Democratic candidates.[2]

Once phases 2 and 3 have been completed, the final phase of the voting process is to vote. This is the phase most familiar to voters because it is the one most covered in the media, the one most studied by political scientists, and the only one for which we get the coveted "I VOTED" sticker, signaling to others our participation in our democratic system.

While the process is mostly linear, phases two and three—deciding to vote and deciding for whom to vote—are cyclical. Take, for instance, a citizen who is registered to vote and has decided to vote in an upcoming election. She has thus completed phases 1 and 2. However, after reviewing the candidates, she doesn't like or trust any of them. So, in phase 3, she has decided that she doesn't want to vote for any of the available candidates, leading her to revisit her decision in phase 2. Unless something subsequently changes her mind about one of the candidates, she may decide not to vote. However, if something does change her perception of the candidates, she may once again revisit the decision in phase 2 and decide, once again, to vote. The cycle of repeating phase 2 and phase 3 may continue ad infinitum until the polls close on Election Day.

This chapter will cover phases 1 and 4. Again, these are action phases rather than decisional phases, and this book is about action. While phases 2 and 3 are important steps leading up to phase 4, I can't really encourage you to engage in those decisions beyond encouraging you to get involved in phase 4. If I can encourage you to get involved in phase 4 (voting), I have in effect activated phase 2 (deciding to vote) for you. In phase 3, you're on your own. But there are resources to help you make those decisions, and I will list them at the end of the chapter.

Another way to visualize the process, and one that will set the stage for the data that will come in this chapter, is to think of voting like a funnel (see figure 1.2). Let's say you have a population of 100 people who meet all of the eligibility criteria to register to vote. What we will see later in the chapter is that only about 67 of those people will register to vote. Then, turnout—the people who are registered and actually show up to vote—is about 50 to 60 percent, or between 34 and 40 people. And that's in a high-turnout election, like for president. In a local race, that number might be 10 percent, or six or seven people.

Let me net that out for you. About 40 people are making national decisions for 100 people, while seven people make important local decisions for all 100 people. And that's just the 100 adults who are eligible to vote, to say nothing of the adults who are not eligible and the minors who haven't yet reached the age of being able to vote.

That's the critical threat to democracy we're talking about in this chapter. We're not dealing with power in the hands of all people; the power to elect government leaders is in the hands of less than half of the population.

Figure 1.2: The Voting Funnel

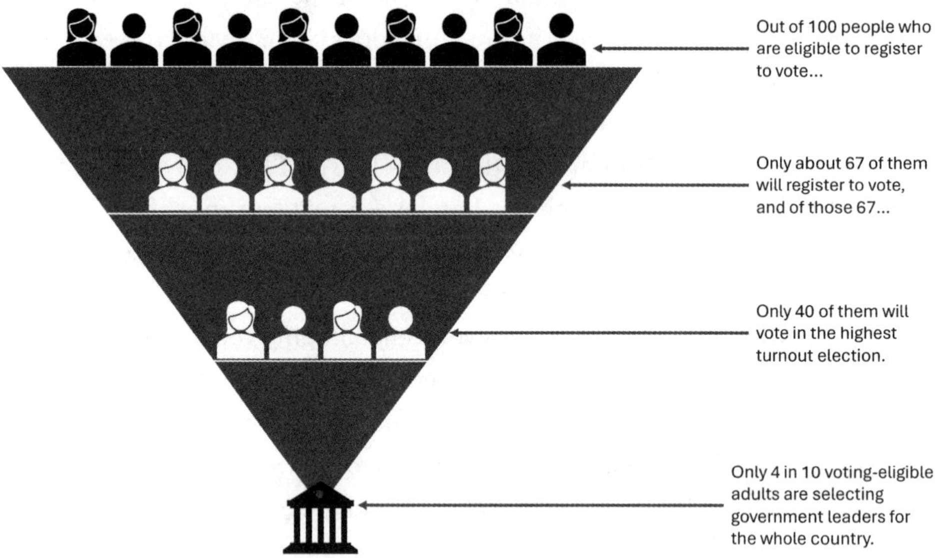

Out of 100 people who are eligible to register to vote...

Only about 67 of them will register to vote, and of those 67...

Only 40 of them will vote in the highest turnout election.

Only 4 in 10 voting-eligible adults are selecting government leaders for the whole country.

When citizens who are eligible to register to vote are funneled through the four-step voting process, only about 4 in 10 voting-eligible adults are selecting government leaders for the whole country.

Why Voter Registration Matters for Democracy

As we've seen, to vote in the US, one must first register to vote. Registration is the first step in the voting process, inextricably tying its democratic importance to the act of voting itself. We see the importance of registration reflected in both policy and activism.

Anyone who has gone to the DMV to get a driver's license in the past thirty years has been asked by the clerk, "Would you like to register to vote at that address?" That is the direct result of the National Voter Registration Act (NVRA), passed by Congress in 1993. Commonly called the "motor voter law," the NVRA requires states to provide more points of access to voter registration. The law's nickname derives from the section that requires states to provide citizens with the opportunity to register to vote in their motor vehicle offices. In addition, states provide voter registration opportunities at other public agencies, such as welfare offices, and through mail-in applications. The NVRA was passed to apply to federal elections, but many states have adopted its requirements for state elections as well.[3] Although some research has shown that the NVRA has not had the intended effects on voter participation,[4] its passage nonetheless demonstrates that policymakers believe voter registration is important.

Beyond implementing the provisions of the NVRA, states have worked to make registering to vote an easier process, further showing its importance. For example, building upon the provisions of the NVRA, many states have incorporated automatic voter registration (AVR).[5] AVR is also triggered by a citizen's visit to a public agency, such as the DMV or welfare office. Rather than having a clerk ask if they want to register to vote (opting *into* registration), citizens are automatically registered and instead must be asked if they want to refrain from doing so—they must opt *out* of registration. In the parlance of the Nobel-winning economist Richard H. Thaler and legal scholar Cass R. Sunstein, AVR "nudges" citizens into registration, the state's preferred action for them.[6] In addition, at the time of this writing, forty-three states plus Washington, DC, have mechanisms in place for citizens to register to vote online.[7]

In addition to policymakers, activists also place a premium on voter registration. For example, the far-left activist group Dēmos released a policy paper in December 2020 in which it encouraged the newly elected Biden administration to "direct federal agencies to provide voter registration services."[8] Following the inauguration of Joe Biden as president, his administration hired several high-ranking activists from Dēmos and implemented the group's plan through the issuance of Executive Order 14019.[9] E.O. 14019 essentially turned many federal agencies, especially those that provide welfare services, into voter registration agencies, diverting funding and other resources away from the agencies' core functions in order to register new voters who are likely, according to research from the Foundation for Government Accountability, to vote, primarily, for Democratic candidates.[10]

But liberals aren't the only activists who want to make sure their supporters are registered to vote. Conservative activist groups also provide information on voter registration, especially to people online. For example, FRC Action, the activist arm of the socially conservative Family Research Council, provides a link to voter registration information on the "Voter Resources" section of its website.[11] And the American Family Association Action website includes instructions on how to register people to vote, including a suite of outreach materials designed to encourage others to register.[12] Meanwhile, Faith Wins, a group dedicated to helping Christians engage in politics, includes a link to register to vote on its website[13] and at events[14] and brags about its efforts to register more than one million new "faith voters."

Policymakers and activists (and sometimes an overlap of the two) take seriously the need to register to vote. But why? Registration itself is not crucial to democratic survival, is it? It is, in fact, and for two reasons. First, registration is a mechanism for protecting the integrity of the vote. Voting is a fundamental right, and when bad actors take away an individual's right to vote through some sort of voter fraud, democracy suffers.[15]

Second, voter registration is part of the voting process. Most Americans cannot vote without having registered to do so, making registration the first step to voting. If voting is fundamental to democracy, and registration is essential to voting, then registration is also a critical function of democratic citizens. Are Americans living up to that critical function?

Registering to Vote

American voters must meet certain qualifications to be counted as eligible voters. Nationally, any citizen who is eighteen years old or older is qualified to vote, although in some localities, residents as young as sixteen enjoy the franchise, at least in some, if not all, elections.[16] Moreover, some states permit seventeen-year-olds who will turn eighteen by the date of the general elections to vote in primary elections.[17] Some states disallow convicted felons from voting.[18] Only US citizens can vote in federal elections (although there is currently no federal law requiring an individual to provide proof of citizenship when registering to vote), while states enforce residency requirements that mandate voters be legal residents of a state before voting in that state. Thus, the barriers to registering are low—there are restrictions regarding one's age, residency, and criminal history. As political scientist Lindsey Cormack puts it, "Many people anticipate voter registration to be cumbersome, but it's often straightforward—more akin to checking in for a doctor's appointment than navigating DMV procedures."[19]

Once those low bars are cleared, one can register to vote by simply filling out a one-page registration form. It would seem, then, that voter registration would be universal—that everyone who is eligible to vote would at least register. However, that is simply not the case. According to data from the US Census Bureau, voter registration is far from universal. In mid-term elections since 1978, an average of only 67.1 percent of citizens eighteen and older are registered to vote.[20] In presidential election years, the number is only marginally higher, at 71.9 percent.[21]

Those numbers likely misrepresent true registration statistics for at least two reasons. First, the Census registration statistics do not account for state-based restrictions such as, for example, allowing individuals convicted of a felony to vote. Thus, the census data reflect what might more accurately be called "voting age registration" rather than "voting-eligible registration."

Second, the statistics rely on self-reported registration. Self-reported behavior is notoriously flawed. One major reason to treat self-reported behavior with skepticism is because of what social psychologists and others call "social desirability bias." As psychologists Mahzarin Banaji and Larisa Heiphetz write, "Not all attitudes are equally socially desirable."[22] The same is true of behavior. Social desirability bias leads people to, often unwittingly, answer a question in a way that is socially acceptable, that places the respondent in a favorable light in the eyes of the person asking the questions. Because voting (and thus, registering to vote) is the socially "right" thing to do, while failing to register and refraining from voting are socially "wrong," individuals are more likely to falsely tell surveyors (in this case, those collecting census data) that they are registered to vote than they are to admit they are not.

We should, then, approach the Census data understanding that it likely misstates registration levels. Even taken at face value, however, the Census Bureau's figures are not promising for democracy. An activity with such a low barrier to entry should see more participation. Think about it this way. The National Football League's 2024 Super Bowl was held at Allegiant Stadium in Las Vegas, Nevada, which seats 65,000 fans. Assuming a full stadium, that means 21,385 people present for the Super Bowl were not registered to vote. More locally, go down to the grocery store and watch people walk in. Every third person, statistically, has not taken even the bare minimum steps necessary to vote.

Looking at figures 1.3, which shows non-registration in presidential election years, and 1.4, which shows non-registration in mid-term election years, two trends are immediately visible. First, no substantial difference between the two figures exists. Non-registration is essentially the same in both presidential and mid-term years. Second, there is little variation over time. Non-registration remains basically the same—around one-third—for the entirety of the time series. It is worth noting, too, that these figures represent what I call the "modern era." By the beginning of the time in these figures (the time when the Census Bureau began collecting this information), the franchise had been constitutionally expanded to include racial minorities, women, and eighteen-year-olds.

Turning Out to Vote

Once registered, and the phase 2 and 3 decisions are made, the final step in the voting process is turning out to vote in the election. Here's why elections matter.

Elections are one way citizens exercise control over public policy, by bringing policy into alignment with citizens' preferences through electoral replacement. But how does it work? Electoral replacement rests on the theory of retrospective voting. It is the age-old wisdom that hindsight is 20/20.

Step one is that voters select a representative. This is accomplished through a series of steps in which partisan voters—i.e., Republicans and Democrats—select a candidate to represent their party in a primary election or, less frequently, a caucus. Candidates from the opposing parties, candidates from third parties (e.g., Green or Libertarian), and other independent candidates (those who do not belong to either of the major parties or to any other minor, third parties) compete against one another in the general election. The winner of the general election becomes the representative. There are places where the partisan balance is so lopsided that an election is effectively decided in the primary election, and of

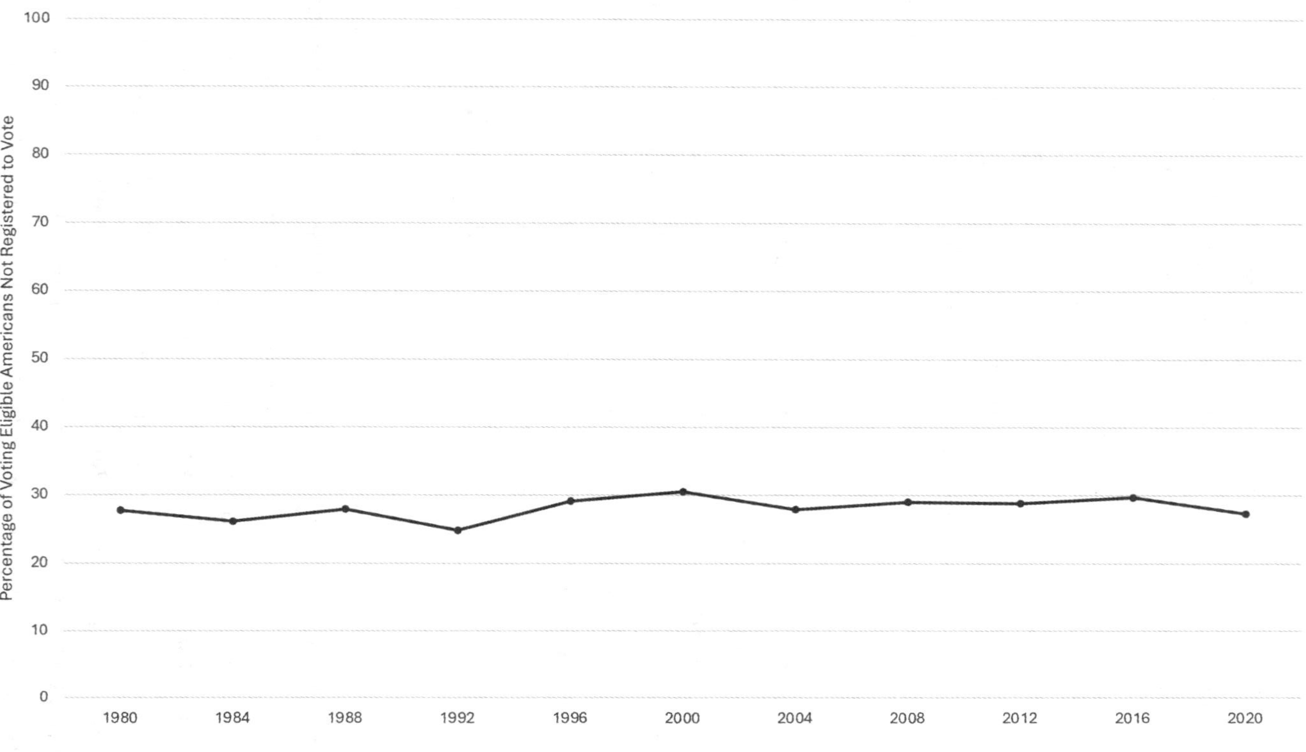

Source: US Census Bureau

Figure 1.4 Non-Registration in Mid-Term Election Years, 1978–2022

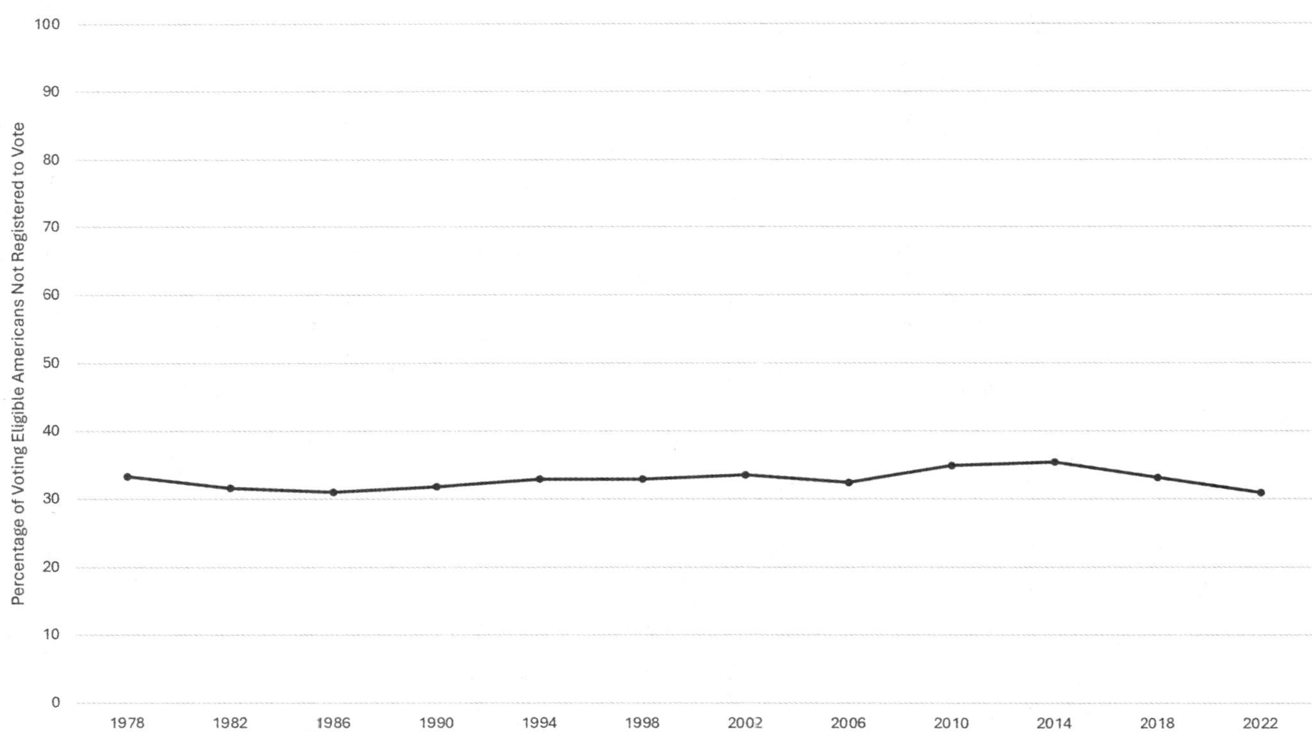

Source: US Census Bureau

course, the presidential election is decided by the Electoral College. But in most places and for most offices, representatives are selected in this primary-then-general-election paradigm.

Once that representative takes office, he or she begins to make policy decisions. Legislators engage in debate and pass or reject proposed laws. Executives, such as governors, secretaries of state, and attorneys general, enforce laws passed by the legislature and issue rules, guidance, and other executive actions with the policy force of law. Elected judges settle disputes between parties and decide cases, leading to what is called case law. Regardless of whether an elected official adheres to the delegate or trustee theory of representation, they must take policy positions and make policy decisions.

Some of those policy decisions are so far outside the range of what citizens are willing to accept, often called the Overton Window, that voters take notice. Elected officials tend to stray away from the promises they made when campaigning, or away from what voters expected them to do in office. And sometimes they just get caught up in the proverbial "swamp" of Washington or the state capitol, or city hall, and their focus shifts away from voters and toward special interests and activists. The late American critic George Jean Nathan once opined that "bad officials are elected by good citizens who don't vote." In other words, we have not only a responsibility to vote, but there are also serious consequences when we don't. When an elected official has strayed too far from the mainstream of their citizens, voters can vote for another candidate in a subsequent election—a candidate who is, in campaign promises at least, more in line with the voters' preferences. When a candidate who is more in tune with voters defeats an incumbent who is not on the same page, policy (or, more accurately, that representative's legislative record) is brought into alignment with voter preferences.

All of this hinges, of course, on citizens taking action. As University of Virginia political scientist Larry Sabato says, "Every election is determined by the people who show up." Set aside for now the fact that to make this work, voters must either pay close enough attention to politics in real time or take time ahead of an election to evaluate their representative's performance. To make electoral replacement possible, citizens must, *at a bare minimum,* show up to vote.

The evidence, however, demonstrates that many people don't vote. Take the example of presidential non-participation trends in figure 1.5. This figure, based on data from the US Elections Project,[23] shows the percentage of eligible citizens who didn't vote in presidential elections from the founding through 2024. Even though these data reflect non-participation among the voting-eligible population, some caution is warranted in exploring this data over such a wide range of time because the criteria for voter eligibility have changed over the past 250 years. In the earliest elections, only white men were eligible to vote. With the ratification of the 15th Amendment in 1870, five years after the end of the Civil War, black men were granted the constitutional right to vote, though many barriers still existed for them. The franchise was then expanded again in 1920 with the passage of the 19th Amendment, protecting women's right to vote, and again in 1971 when the 26th Amendment granted eighteen-year-old citizens the right. Moreover, denial of the franchise to felons has limited the eligible population at various points in time.

Still yet, presidential elections represent the high-water mark for voter turnout. The contest for president is high profile and usually hotly contested. These features are a draw to many Americans, even those who participate in no other election or civic life whatsoever. Nonetheless, as you can see clearly, voter turnout is far from universal. A figure that indicates universal or nearly universal voter turnout would have the trendline at or near zero.

In the first part of the twentieth century, non-participation spiked. In fact, in the presidential elections of 1920 and 1924, non-participation was above 50 percent. That means William Harding and Calvin Coolidge, respectively, won their presidential elections with less than half of eligible Americans casting a vote. Following that high-water mark, non-participation leveled off and has almost consistently hovered between 40 and 50 percent.

To account for the expansion of the franchise mentioned earlier, let us take a closer look at the data by focusing on what might be called the "modern era." By that, I mean elections post-1971, by which time all American citizens eighteen years old or older, regardless of race or gender, have been eligible to vote except for felons in some states.[24] Limiting the analysis to that modern era, starting with the presidential election of 1972, non-participation in presidential elections has averaged 43 percent. Put another way, four out of every ten Americans who are eligible to vote regularly refuse to participate in selecting who will hold the most powerful and influential office in the world.

What kind of difference does that make? Let's look at the last three presidential elections. In 2016, approximately 100 million voter-eligible Americans chose not to vote. That's more people refraining than people voting for either of the two major-party candidates. In 2020, it was similar. The non-voting number of approximately 80 million was only slightly smaller than the share of voters who selected Joe Biden (81.2 million) and was still larger than Donald Trump's vote share (74.2 million). Most recently, in the 2024 presidential election, non-voters numbered 88.4 million compared to Kamala Harris' 75 million and Trump's 77.3 million. Figure 1.6 shows that if Not Voting were a candidate for president, they would have won the nationwide popular vote in the last three presidential elections.

Figure 1.5: Presidential Election Non-Participation, 1798–2024

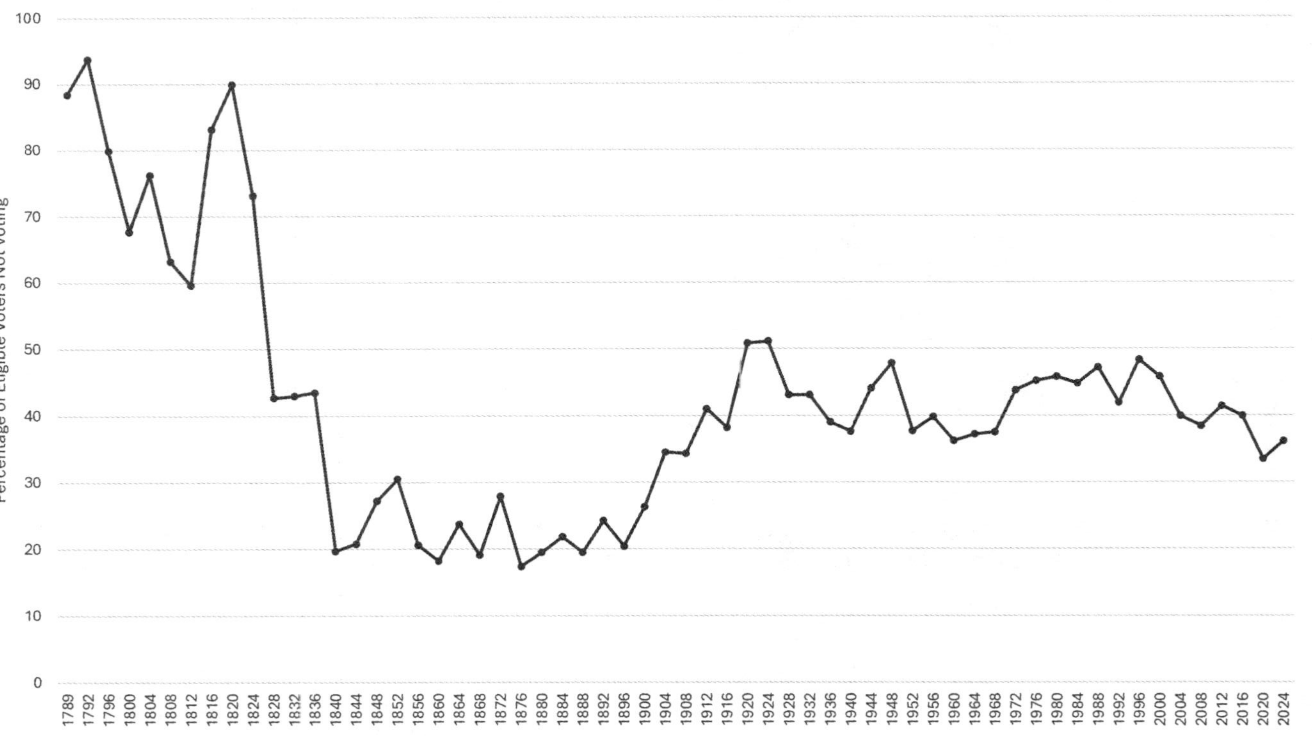

Source: US Elections Project

Figure 1.6: Number of Votes Cast for Each Major Party Presidential Candidate Compared to Number of Non-Voters, 2016–2024

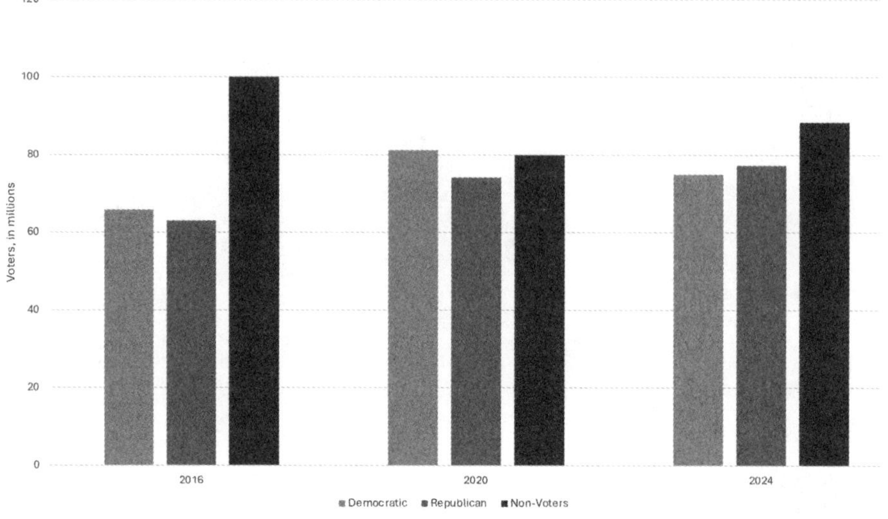

Source: Author calculations

Things are even worse in election years when a presidential contest is not on the ballot. Figure 1.7 shows non-participation rates among voting-eligible citizens from 1790, the first mid-term election under our Constitution, to 2022, the most recent mid-term election, as of this writing. Non-participation is even higher than in presidential elections. We also see a familiar spike in non-participation around the quarter-century mark of the twentieth century. However, that spike does not dissipate in quite the same way it did in presidential election years. Mid-term non-participation remains nearly as high today (54 percent in 2022) as it was a century ago (64 percent in 1922), which was (and is) twice as high as it was nearly 200 years ago (29 percent in 1838). Limiting the analysis to the modern era, non-participation averages 59 percent. That means our members of Congress, since 1974, have been elected by only four out of ten eligible voters.

Figure 1.7: Mid-term Election Non-Participation, 1790–2022

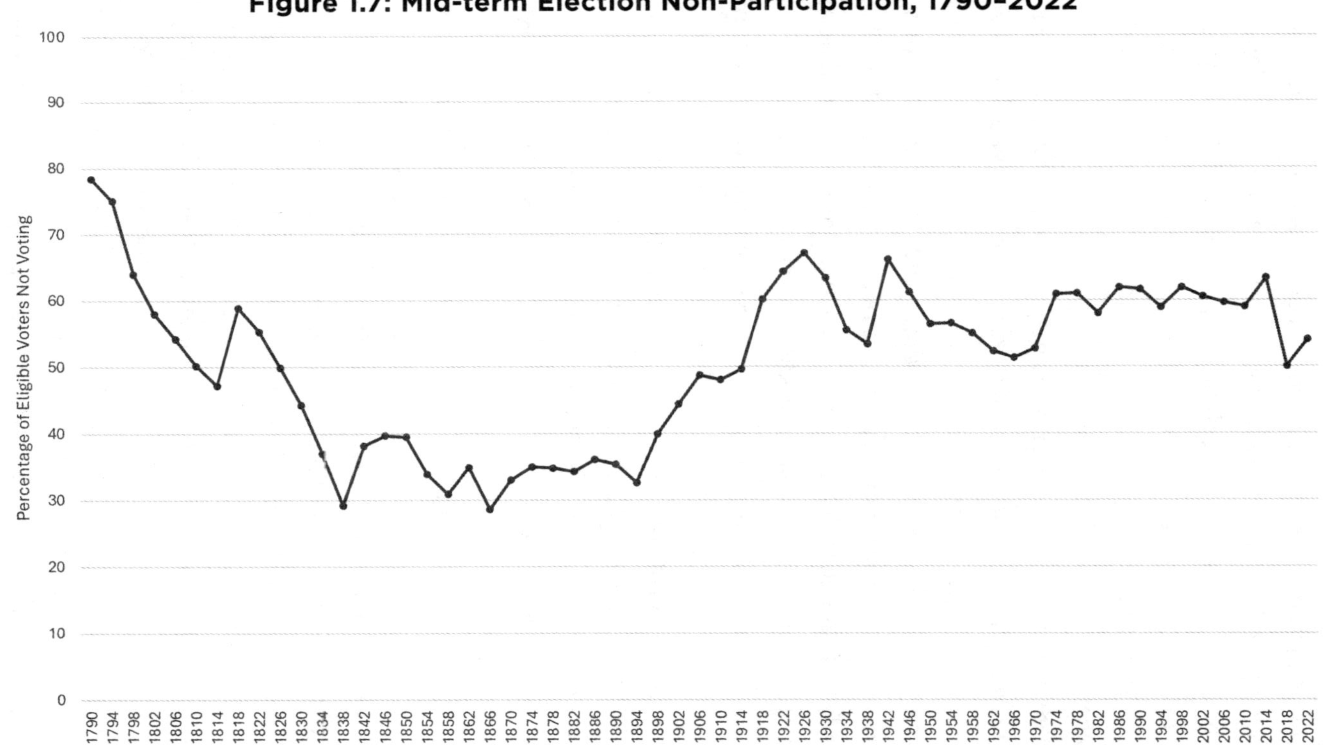

Source: US Elections Project

And all of this doesn't even get into the lamentable situation of local elections, which draw headlines like, "Voter Turnout Plummeting in Local Elections."[25] In that article, the reporter cites turnout data from more than 100 cities, showing that non-participation in elections for mayor in America's largest municipalities hovers between 75 and 80 percent. More than three out of four Americans don't take the opportunity to have a say in who runs their city.

There are myriad reasons citizens may not vote. When you net out all the reasons, though, they boil down to three themes, which were summarized, in a quite memorable way, in a seminal piece of scholarly research by political scientist Henry E. Brady and his colleagues: "because they can't, because they don't want to, or because nobody asked."[26]

Brady and his colleagues find that political interest is the attitude most predictive of voting participation, indicating that many people who do not vote refrain simply because "they don't want to" vote. Of course, there are issues of inability (the "can't" bucket) that have to do with political knowledge, which we discussed in the introduction. And there is still an issue of "nobody ask[ing]," which we will cover in chapter 2 on campaign volunteerism. However, the key takeaway from the Brady et al. research is that voter apathy plays a key role. Put simply, many voters don't want to vote.

That raises an important question. *If voting is so important to democracy, why don't people want to do it?* In a 2020 news article, CNBC journalist Catherine Clifford told the stories of several people who choose not to vote.[27] Through quotes from people who made that choice and experts cited in the reporting, I identified two themes.

First is indifference, both to the outcome and toward politics in general. One non-voter told Clifford that she didn't "care who wins the election." This shows a deep indifference to the outcome of the election. Perhaps this indifference is driven by a dislike of the candidates or because of a lack of efficacy—that there was no effective difference between the candidates and thus her vote would not have changed the course of public policy in any meaningful way. Citing an indifference toward politics in general, political scientist Christopher Federico told Clifford that "some people care about politics . . . others do not."

A second theme is related to outcome indifference. Some citizens abstain from voting simply because they don't like the choices. Citing a writer on *The Doe*, "which shares 'anonymous narratives to promote civil discourse,'" Clifford writes that the user doesn't "feel represented by the candidates the parties in power keep offering up." That user goes on to say that "until and unless there is a candidate who I feel I could vote for in good conscience, I'm not voting." Disliking the candidates is distinct from indifference in at least one critical way. A non-voter who doesn't like the candidates still cares about politics, at least enough to be informed about the current options, and about the outcome of the election. Rather than being a passive abstention, this is more of a principled abstention.

Beyond the themes identified in Clifford's reporting, political science research has uncovered factors that help explain non-participation. As we've already seen, a lack of political knowledge is a major driver in the choice to not participate. To restate Delli Carpini and Keeter, "a central resource for democratic participation is political information."[28]

For more than 70 years, political scientists have debated the effect of efficacy on political participation.[29] More recent research from psychology confirms what political scientists have long known: A sense of efficacy increases an individual's likelihood of voting.[30] Efficacy, defined simply, is the belief that one's actions can make a difference in some outcome. Political efficacy, then, is a citizen's sense that she can, by voting, change either the outcome of the election or the trajectory of public policy. Those with lower efficacy are less likely to vote.

As are individuals with lower levels of trust. Maybe. There should be no doubt that trust in American government is hovering near all-time lows.[31] For example, State Policy Network's Trust Tracker found that, in December 2023, only 24 percent of Americans said they trust (either completely or a great deal) the government. Compare that to 1958, when

Pew Research Center reported that trust in government was three times as high—73 percent.[32] But how does trust affect voting?

Older research in American politics demonstrated that lower trust plays no role in whether someone votes or not. However, trust may impact vote choice, leading individuals with lower levels of trust to choose outsiders or non-incumbents.[33] However, more recent research in the European context demonstrates that trust in institutions (rather than actors) does affect whether someone decides to vote or abstain.[34]

Regardless, because voting is a four-step process, in phase 3, if a voter does not trust either candidate and refuses to vote for either one, she may cycle back to phase 2 and decide to abstain. Thus, a person with low levels of trust may decide to vote but ultimately change his or her mind when forced to choose a candidate. For that reason, I believe a lack of trust may have some impact on non-participation, even if we as political scientists have thus far failed to measure its impact.

Democracy InAction Survey

So, what does my research show? Recall that I conducted a survey of American adults to evaluate their feelings of apathy and alienation as well as find out about which civic behaviors they engage in or abstain from. The results of that survey and the regression analyses of that data are presented in this section.

What comes next is going to be the technical discussion of the regression models. If you want to skip that discussion and jump ahead to the conclusion, feel free to do so. But before you do, let me give you a quick summary of the statistical findings.

Across three statistical models with three different outcomes of interest, I find that apathy plays a consistent and expected role in civic life. Increased feelings of apathy are associated with higher levels of electoral avoidance (engaging in behaviors that avoid registration and voting) and with lower levels of personal responsibility toward registration and voting. Alienation plays an inconsistent role, impacting only avoidance behaviors, but not personal feelings of responsibility. Put simply, apathy has a detrimental impact on civic attitudes and behaviors.

Okay, now you have the short version of the results. If you want the detailed version, keep reading. If not, you can skip ahead to the conclusion.

Electoral Avoidance

Let's begin our exploration into the results by considering electoral non-participation, using an outcome variable called Electoral Avoidance. This variable is what is called an additive index variable, which is a fancy way of saying it takes several other variables and adds them together. This variable adds five other variables: if the respondent is not registered to vote, has not updated his or her voter registration to their current address, has not voted in the past five years, has intentionally skipped an election in the past five years, or has accidentally missed an election in the past five years. Each of these variables is coded 1 if it is true of the respondent and 0 if it is false. So, for example, a respondent who is not registered would be coded 1 and someone who is registered to vote is coded 0. In other words, if they engage in an avoidance behavior, they get a 1. When you add those variables together, a respondent who has engaged in none of the avoidance behaviors would have a 0 on the Electoral Avoidance variable, while someone who has done all five would be coded as a 5. The higher the number, the more electoral avoidance someone engages in.

First, let's look at Apathy. Recall from the introduction that apathy is an internal feeling of not caring about engaging in civic life. In the regression models, it is also an additive variable, the sum of several questions used to gauge apathy. So, again, the higher the number, the more apathetic a respondent feels. When we look at the point estimate (that's the circle on the Apathy line), we see that it is to the right of the 0 line and that the confidence intervals (those whiskers on either side of the circle) do not cross the 0 line, meaning Apathy has a positive and statistically significant relationship (also note the * next to the variable name, which indicates statistical significance) with Electoral Avoidance.

But what does that mean? In short, it confirms exactly what I expected: Apathy leads to civic non-participation. The more apathetic one feels toward government, the more likely they are to avoid participating in elections. Put another way, the less someone cares, the less they participate. Higher levels of apathy are associated with being unregistered and not voting, even when controlling for other factors.

The same is true of Alienation, another additive index variable that measures how excluded one feels from civic life. Higher levels of alienation are also associated with more electoral avoidance. The more one feels like they don't belong in American civic life, the less they participate in elections—less registration and less voting. Apathy and Alienation work separately and independently of one another to drive down electoral participation.

Of the control variables included in the model that exhibit a significant relationship with Electoral Avoidance, all of them behave as expected. Higher levels of trust and more political knowledge are both associated with lower avoidance. An increase in age leads to lower levels of avoidance, as does an increase in income. And women are significantly more likely to participate (less likely to avoid) than men. Finally, the more conservative one is, the less electoral avoidance they engage in.

Figure 1.8: Electoral Avoidance

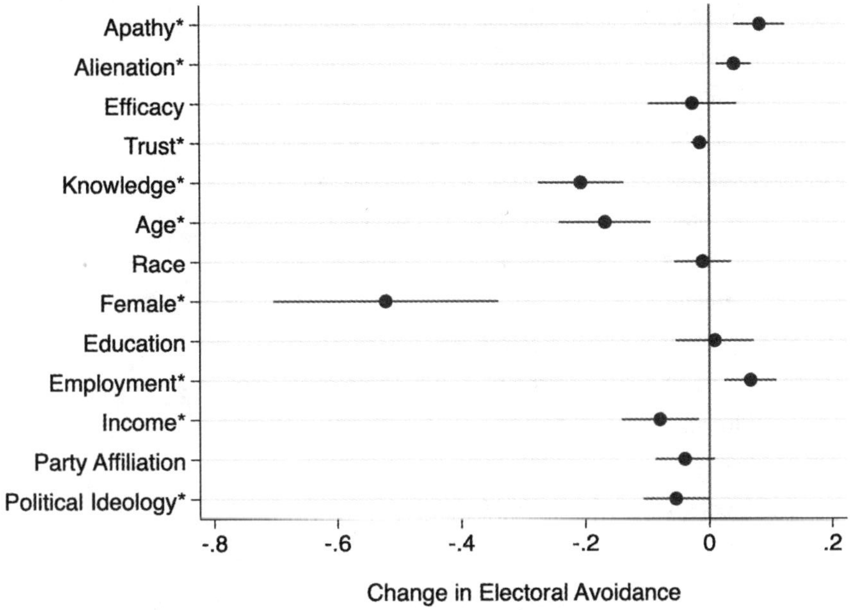

Apathy*
Alienation*
Efficacy
Trust*
Knowledge*
Age*
Race
Female*
Education
Employment*
Income*
Party Affiliation
Political Ideology*
-.8 -.6 -.4 -.2 0 .2
Change in Electoral Avoidance

Apathy and Alienation both increase electoral avoidance. See Appendix D for methodological and modeling information.

Feelings of Personal Responsibility

Turning now from actions to beliefs, we look at whether Apathy or Alienation impacts how Americans feel about their personal responsibilities to participate in elections. We start with feelings of personal responsibility to register to vote. Higher values indicate a greater feeling of responsibility. We would expect Apathy to drive down feelings of responsibility toward voter registration.

And that is precisely what we see. An increase in apathy results in a decreased feeling of personal responsibility to register to vote. The less one cares about civics and government, the less they feel responsible to register to vote. Here, though, alienation plays no role; apathy does all the work, while the control variables perform once again as expected.

Figure 1.9: Personal Responsibility to Register to Vote

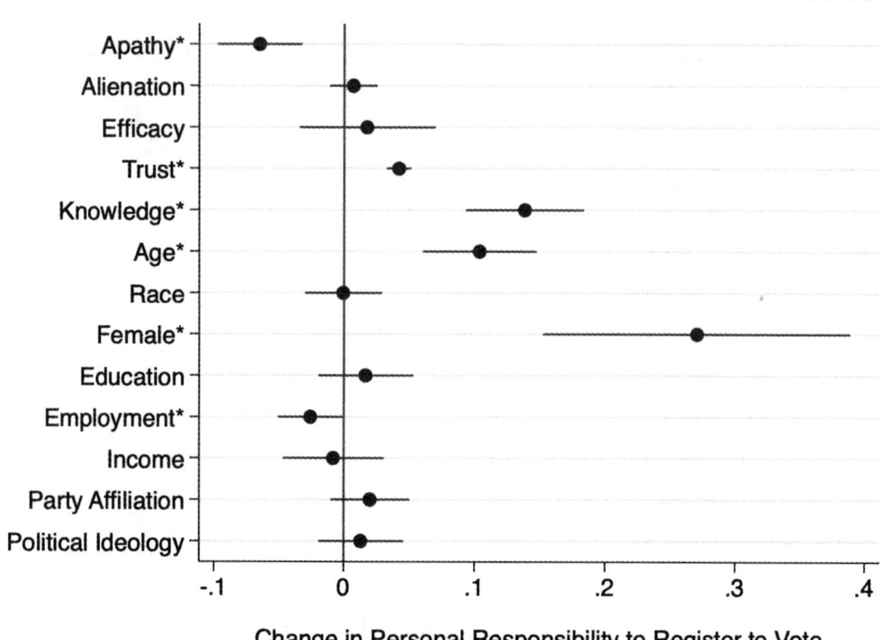

Apathy decreases an individual's feelings of personal responsibility to register to vote. See Appendix D for methodological and modeling information.

Similarly, when we consider the personal responsibility to vote, Apathy plays a starring role. The more apathetic a respondent is, the less of a responsibility they feel toward voting, while alienation remains not statistically significant, and the control variables perform as anticipated.

Figure 1.10: Personal Responsibility to Vote

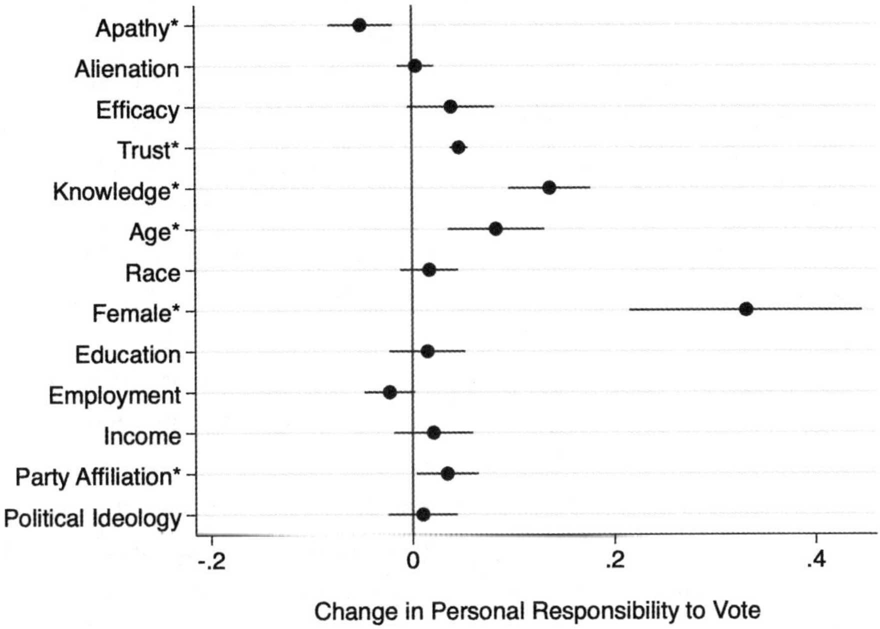

Apathy decreases an individual's feelings of personal responsibility to vote. See Appendix D for methodological and modeling information.

Conclusion

We have covered a lot in this chapter. We started with a conceptualization of voting as a four-phase process. Voting is not just showing up on Election Day and casting a ballot. That is the end of the process. Voting begins with registration, at least for the vast majority of Americans. Then, one must decide to vote in an upcoming election and then decide for whom they will vote. Only once those three steps are completed does the culmination come—casting a ballot.

But not everyone in America takes part in that process. I have shown you that, in the United States, voter registration (phase 1) and voting (phase 4) are far from universal. In a good year, only about two out of every three eligible Americans are registered and actually vote. This is true of both mid-term elections and presidential elections, although more Americans participate in the latter than the former.

Along the way, I have tried to convince you that these are important acts. Registration is important because without it, you cannot vote. And voting is important because it is the mechanism through which you (yes, *you*) and the rest of your community hold elected officials accountable. If you think government sucks, you (again, yes, *you*) can do something about it. But doing it is up to you. Don't rely on others, because they are the ones who voted for the government that you think sucks. As novelist David Foster Wallace said, "In reality, there is no such thing as not voting: you either vote by voting, or you vote by staying home and tacitly doubling the value of some Diehard's vote."

Apathy is a feeling of not caring about government and politics, and it leads people to engage in undemocratic thinking and actions. A lot of people don't care, and everyone has his or her own reasons for feeling that way. You're not alone, either in your thoughts, feelings, or abstention.

If that's you, I hope this chapter has encouraged you. But let me encourage you further. Politics can be interesting. Government can be fascinating. It's not something you have to immerse yourself in. Who has time for that, besides those of us who do this for a living? Here's one way to start. Think about something you care about, perhaps even something you care *a lot* about. Maybe it's children and education. Perhaps it's animal welfare. Or maybe it's the potholes on your street or the ever-increasing national debt. Got it? Good. Now, chances are very good that in some way, politics and government touch what you care about, and if you think through it, you'll probably find it pretty quickly. Maybe it's through funding, regulation, or prohibition. Find government's touchpoint on what you care about and use that to motivate you.

Let me offer a word of caution. Once you have found what you care about and how government impacts it, and have used it to motivate you to get involved in voting on that issue, don't give up. Government is a behemoth. It's huge. And it's headed in one direction. You're not going to turn it on a dime. It will take time, so keep at it. And one thing about voting is that it is habit-forming.[35] Once you do it, chances are you'll do it again. And again. And again.

And just remember that on the other side of the thing you care about is someone who cares too, and they are working against you. Are you going to let them win?

Three Questions

1. If we value voter participation, should we make voter registration automatic? Why or why not?
2. Even though voter turnout is low, there are still a lot of votes cast in any given election. Does it really matter, then, if you vote?
3. Some countries, like Australia, have compulsory voting, legally requiring citizens to vote. Should the US or individual states require citizens to vote? Why or why not?

Three Actions

1. Register to vote if you haven't already. You can do this wherever you get your driver's license or at your local elections office. An Internet search can help you find out where that is. If you are already registered, make sure you are registered to vote at your current address. In most places, this can be done by going to your state or local election official's website.

2. Find a list of all the elections in your area this year and put them on your calendar. Then, plan for Election Day—know what time you're going to vote and where you're going, make sure you have coverage at work, and know who's going to watch the kids and let the dog out. Think about every aspect of your daily life that could be changed and make a plan for it. Also, you can print a sample ballot ahead of time and take it with you, so when you get in the voting booth, you'll already know who you're voting for; this will reduce the time you have to spend at your polling place.
3. Talk to your local elections office about becoming a poll worker. Poll workers are the folks who make voting happen, and they are always in short supply.

Additional Resources

1. Getting started with politics can be incredibly daunting for someone who has never been involved. Maybe you don't even know the difference between a Democrat and a Republican. Who should you vote for? What do they even stand for, and how does that align with what you believe? I Side With is an excellent tool for getting started. Go to ISideWith.com and take the quiz. At the end, it will tell you which party your views most closely align with. Then, when you look at your ballot, see which candidate represents that party. Chances are, they'll be the best candidate for you. If you have doubts, do some more research.
2. Another excellent resource is Ballotpedia. If you have a question about anything related to American politics, chances are very good that they have some information on

it. Whether you want to find out how to vote, who's running in an election, who won the last election, or even election-specific registration information and deadlines in your state, Ballotpedia is a one-stop shop: BallotPedia.org.

CHAPTER 2

CAMPAIGN ACTIVITIES

"Volunteerism is the voice of the people put into action. These actions shape and mold the present into a future of which we can all be proud."

HELEN DYER

What if I told you I have a great plan to reduce the amount of time you spend doomscrolling? That you could get out, meet new people with shared interests. Maybe even make some new drinking buddies. Or that you could put your skills to work for a cause you care about or develop new skills.

Well, I do. And that's what this chapter is about. You'll read these words repeatedly in this chapter: Volunteers are the lifeblood of a campaign. They make the campaign run. But they also make the campaign fun.

• • •

I was working on my third campaign ever and managing my second. It was a high-profile state legislative race, and we planned to spend half a million dollars. We were also fully expecting our only competitor to spend even more. Oh, the joys of facing a wealthy, self-funded opponent.

That is a lot of money for any state legislative race, but especially for a rural one that would feature little to no television advertising. It was an old-fashioned, shoe-leather, grassroots effort. We had a candidate who was willing to work hard. He had a teenage son with the seemingly boundless energy that only teenagers can exhibit, who was excited to beat the streets for his dad. The candidate's mom would have licked a million stamps if I had asked her to. Fortunately, we were well into the era of peel-and-stick postage stamps, so no licking was required.

We also had a core volunteer group, with no blood relationship to the candidate, of about half a dozen souls who were instrumental in the campaign. These volunteers wanted no credit, no recognition. They were not show horses. They were workhorses. What we lacked, however, was a robust volunteer operation. We had our starters and no bench. It was me and a gang of eight. Heck, I even had trouble recruiting a paid intern from the local university. (I did eventually hire one, and she was invaluable!) Unfortunately, that was not my first such experience. The previous year, I had a very similar experience on my first campaign management gig, a congressional campaign—a family who was fully supportive of the candidate and worked their butts off, a few volunteers who would do whatever we asked of them, and . . . no one else.

I know I'm not alone in my frustrations. Many campaign managers and grassroots directors have similar experiences. Finding, recruiting, and retaining campaign volunteers is incredibly challenging. While local political parties and interest groups were once a rich source of volunteer labor, many of those wells have run dry. Consider what scholars Daniel Shea and Michael John Burton write in their practical handbook for political campaign managers: "Local party volunteers are not the force they once were," leading the authors to muse whether recruiting volunteers is "easier said than done."[1] Political scientist Michael Cohen surmises that this is because of the shift to candidate-centered campaigns: "Political parties have become adjunct organizations to the core of modern campaigns: the candidates themselves."[2]

Campaigns, like the ones I previously managed, tend to be staffed by volunteers who are connected in some way to the candidate. Many are family members. Others are friends, coworkers, and community connections. In fact, most handbooks for campaign managers offer the contact list on the candidates' smartphone as the jumping-off point for finding volunteers.[3] Beyond this (rather obvious) starting point, few other meaningful avenues of recruitment are offered. They include local political parties, community groups, student groups, and senior citizens. I'm not even kidding about that last one. In concluding their paragraph on potential sources of volunteer recruitment, Shea and Burton write, "Older Americans are a rapidly growing demographic group, are politically active, and often have a good deal of time to spare."[4]

Why Volunteering is Important

Campaigns matter. And by campaign, I don't just mean all the television ads and direct mail pieces. Political science research shows that those kinds of campaign expenditures are relatively benign; they have little to no discernible impact on the outcome of an election, except in the closest of races.[5] They do not increase turnout, and they do little to persuade people to support one candidate over the other. That's not to say they don't have a place in campaigning. I believe they do, and I have written about that previously.[6] But what matters most is the kind of campaign work we discuss in this chapter. It is the hard work and effort put in by volunteers that swing elections.

Consider one of the major studies on get-out-the-vote (GOTV) efforts, *Get Out the Vote: How to Increase Voter Turnout* by political scientists Donald P. Green and Alan S. Gerber. What it lacks in creative titling, it makes up for in impact. Green and Gerber's work truly has shaped how many political scientists (including me) and campaign managers (again, including me) think about and practice politics. In it, the researchers explore the effects of a wide range of campaign activities, from hosting and attending political events to mass media campaigning. And they consistently find that the most impactful methods of increasing turnout are door-to-door canvassing and, to a lesser extent, person-to-person phone calls.[7] And guess what canvassing and phone calls require? If you guessed voter lists, you'd be right. But that wouldn't fit the purpose of this chapter. They also require volunteers. And, often, lots of them. In his book on running professional campaigns, political scientist Michael Cohen writes, "Whether it is organizing a team of volunteers to make calls, knock on doors, or bring people together to maximize turnout on Election Day, people make campaigns move."[8]

Political campaigns matter because they educate voters, leading to voting for the candidate who most closely matches a voter's preferences. And, put simply, campaigns would implode without volunteers. If campaigns do not have the people necessary to run a campaign, that campaign's message does not get to voters who are, in turn, left uninformed and may make poor choices at the ballot box.

We will see in the data later in this chapter that relatively few people volunteer, especially for campaigns. They don't, despite the evidence that volunteer efforts matter a lot. So, then, why don't more Americans step up and volunteer for campaigns? I can think of several reasons.

One reason is that it can be uncomfortable. When considering that, it makes sense that most people would be unwilling to volunteer for a campaign. To make phone calls or knock on doors—two of the most labor-intensive tasks on any campaign and thus where the most volunteers are needed—can put people in awkward positions, having to answer tough questions from voters. Or deal with passive-aggressive hangups and aggressive-aggressive door-slams. People like comfort more than conflict. When one considers all that might be asked of them in a volunteer situation, it seems unsurprising that a vast majority of them would, rationally, decline.

Another reason is that doing so is a major time commitment. Americans live busy lives. We work for a third of the week and sleep for a third of it. Then, we cram everything else into the remaining eight hours a day, Monday through Friday, and thirty-two hours (when subtracting sleeping hours) on the weekends. We have to commute to and from work, cook, eat, take kids to piano and tae kwon do and soccer, go to church, attend family functions, go on dates, go on vacations, spend time with friends, binge the latest season of whatever show we're into, read a book or a magazine. When are we supposed to find time to volunteer for a campaign? For many—indeed for most—Americans, the answer is clearly *never.* Life is simply all-consuming, and there is no time left for something that isn't even a blip on the radar.

Which brings me to my next point: Many Americans don't volunteer for campaigns because they simply don't know about them. Politics, when it occurs to them at all, only comes front of mind in the days leading up to an election. They're not paying attention. As a campaign manager, I always told my candidates that everything they do before Labor Day is just laying the foundation. The real campaign officially starts when summer officially ends, mere weeks before Election Day. Nobody is paying attention before that. So, without knowledge that a campaign is even being waged, how can they know about volunteer opportunities?

Besides not knowing about volunteer opportunities because they are not paying attention to politics, people likely don't know that campaigns need volunteers. Many Americans may simply believe that campaigns operate with nothing but a paid, full-time staff. That's an understandable assumption considering all the talk in the media about money in politics and the costs associated with running a campaign. But volunteers are the lifeblood of a campaign. And most campaigns operate on shoestring budgets, not the multi-million-dollar balance sheets of congressional, gubernatorial, or presidential races. They can rarely afford to pay for one employee, let alone a full staff. But the fact remains that, because of faulty assumptions, many people may not volunteer because they don't know that they can.

Relatedly, some people may not volunteer simply because no one asked them to. Recall the quippy opening to the research paper I wrote about in chapter 1—that people don't vote because they can't, because they don't want to, or because nobody asked. Those reasons apply here, too. I've covered the can't (time constraints and lack of knowledge), and now we are on to the nobody asked. Previous research has shown that part of the decline in campaign volunteerism is due to a reduction in mobilization. Candidates and parties are not doing the work of recruiting volunteers—they're not asking, so nobody's volunteering.[9] Candidates, campaigns, and their supporters can do a better job here, spreading the message and inviting people to participate in campaigns, to pitch in a few hours when and how they are able.

What Volunteers Do

Perhaps you are one of the 97 percent of Americans who have never volunteered for a campaign. You have no clue what that would even look like. You might be asking, *What, exactly, do campaign volunteers do anyway?* Even though my mom always told me it is bad manners to answer a question with a question, I'll do that here. What do campaign volunteers *not* do?

Of course, I say that tongue in cheek, but the point is serious. Campaign volunteers do it all! And here's why. Every volunteer brings something to the table. Some have the gift of gab, and some don't. Others are data whizzes, while some cringe at the mere mention of a spreadsheet. Some are introverts, others are extroverts. Some can plan a heck of a party, while others are skilled at working the room at that party. No two volunteers are the same, so they can all be put to work using the skills that they are most comfortable with.

Likewise, no two campaigns are the same. Some campaigns will put volunteers to work every day of the week, while others work mostly on the weekends. Some will use volunteers extensively, while others rely almost exclusively on the candidate and paid staff. Some campaigns will use volunteers in all the tasks I list below, while others will employ only one or a few of these tactics.

Here is the key takeaway for you in this section: Figure out what *your* skills are and how you can put them to use for a campaign. Then call one up and offer your skills. The rest of this section explains some of the common ways campaigns put volunteers to work. Maybe one or more of these tasks sound appealing to you, and maybe they don't. If not, you are probably in an excellent position to see what's missing and how your skill set can fill a void. Speaking as a former campaign manager, I can tell you that I would have jumped on an opportunity like that in a heartbeat.

Canvassing and Lit Drops

Canvassing is a fancy campaign word for going door to door. Volunteers, under the direction of a volunteer coordinator or paid campaign staffer, such as a grassroots director or campaign manager, will fan out across a targeted area, knock on the doors of targeted voters, and talk to the voters about the candidate. Canvassing can serve several purposes, but the two primary purposes are persuasion (attempting to convince the voter to support your candidate) and mobilization (attempting to get the voter to go vote). Other efforts might include disseminating absentee ballot applications, identifying favorable and unfavorable voters, and "harvesting" ballots (where it's legal), among others.[10]

This is the kind of support many outside political groups, like teachers' unions, lend to preferred or endorsed candidates. The problem, though, is that many times those activist groups will bus in doorknockers from other places, which means the person knocking on the door and talking to a voter has no real connection to the place, no real interest in the outcome of the election. As Green and Gerber put it, "any organization that becomes an ally has its own agenda."[11] Many times, that agenda does not align with the values or interests of a community. They're there because they are activists. I don't want you to become an activist. I want you to have a stake in *your* community, to impact the lives of *your* family and *your* neighbors.

Yes, talking to people can be a challenge for some of us. Talking to them about *politics* is downright scary. But, as we will see later in this chapter, it is far and away one of the most effective methods of campaigning.

Literature distribution, known in the industry as "lit drops," is another labor-intensive campaign activity. Volunteers go out in the community and distribute campaign literature, such as push cards (also called palm cards because they fit in the palm of your hand) or doorhangers. These can be placed on the doors of voters in an area but do not require the volunteer to engage directly with a voter (so, in that way, they are similar to, but distinct from, canvassing). Volunteers can also engage in lit drops at malls or supermarkets by simply handing the literature to passersby (with consent from the business owner, of course) or at events, such as football games or even before and after worship services at churches with large congregations, by again handing them out or simply placing the literature on the windshields of cars in the parking lot. Lit drops, depending on the type of activity, may be less intimidating for some volunteers because they require less interaction with voters.

Phone Banking

Calling voters is an effective campaign tactic. Like canvassing, phone banking can serve several purposes, but the two most common are, again, persuasion and mobilization. In phone banking, though, rather than knocking on a voter's door, the volunteer calls the voter, talks to her about the candidate, and encourages her to either support the candidate or go vote. These calls can be especially powerful when the volunteer speaks a language other than English that is predominant in an area, allowing non-English-speaking voters to receive calls from the campaign in their native language.

Phone banking has come a long way from the days of volunteers gathering in a room at campaign headquarters and calling voters from one of the campaign phones. While this still may happen, with updated technology, it is more common that voters can make phone banking calls from the comfort of their own home (or wherever else their cell phone gets a signal. Can you hear me now?).

Again, phone banking requires volunteers to engage with voters directly, so this can be an intimidating task for many volunteers. But they are generally good for producing results for the campaign. These calls are most effective when they come from, in order, the candidate, the candidate's family, a volunteer with a personal connection to the voter, and then any other campaign volunteer. Professional phone banking typically has little to no effect, with live professional calls having a weak effect and prerecorded (robo) calls having almost no impact on voter mobilization.[12]

Events

Events, although they are generally held for people who are already supporting the candidate and thus have little effect on the outcome of a race, are incredibly labor-intensive. Campaign events can run the gamut from meet-and-greets, which are usually relatively informal get-togethers in a supporter's house where the supporter's friends, family, and neighbors are invited to meet the candidate, all the way to massive fundraisers or election night parties.

Campaigns use volunteers in a wide variety of roles at events. Some volunteers might be asked to work a check-in table, where guests are greeted and given a name tag. Others may serve as bartenders or waiters, circulating food and drinks. Volunteers with special skills with audio-visual equipment may be asked to deejay or set up other sound, lighting, or presentation equipment. Volunteers might also be tasked with setting up the venue before the event or cleaning up after everyone else has gone home.

Logistics

So much work goes on behind the scenes of a campaign—I mean, a lot. And it takes a lot of people to get that work done. Because when the logistics and preparation work doesn't happen, the front-and-center stuff doesn't happen. Consider the consequences of having fifty volunteers show up on Saturday morning to canvas (every campaign manager's dream!), but no walking lists have been prepared, no door hangers have been printed, no bottles of water have been purchased, and—worst of all—nobody brought the dang donuts (every campaign manager's nightmare)! You're going to have fifty lost, silent, dehydrated, and hungry volunteers. And frustrated. Oh man, will they be frustrated.

That's why logistics are important. Walking lists have to be prepared. Someone has to pick up the push cards from the printer. Need more stamps? Well, someone has to run to the post office! And let's be honest. Donuts do not deliver themselves. Someone—and preferably a lot of someones—must do the behind-the-scenes work to keep the campaign on track.

Miscellany

I have covered some of the major activities in which campaign volunteers engage. Of course, every campaign will have other tasks that need to be done, and volunteers are the perfect group to do them. Some miscellaneous tasks might include:

- **Running errands.** These might include trips to the bank or to pick up checks from donors. Or, you might have to run to the office supply store to pick up more printer paper. Perhaps the candidate's call time (when the candidate is calling prospective donors to raise more money) falls during lunch, and he needs someone to bring him a burger. Think of the errands you might run for yourself, your own household, or your business. Chances are, campaigns need someone to play gopher for those same types of tasks, too.
- **Maintaining lists.** Campaigns are list central. Voter lists. Donor lists. Volunteer lists. Lists of supporters. Lists of

events. Lists of lists. Maybe spreadsheets are your jam, and this is something you could get behind. Someone has to help keep those lists in tip-top shape, and a volunteer who knows his or her way around a spreadsheet is often a godsend for a campaign.

- **Answering phones.** Imagine if you called a barber shop or salon to book an appointment for a haircut, and the phone just rang and rang. And rang. That'd be annoying, right? And you might even find somewhere else to get a haircut. Now, imagine someone calling a campaign headquarters to get a yard sign, but no one answers the call. They might decide not to vote (or worse, vote for the other candidate). Or a reporter calls for an interview, but no one answers. Incoming hit piece! Campaigns need people to answer the phone. And it's something you can do while still scrolling on your own phone.
- **Recruiting more volunteers.** Judge Lawrence Gray tells an amusing story about one volunteer for his campaign when he ran for prosecutor. This volunteer could "raise other volunteers on a moment's notice."[13] Turns out that was because this (male) volunteer was viewed by (female) volunteers as quite attractive. Gray writes, "That had not occurred to me. Sure enough, I took a second look at his volunteers and saw they were all college women, and every now and then one would look at him and smile."[14] The point is that volunteers beget volunteers.
- **Driving the candidate.** Candidates have a lot of work to do. They are on the phone almost constantly—talking to staff, donors, reporters, you name it. If they're not on the phone, they may be writing thank-you notes. Or studying policy to prepare for an upcoming debate. The problem is, they cannot be stuck in an office all day to get work done, so quite

often they have to do it on the road between one campaign stop and another—after that candidate forum but before their daughter's volleyball game. So, to get work done, they need someone to drive them. Rideshares get expensive, so volunteers are a great resource for driving the candidate.

- **Dropping off campaign signs.** This one seems pretty self-explanatory. Supporters want yard signs, and the campaign needs to get them to the supporters. So, someone has to drop them off. In addition, campaigns often use 4x8-foot signs that are put up on posts in fields or hung on fences in high-traffic areas. Those things are a beast to put up, especially when fighting a strong gust of wind.

As I said earlier, this is far from a comprehensive list. Grassroots expert Christopher Kush provides a list of things you can do to help campaigns get out the vote that don't even require coordinating with a campaign, everything from driving an elderly neighbor to the polls to having breakfast with a friend before going to vote.[15] But, as you can see, there is a lot of work to be done on a campaign, so campaigns need volunteers. Volunteers truly are the lifeblood of any campaign organization. And they are an indicator of a successful campaign. As one campaign manager told researchers, "A venerable test of a campaign's viability is 'whether they've found enough volunteers . . . to . . . generate momentum on a grassroots level.'"[16]

Campaign Volunteers: What the Data Say

Given the importance of campaign volunteers and the work they do, it seems surprising that relatively little data exist on campaign volunteering. However, there are some reliable sources of data that show just how rare it is. In one of the most comprehensive studies of citizen participation, political scientists Steven Rosenstone and John Mark Hansen write that "from the 1960s to the 1980s, the percentage of Americans who volunteered to work for political parties or candidates dropped 1.9 percentage points."[17] They report that, on average, from 1952 to 1990, only 4 to 5 percent of Americans worked for a candidate or party.[18]

It has only gotten worse since then. According to the American National Election Study (ANES), campaign volunteerism has dropped to an average of only 3 percent.[19] In an average election year, 97 out of 100 Americans report not volunteering for a campaign. Figure 2.1 shows the trend in the number of people who told ANES researchers that they had not worked for a party or candidate during a given election cycle.

These numbers seem especially abysmal when you consider that Americans do not seem to be volunteer-averse overall. According to a 2021 analysis of US Census data by Civic, a company that "work[s] to . . . increase civic participation,"[20] volunteerism among Americans remained fairly consistent from 2002 through 2018, hovering around 27 percent.[21] Granted, only one-quarter of Americans bothering to give of their time is nothing to brag about. But it does show quite a chasm between Americans' willingness to volunteer in general and Americans' willingness to volunteer for a political campaign.

Democracy InAction Survey

As we've seen thus far, campaign volunteers are important to the political process because they provide the services that matter most in swinging elections. We've also seen that relatively few people volunteer, and I talked about some of the reasons why they may not. Those reasons covered the "can't" and "nobody asked" issues. Now, to address the "don't want to," let's turn to the Democracy InAction Survey and explore the impact of apathy and alienation on campaign activities.

Before we dig into the details, let me brief you on the key findings. Apathy exerts exactly the power I expect it to. Apathy drives up nonparticipation in campaigns and drives down feelings of personal responsibility to volunteer for a campaign. Apathy breeds undemocratic attitudes and behaviors. Alienation unexpectedly cuts against the grain, increasing participation and feelings of personal responsibility. I will discuss some possible explanations for this in the conclusion.

Now you know the key points. If you want to avoid the nitty-gritty of the regression models, you can skip ahead to the conclusion. If you want the deep dive, read on.

Campaign Avoidance

Recall that apathy is simply not caring about the political process. If one does not care about politics, we would expect them to avoid participating in campaign activities. And that's exactly what the results of the Democracy InAction Survey show. Higher levels of apathy are associated with campaign avoidance. See figure 2.2. More apathetic respondents avoid campaign volunteering at a level that is statistically significantly higher than respondents who express lower levels of apathy.

Alienation, on the other hand, plays a countervailing role. The more alienated one feels, they less they avoid politics. Put another way, the more one feels like they don't belong, the more they volunteer for campaigns. This is a counterintuitive finding. Perhaps the alienated are looking for ways to belong, and participating in campaign activities is an effort at belonging. Still yet, the detrimental effect of apathy ($\beta = 0.060$) is nearly twice as large as the positive impact of alienation ($\beta = -0.033$).

The other psychological and demographic control variables that reach statistical significance perform as expected. Higher levels of trust, education, and income are all associated with less campaign avoidance. More trusting people and those with more formal education and higher incomes volunteer for campaigns at significantly higher levels than those with lower levels of trust, less formal education, and lower incomes.

Political ideology also plays a significant role in campaign avoidance. The more conservative a respondent is, the more they avoid campaign activities. This make sense when you consider that most political activism

Figure 2.1: Percent of Americans Who Did Not Volunteer for a Party or Candidate, by Election Year

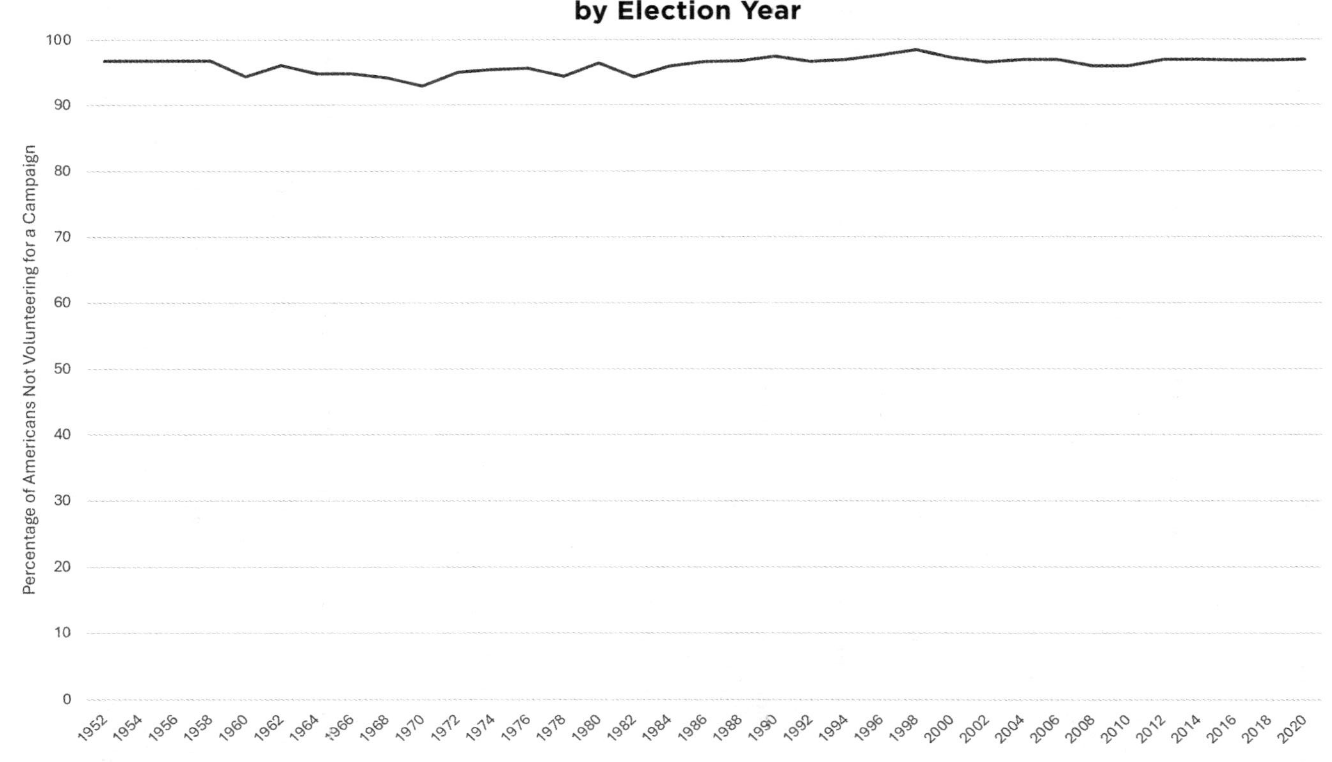

Data from American National Election Study Data Center. https://electionstudies.org/data-tools/anes-guide/anes-guide.html?chart=worked_for_party.

is undertaken by the political left, while conservatives are more likely to engage in more traditional political behavior, like voting, as we saw in chapter 1.

Figure 2.2: Campaign Avoidance

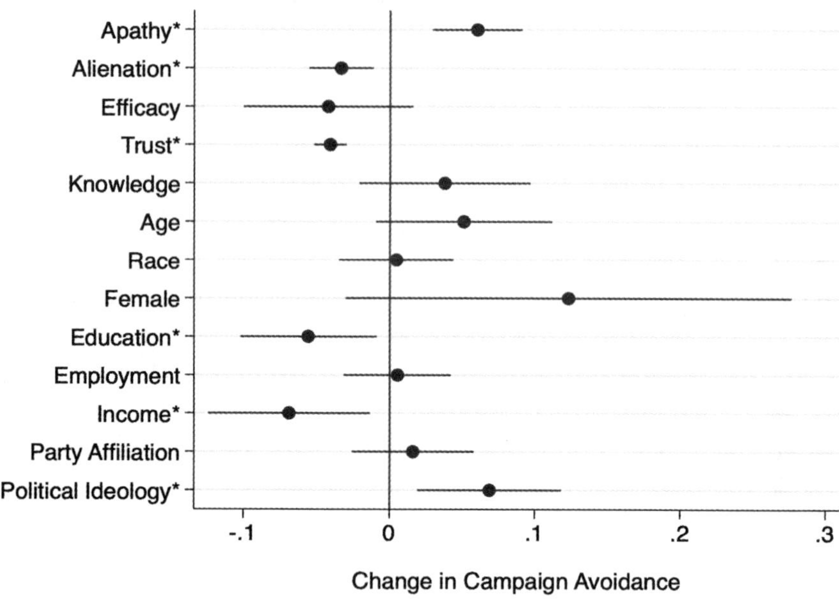

Apathy and Alienation play countervailing roles in campaign avoidance, with Apathy increasing avoidance and Alienation decreasing it. See Appendix D for methodological and modeling information.

Personal Responsibility to Volunteer for a Campaign

Turning now to figure 2.3, we see that apathy significantly reduces an individual's feelings of personal responsibility for volunteering for a campaign. The less one cares about civic affairs, the less personal responsibility they feel to engage in campaign activities. Alienation, once again, acts as a countervailing force, increasing personal responsibility for volunteering in the same way that it increases participation. While alienation played no role in attitudes toward voting and increased voting avoidance, it is playing the opposite, unexpected role in non-electoral political behavior.

Figure 2.3: Personal Responsibility to Volunteer for a Campaign

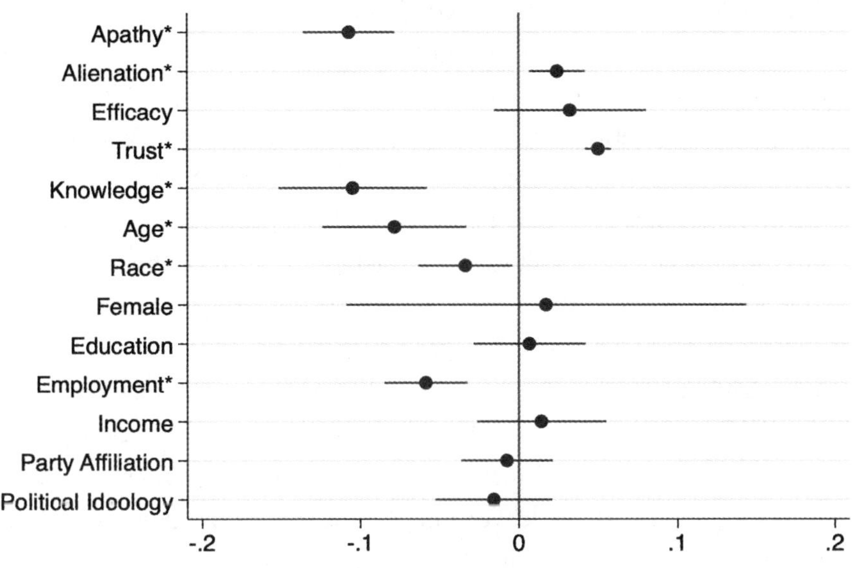

Apathy and Alienation play countervailing roles in an individual's feelings of personal responsibility to volunteer for a campaign, with Apathy decreasing personal responsibility and Alienation increasing it. See Appendix D for methodological and modeling information.

The control variables in this personal responsibility model produce some intriguing results. Let's start with Trust, the one control variable that performs as expected. Looking again at figure 2.3, we see the point estimate is in the positive territory with error bars that do not cross zero, indicating that more trusting individuals feel significantly more responsible to volunteer for a campaign. Again, this is what we should anticipate. Beyond this finding for trust, however, the results are not as expected.

Greater political knowledge reduces feelings of personal responsibility for campaign volunteering. This runs counter to the idea that political knowledge increases civic-mindedness. Maybe it reflects a rational approach to civic participation. Knowledge increases democratic beliefs related to voting, a finding from chapter 1, but decreases feelings of campaign responsibility, as we see here. So, perhaps knowledgeable participants believe their greatest impact is voting and thus feel responsible to vote but do not consider engagement beyond voting as an obligation.

If this explanation is accurate, they are simply wrong. Voting is one of the *least* rational forms of political participation.[22] As political science research has shown, and as I covered earlier in this chapter, campaign activities provided by volunteers translate into a huge benefit for the campaigns. Yes, for all the reasons covered in chapter 1, Americans should vote. But from a standpoint of pure rationality, volunteering for a campaign is a more beneficial activity. Rationality is when the benefits of an activity outweigh the costs. The bigger the bang for the buck, the more rational something is. Volunteers—whether they are knocking on doors or making phone calls—deliver a huge bang for the campaign's bucks by increasing turnout. Canvassing, particularly, produces one additional vote for every fourteen contacts.[23] That's about an hour's worth of canvassing. So, if you spend one weekend canvassing for a campaign, you could produce an extra fifteen to twenty voters. Multiply that by ten volunteers and about ten solid weeks of campaigning between Labor Day and Election Day, and you're talking about thousands of voters. That is a huge boon to democracy. Much more than one person's one vote (which, by the way, is also *very* important!).

Age and race are also significantly and negatively associated with feelings of personal responsibility to volunteer for a campaign. Starting with age, older individuals do not feel the civic pull of campaigning, relative to younger respondents. *Leave that to the young folks.* This is an intriguing finding for me for a couple of reasons. First, it is at odds with my own personal experience on campaigns. The majority (by a lot) of my most loyal and hardworking volunteers were older. Sure, we had some younger volunteers, but they were itinerant; they had other obligations that older, retired folks were unencumbered by. Second, recall the line from Shea and

Burton about sources of volunteers that I quoted earlier? Let me refresh your memory: "Older Americans are a rapidly growing demographic group, are politically active, and often have a good deal of time to spare."[24] The campaign handbooks instruct campaign managers explicitly to recruit older volunteers. These results show that it may not be such sound advice.

Turning to the effect of race, we again see a significant and negative relationship. However, Race is a categorical variable that does not have a natural order, like age. So, to understand the effect of race, I undertook a more detailed examination of the data. I started by comparing all other races to Asians (coded 1) and then rotated the baseline category (the point of comparison) through each of the eight race categories. I also created a new variable that compared non-White respondents to White respondents. I found only two significant differences between racial groups, both when Hispanics are the baseline group. What I found is that, compared to Hispanic or Latino (coded 3) respondents, Whites (coded 7) and participants who claimed another race (coded 8) are significantly less likely to feel a personal responsibility. The regression model shows that the higher the number for race, the lower the feelings of personal responsibility. Since both White and Another Race are coded with higher numbers than Hispanics, this deeper dive makes sense of the regression result. There is not a significant difference at *every* step of the racial category, only between one baseline group and two others, but it was enough for the model to identify it as significant.

Employment is also negative and significant. As with race, however, employment is a categorical variable, so a more detailed look at the data is in order. Unlike race, an explanation for the employment result was immediately apparent when using the category coded 1 as the baseline. Compared to respondents working full time, every other category of employment was associated with lower feelings of personal responsibility to volunteer for a campaign. All but two (part-time workers and students) were statistically significant. Looking at figure 2.4, you can see the distinct decline in volunteerism as one moves away from full-time employment.

This finding makes sense. In the introduction, I cited a study that found strong correlations between civic engagement within a community and the community's unemployment rate. In that study, researchers determined that, even controlling for economic factors, civic health significantly reduced unemployment. When looking at volunteerism, the study's authors write, "An increase of one point in volunteering was associated with 0.192 percentage points less unemployment, controlling for the eight economic variables."[25] At the macro level, employment is associated with volunteerism—states and cities with high rates of volunteering have higher rates of employment. So, it stands to reason that this relationship would hold at the micro level—that people who are employed feel the greatest responsibility to volunteer. That's precisely what the results of this regression model show.

Figure 2.4: Personal Responsibility to Volunteer for a Campaign, by Employment

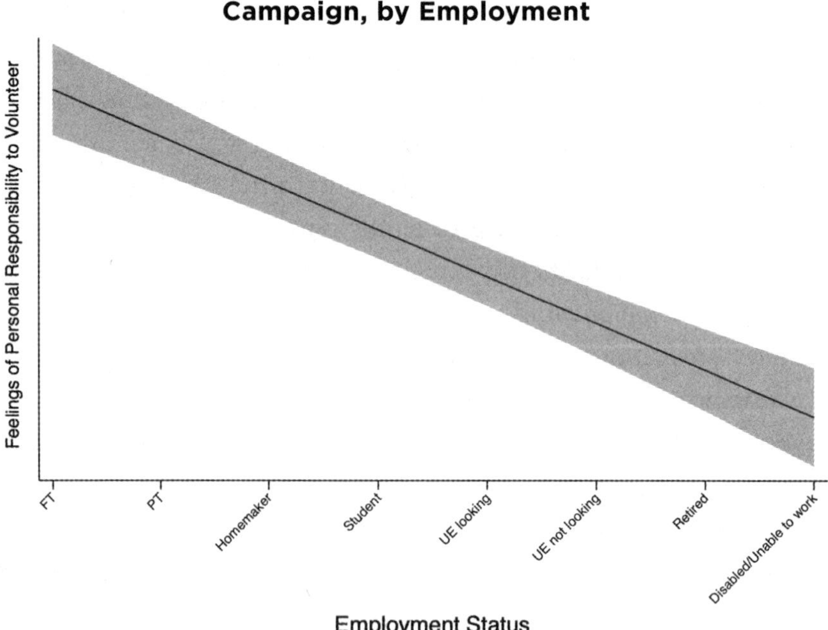

Employment status plays a significant role in an individual's feelings of personal responsibility to volunteer for a campaign.

Conclusion

Volunteering is critical to the operations of political campaigns. As I have written repeatedly throughout this chapter, volunteers are a campaign's lifeblood. Volunteers perform dozens of various tasks for campaigns. Tic Tac, the breath mint, once had a tagline: "Can you breathe without a Tic Tac? Sure, but I wouldn't recommend it." That's how I feel about campaign volunteers. Yes, you can run a campaign without them, but I wouldn't recommend it.

Unfortunately, the vast majority of Americans don't volunteer for campaigns, despite their seeming willingness to volunteer more broadly. This chapter explored several potential reasons why Americans are disinclined to volunteer for political campaigns, and the data pointed very clearly to one explanation: apathy. People who don't care about politics don't volunteer, and they don't believe they have a personal responsibility to volunteer.

If that's you, the data show you are far from alone. And I get it; I truly do. I'm busy with work, family, church, and so much else. I am an introvert, and I am physically exhausted by spending extended time around people. I'm somewhat socially awkward and sometimes (okay, fine, you caught me, I *often*) make inappropriate jokes at inappropriate times. I know that this describes the lives of many people out there, maybe even you.

But the truth is that Americans have always been busy. The eighteenth-century American farmer's field didn't plow, plant, or harvest itself. But they found time, and so can we. Introverts have always been in our midst, and they've found ways to overcome the draining nature of social interaction. And if I can find a filter for my inappropriate jokes, I know you can find a way to get involved, even if for just a little while.

Of course, you can find a reason to do it for yourself. Find that thing you are passionate about. Find a candidate you can really get behind. But, even if not, do it for your community. As we saw earlier in the chapter, robust civic engagement is associated with better economic health in the community. The National Conference on Citizenship calls areas without opportunities to volunteer "civic deserts." Matthew Atwell and his colleagues write in a 2017 report that "'Civic Deserts' . . . are increasingly common in the United States. The continued decline in a wide range of important indicators of civic health and connectivity threatens our prosperity, safety, and democracy."[26] Don't let that happen to your community. As an unknown author once put it, "Volunteering is the ultimate exercise in democracy. You vote in elections once a year, but when you volunteer, you vote every day about the kind of community you want to live in."

Maybe you don't know where to start. Well, your first step was reading this chapter and understanding that campaigns need volunteers. If I could give you a certificate of completion, I would. Now, it's time for step two. Maybe, in reading this chapter, you even thought of a particular skill you have that might be valuable to a candidate. Below, I list three concrete baby steps you can take on your path to becoming a campaign volunteer. Remember, I'm not asking you to become an activist. We have enough of those running around. I'm asking you to take an interest in your community and the people who represent you, your family, and your neighbors. You will all be better off for it.

Three Questions

1. How important or unimportant is it for campaigns to have volunteers willing to help? Why?
2. In your view, how important is it for Americans to volunteer for a political campaign? For what reasons do you say that?
3. If you were working as a campaign manager or volunteer director, where would you go to try and find volunteers?

Three Actions

1. Research the candidates for office and find one you're particularly excited to vote for. Contact that candidate's campaign office and request a yard sign or bumper sticker.
2. Ask the volunteer coordinator or grassroots director how you can help the campaign. If you're a people person, ask if you can make phone calls or knock on doors. If you're the shy, quiet type, tell them you'd prefer to stuff envelopes or help set up for events. There are plenty of opportunities, regardless of your experience, skills, or preferred level of interaction with other people.
3. Campaigns run on sweat and cash. In addition to investing your sweat equity, consider making a small financial donation to the candidate.

CHAPTER 3

RESPONDING TO POLLS

"Polling is merely an instrument for gauging public opinion. When a president or any other leader pays attention to poll results, he is, in effect, paying attention to the views of the people. Any other interpretation is nonsense."

GEORGE GALLUP

Little room for doubt exists that polling has faced its share of criticism over the past decade. From the surprise victory of Donald Trump in 2016 to the smaller-than-expected win by Joe Biden in 2020, polling has faced a crisis of credibility in the eyes of many Americans. Even in 2024, quite a bit of consternation still existed from both the national[1] and international press.[2] And although the 2024 polls showed the presidential race between Vice President Kamala Harris and former president Donald Trump as a statistical tie,[3] the polls ended up performing quite well, according to Scott Rasmussen, a conservative pollster who is considered by many to be one of the modern leaders of the polling field.[4]

But to say the polls performed better in 2024 than in the previous two cycles is not a partisan claim. Democratic pollster Natalie Jackson agrees, writing about polls in the 2024 presidential election, "The roughly 3-percentage point bias among national polls—and about 2 percentage points in the battleground states—was well within the margin of expected error for polls."[5] She went on to say that 2024 polling "did a better job of showing the state of the race and the possibility of a Trump win than in either of his previous campaigns."[6] A report on 2024 polls from the American Association for Public Opinion Research, one of the nation's leading professional organizations for pollsters and academic survey researchers, reached similar conclusions.[7] The authors of that report, while noting that 2024 was "the third straight presidential cycle [in which] pre-election polls underestimated Republican vote shares relative to Democrats'."[8] it "marked a substantial recovery in overall polling accuracy."[9] Moreover, the AAPOR report authors noted that 2024 was "the most accurate cycle for presidential polling at the state level since 1944."[10]

Whether or not criticism of the polls is warranted remains a matter of much debate. AAPOR released post-election reports, similar to the one cited above, on the state of polling after both the 2016 and 2020 elections. Those earlier reports lay some blame at the feet of pollsters. On the other hand, practitioners themselves point out that the polls didn't get the elections *that* wrong. And besides, polls are a snapshot in time and are not meant to be predictive of election outcomes.

As a pollster myself, I am concerned about getting reliable and valid measures of public opinion. I want my organization, the Center for Excellence in Polling at the Foundation for Government Accountability, and my consulting clients to have good data with which to make decisions. But what is more troubling to me than whether "the polls" got an election right or wrong, or whether my estimate of support for a given public policy is right, is how few people are willing to participate in the process. To be sure, there is no dearth of pollsters. What is missing from the equation, however, is people on the other end of the phone. I want (and need) to be right. But for *me* to be right requires *you* to participate.

For years, pollsters have lamented abysmal and worsening survey response rates. Citizens simply don't respond to polls in the numbers they once did. The irony of diminishing response rates to political polling is that the retort from voters to the publication of a poll they don't like has remained constant: "Who are they polling? I never get called!"

Well, maybe you did. And instead of staying on the phone to answer a few questions about politics, you hung up. Or maybe you sent that call from an unknown number to voicemail, and the pollster moved on to another phone number on her list.[11] Or maybe you ignored the text message that read, "We're surveying voters in your area . . ." The ones who hang up on the pollster, send the pollster's call to voicemail, or ignore the pollster's text message are in a crowded field—they vastly outnumber the ones who answer the call, stay on the phone, or click on the link in the text message. In fact, about 98 to 99 percent of Americans are in the former group. Only 1 to 2 percent of individuals who are contacted to participate in a poll actually answer the pollster's questions.

Pollsters, unlike Occupy Wall Street, are thankful for the one percent.

But what does polling matter for democracy? I'm glad you asked. The short answer is, "everything." The long answer is, well, more complex. Providing a more complex answer is the purpose of this chapter. In it, I will dive into the importance of polling data, why citizens should respond to polls, why they don't, and why that lack of response is detrimental to representative democracy.

Polling as a Tool of Democracy

Many commentators lament politicians' reliance on polling. Their reasoning relies on the trustee theory of representation.[12] Recall that, under this theory, elected officials are selected by the people and then turned loose to do as the official sees best.

However, under the delegate theory, representatives must carry out their duties in a way that would enact public policy that aligns with the preferences of the people who put them in office in the first place.

To do so, elected officials must rely on some mechanism for learning public opinion, and most politicians—especially those who want to get reelected (which most of them do[13])—are tuned in to polls, even when they claim they aren't. There is much debate in political science about whether politicians follow public opinion or, through their actions, they are instead swaying public opinion.[14] Setting aside that empirical debate for now, the question becomes, how do representatives learn what citizens want so that they, as delegates, can enact the preferences of the people? Certainly, they can rely on approaches like town halls, listening tours, or social media monitoring. These mechanisms have their benefits. Town halls and listening tours put politicians in front of voters to smile, shake hands, and kiss babies. They are great venues for politicking. Social media monitoring can help politicians learn about what issues are garnering attention online.

However, these ways of hearing from the voters share a common fatal flaw. While social media usage is ubiquitous in the United States, not everyone is on Facebook or X to share their political views. And, as we will discuss in the next chapter, very few people take the time to attend a meeting with an elected official. The people who engage in political discussion and debate on social media, and the people who attend town halls, are more engaged than the vast majority of Americans. Because these venues for civic discussion are driven by the loudest and most politically active citizens, they usually do not properly reflect the attitudes and beliefs of the larger community. In scientific terms, these fora are unrepresentative.

Elected officials, therefore, are better off when they listen to valid public opinion polls.[15] Because well-constructed surveys rely on decades of scientific work in sampling, statistics, psychology, and other fields, they offer representatives a more reliable and valid measure of public opinion. Polls provide elected officials with the information they need to execute their duties as delegates.

How Polling Works

Polling is simple and it's complicated. It is simple in that, when done correctly, it can provide an accurate, if imperfect, reading of public opinion.

However, getting it right—doing it correctly—can be quite complicated. Let's walk through a simplified explanation of the process.

First, as elementary as it may seem to some readers, let's cover what a public opinion poll is and what it's not. A public opinion poll is a series of questions about matters of public interest—typically politics, policy, or government—asked of a fairly large sample of people who are representative of a larger population of interest. We will cover many of these concepts in this section. A public opinion poll, as we use it here, is not a survey of consumers. There are many similarities between a consumer survey and a public opinion poll, but there are myriad differences, such as topics (Pepsi versus policy) and respondents (consumers versus voters).

Focus groups are also not polls. Focus groups are a qualitative research method used to uncover emotional reasons for behaviors or preferences—they ask "why," whereas polls are quantitative. Focus groups also have much smaller samples than polls, typically about eight participants, are conducted in an interactive or conversational way, and are rarely representative. For these reasons, focus group findings are limited and should almost never be reported quantitatively (for example, it would be inappropriate to say that 50 percent of focus group participants said they support building a wall on the southern border). That, of course, is not to say that focus groups are unimportant as a public opinion tool; they are very important and have their rightful place in public opinion research. For example, when the purpose is to develop messages that resonate with voters, it is important to hear voters discuss issues in their own words. Or when one wants to understand the emotional impact of a policy, getting voters to open up is a powerful tool.

A public opinion poll begins with a question that is translated into an objective. For example, a candidate might ask, "Where can I get more support for my campaign?" The pollster's objective is to "determine areas where the candidate's support is strongest and where it can be improved." Most readers will be familiar with polls commissioned and reported by major media outlets, such as the *Wall Street Journal*/NORC poll or the ABC News/YouGov poll. These polls typically start with the question, "Who is leading the presidential race?" or "What is the president's approval rating?"

Once the objectives for a poll have been defined, a pollster must write the questionnaire. The old cliché is that this is both art and science, and there is some truth to that. However, writing a good poll focuses more on the science than on the art. Research from several different fields of study converges here as pollsters formulate questions that are easy to read (educational science of reading and reading scores), easy to answer (survey science on response options that are comprehensive, non-overlapping, and match how people think about an issue), and unbiased (psychological research on bias). In addition to making sure the *questions* in a survey are right, pollsters must ensure the questionnaire itself is right, avoiding (to the extent possible) issues such as order bias, where one question alters or has the potential to alter the way respondents answer subsequent questions.

After a questionnaire is written, the questions are then asked of people called respondents; we call this sending the poll to the field. As with the other phases of conducting a poll, a host of decisions go into fielding a poll. Pollsters must make decisions such as how long will we leave our poll in the field, what is the population we want to understand (e.g., American adults, registered voters in a particular state), how many respondents do we need to answer our questions (what we call the sample size), how can we ensure the sample is representative of the population, and how do we want to deliver the questionnaire (by phone, on the web, by text message, or some combination of these). We must also determine which voters are most likely to show up to vote on Election Day, developing a so-called likely voter model.

When our raw data come back at the conclusion of our time in the field, we have yet more work to do. First, we have to remove bad data. Despite our best efforts, sometimes we get respondents who simply don't take a poll seriously—for example providing the same answer throughout the entire survey, speeding through it, or providing irrelevant answers to open-ended questions—and we have to remove them from the sample. Then we check to see if our sample is representative. Rarely do we actually collect a sample that reflects the population. Perhaps we have a sample that is 60 percent female from a state where women make up 54 percent of the population. Or we have too many older voters. Or too many Democrats. To ensure the final results are our best estimate of public opinion, we have to ensure our sample is representative of the population. To do so after we've completed the field time and have the raw data, we do what is called "weighting," a procedure in which we statistically adjust each response to make the final results reflect the actual composition of the population. So, in our example of a poll with 60 percent women in a state that is only 54 percent female, the responses of women will be given a slightly lower statistical weight so that the weighted sample is 54 percent women.

The final step is conducting an analysis. This may be as simple as reporting the toplines (75 percent of likely voters support work requirements for food stamp recipients) or some basic crosstabs (60 percent of men support the death penalty while only 52 percent of women do). It may also be as complex as conducting multiple regression analyses to determine how different factors impact a question independently of other factors. Only once all of this is done is a poll ready to be released.

As I said, this is a simplified explanation of how polling works. If you are interested in learning more about polling, I encourage you to read *How Did You Get This Number* by Anthony Salvanto, the head of polling for CBS News, or *Strength in Numbers* by G. Elliott Morris.

Types of Polls

In the previous section, I covered what a public opinion poll is and what it's not. But did you know there are several types of polls? There are, and they serve different purposes.

The polls that you may be most familiar with are media polls. These types of polls might include a horserace poll or an approval poll. Horserace polls are generally what come to mind when people hear about "the polls." They tell us which candidate is leading and which one is trailing in a given campaign. Approval polls tell us to what extent people approve or disapprove of the job an elected official is doing. These types of polls are widely reported in the media, hence their familiarity.

Candidates and campaigns also use several types of polls, and they are used primarily for strategic purposes—to make smarter campaign decisions. The most common ones are benchmark polls, brushfire polls, and tracking polls. Benchmark polls are lengthy surveys fielded at the beginning of a campaign, often before a candidate has officially declared that he or she is running. They provide the campaign information on the baseline state of the race such as the candidate's name ID (how well he or she is known) and the name ID of any competitors, what issues are important to the voters in the upcoming election, and message testing to determine the candidate's strengths and weaknesses and how to talk about the key issues.

Brushfire polls are short and focus on gathering information like movement in ballot choice and testing the impact of campaign events and communications, or things that happen beyond the campaigns' control, such as natural disasters or a spike in crime rates. Brushfire polls are run during the campaign to keep tabs on how things are going.

Campaigns also run tracking polls. These are very short surveys conducted on a rolling basis toward the end of the campaign. They provide key information about where a candidate stands in the horserace, what kind of late movement is happening, and where resources should be allocated or reallocated in the closing days and weeks of the campaign.

While candidates use polls to make strategic campaign decisions, elected officials and interest groups use polls to make governing decisions. These polls gather insights on citizens' support or opposition to certain policy proposals. Such policy polls can give elected officials an important glimpse into the minds of the people they represent. While your participation in all types of polls is important because each one provides candidates and elected officials with a critical link to the people, policy polls are the most important because they are the ones officeholders use to provide substantive representation.

How to Read Polls

Chances are you'll never have to read a benchmark or brushfire poll (unless you take my advice from chapter 2 and get involved in political campaigning). But you are likely to encounter the media polls on a regular basis. And a wise citizen is one who can deftly read a media poll and determine whether it's worth the paper it's written on. Because the truth of the matter is that many of them are not.

Before I get into reading a single poll, let me offer a few words of caution. It has become cliché to say it at this point, but there is a lot of truth in the adage that a single poll is just a snapshot in time. A single poll serves little predictive value, especially in trying to forecast something as unpredictable as an election. Rather than focusing on one single poll, a wise observer will pay more attention to polling trends and averages, in that order. Trends show the direction of movement. For example, if the Democratic candidate is leading for months on end but the Republican surges in the last few weeks of a campaign and approaches parity with the Democrat, that's more indicative of the state of the race than what any one poll can tell you.

Averages are not as good as trends but are still better than a single poll. Averages, such as those reported by RealClearPolitics or Ballotpedia, simply report the mean margin of all credible public polls, e.g., by how much one candidate is leading in the polls on average. Because of a statistical concept called regression to the mean, in which extreme findings are attenuated with more reasonable results upon repeated measurement, when you have polls that show a candidate down by a lot and the ones that show that same candidate leading by a lot, the truth is somewhere in between. A word of caution when considering polling averages: Not all polls are created equal. Even if you average 50 legitimate polls from 10 different reputable pollsters, there are still myriad differences—from turnout models to sampling approaches and more—that make comparing polls not a one-to-one proposition. Fellow pollster Adam Probolsky put it this way to me: Polling averages are "a vanilla, bison, sesame, hot sauce, donut milkshake." In less interesting (and certainly less disgusting) words, each poll is different, and you can't put them all together and get something good out of it. While Adam's correct from a purely statistical standpoint, I am more open to using a polling average to understand the state of the race than I am to using a single poll (and definitely more open to it than Adam is!).

Aside from reading too much into a single poll on the same topic, you would also be wise to look beyond the horserace. Look for other poll questions that indicate how people are thinking about the state of the nation. For example, look for polls that ask not only what people think is the most important issue but also which candidate or party they think is better on that issue. For example, if the economy is the most important issue facing the country, do voters think Republicans or Democrats are more trusted to address the issues facing the economy, such as reducing inflation, increasing employment, or adding jobs? Another key leading indicator is the enthusiasm gap. Which party's voters are more excited to go vote? If Democrats are more motivated to go vote, that does not bode well for Republicans, and vice versa.

One final word of caution when reading a public poll. Make sure you think about whether the poll you're reading is really telling you what you think it is. For example, are you reading a poll that tells you the Democratic candidate for president is ahead in the polls nationally? That poll is telling you very little about the state of the race because the presidency is not decided by a national popular vote but rather by the Electoral College in a series of state-by-state elections with varying electoral rules. The presidential election is not like the Super Bowl with one big contest. It's more akin to the World Series with several contests. You should think about whether the poll you are reading accounts for those kinds of constraints, because if they can't get the fixed features of government correct, how can you trust them to get variable outcomes, like elections, correct?[16]

With those warnings in mind, here are seven things you should consider when evaluating a publicly released poll: the margin of error, the sample, field dates, sponsor, pollster, question wording, and mode of delivery.

Margin of Error

The first thing you should look at when reading a poll is the margin of error. This statistic tells you how close the poll's result is to the real-world outcome based on the fact that the poll tests only a sample of people, not the entire population. When you read the margin of error, it will typically be reported as ± (read, plus or minus) X percentage points—for example, ±4.38 percentage points. What might be better named the margin of *sampling* error, it is the only source of error in a poll that we can quantify because it is calculated using numbers.[17] The reported margin of error is estimated using four numbers (because my colleague, Sarah Coffey, hates math, she made me remove the equation, so you can thank her): Sample size (how many people are surveyed), the population size (how many people are in the universe the pollster wants to make a claim about), the proportion (or percentage) of respondents who answer a question a certain way, and how precise the pollster wants to be (for example, is the pollster using a 95 percent confidence level or a 90 percent level?). Of these four variables, the sample size exerts the largest impact on the margin of error. Larger samples equate to lower margins of error, while smaller samples lead to larger margins of error. It makes sense, right? The more people who are asked, the more confident and precise the results will be.

However, the margin of error reports only one source of error in a poll—the inaccuracies created by sampling. There are, however, other sources of error in a poll that are not reported because they cannot be quantified.[18] One example is the likely voter model used. Different pollsters use different models, and since none of them are perfect, they introduce error into the poll.[19] How a question is phrased and the order in which questions are asked can also introduce bias, leading to unquantifiable error. A nonrepresentative sample can introduce error as well. Here, I am not talking about representation in terms of demographics because we can correct for that; I am talking about the fact that, sometimes, you just draw an odd sample that, despite being demographically identical to the population, does not reflect the larger targets in some important but unmeasurable way. Thus, when you consider a poll's margin of error, understand that it is reporting only one source of error and should not be considered a metric for total error in a poll.[20]

Sample

Sample is a jargony word that means "the people who took the poll." Think about making a pot of soup or sauce. You don't have to taste the whole pot to know how dinner is going to taste. All you need is a sample. Give the pot a good stir, then taste a spoonful. It's the same way in polling. To know what a population (that's the whole "pot" of people) believes, we just need a "spoonful," a small sample. But who makes up that sample can lead to different findings. Just like if you think you're sampling a pot of chicken and sausage gumbo, but you pull out a spoonful and it tastes like beef stew, you need to understand what happened.

Pollsters tend to sample from three different groups: American adults, registered voters, and likely voters. While there is a tremendous amount of overlap in the three populations, these three groups often have very different opinions. Those differences can lead to flawed analysis and decision-making when consuming a poll, so you should always look to see who a pollster sampled to better understand the claims an analyst (be it the pollster or a journalist, for example) makes about that poll. This is especially critical when you are comparing one poll to another. Let's briefly cover each of these three populations, which can be thought of as being contained within concentric circles—all likely voters are contained within the universe of registered voters, and all registered voters are contained within the universe of adults.

The "American adults" sample is the broadest (and arguably the most democratic) sample. And it's relatively straightforward. If the respondent is an American citizen and is eighteen years old or older, they are in the population and can be part of the sample. As I said, it's broad, and that makes sense. However, I also said it's arguably the most democratic sample, and that deserves a bit of explanation. As we covered in the introduction to this book, a democracy is ruled by the people, theoretically (though not often practically) as many people as possible. Thus, government theoretically should represent all people, not just the politically engaged. So, in theory, providing elected officials with the voice of the entire populace would lead to more democratic outcomes.

But, and take it from me, an academic political scientist and a political practitioner, theory and practice rarely align. Policymakers tend to focus on pleasing the people who put them in office: voters. This is where we start to narrow the circumference of our circle, next encountering the registered voter sample. These are all American adults (you have to be a citizen and eighteen or older to register), but they've taken the first step in the four-phase voting approach discussed in chapter 1. They have registered to vote. They are official. Sampling of registered voters often comes directly from the voter rolls, for example, when polling by phone or text messaging (more on modality shortly). Other times, such as when drawing a sample from an online panel, registration status is obtained by self-reporting, which has some drawbacks—especially related to the propensity to lie about being registered that comes from the desire to provide a socially acceptable answer—but those flaws are frequently overlooked.

Sampling likely voters gets tricky because there is no universally accepted definition of a "likely voter." This means that almost every pollster has his or her own definition of a likely voter, built on some kind of probability modeling. Some models are simple. If a voter has a documented (or self-reported) history of voting in three or four of the last four elections, they are considered a likely voter. We like to say that the best predictor of future behavior is past behavior; if people vote regularly in the past, they are likely to vote regularly in the future. Other models are more complex, asking people questions about the upcoming election, such as the date of the election, where their polling place is, what time of day they plan to vote, and others, and determining how serious someone is about voting based on knowing what they need to know to vote and having a plan to do it.

Still other likely voter models attempt to make predictions about the upcoming election to gauge a respondent's likelihood of voting. Will turnout be 45 percent? 55 percent? 65 percent? At each of those levels, what is the profile of the likeliest voters? What's the profile for someone who will vote and push turnout higher but might stay home and keep turnout low, and how does this specific respondent match that profile? Analysts then impute (assign) a likelihood score to each respondent, and only those above a certain score are classified as likely voters.

If it sounds complicated, that's because it can be. For the average consumer of polls, though, knowing the details of a specific pollster's likely voter model is not terribly important. It is certainly less important than understanding that there are often differences in attitudes between the three common samples and that who is sampled can—and, in many cases, likely *does*—alter the outcome of the poll. And the sample should certainly be considered when comparing polls or, as discussed previously, considering their averages.

Field Dates

The next thing you should look for when reading a poll is the field dates. These are the dates that the poll was "in the field," meaning respondents were being contacted and asked to respond to the poll's questions. When looking at the field dates, there are three things you should consider. First, how recent is the poll? Sometimes, older data are okay, especially on a topic you have reason to believe hasn't shifted much. For example, the number of people who support requiring voters to present a photo ID when casting a ballot remains fairly constant, so a poll that is a year old on that topic is probably still pretty accurate. A horserace poll in the governor's race that is a year old is worthless.

Another factor related to field dates you should consider is the duration. How long was the poll in the field? Sometimes, short field times are useful. Consider asking people for their immediate reactions to a debate. A pollster would want to capture those insights as immediately as possible, so a post-debate poll might be in the field for only a few hours, if that long. However, those types of instances are the exception to the rule. A poll that is in the field for only a day can really only tell pollsters what people were thinking on that particular day, or what only people who were available to respond on that day were thinking. Conversely, polls that are in the field for too long run the risk of having too many intervening issues impact respondents' thoughts, attitudes, behaviors, etc. The ideal field time is between three and seven days, preferably with a mix of weekday and weekend responses.

One final consideration vis-à-vis field dates is intervening events. I mentioned them previously for polls that are in the field for too long, but a major event can disrupt the analysis of a poll that is in the field for a reasonable duration. Consider, for example, a presidential approval poll that could have been in the field from September 10 through September 13, 2001. Because of the intervening events of 9/11, how people perceived President Bush's job performance on September 12 would likely have been radically different than their perceptions when that poll went to the field on the tenth. When evaluating a poll, you should know what was happening in the world when the poll was in the field to determine whether any major events may have skewed or shifted the results.

Sponsor

A fourth major concern when evaluating a public poll is its sponsor. Who paid for the poll? Many publicly released polls are sponsored by media organizations, each with their own biases that you should consider. But other polls are sponsored by partisan organizations looking to advance a specific agenda. While not every poll released for public consumption will be used to serve some hidden agenda, a wise polling consumer will still look for the identity of the sponsor and evaluate the poll based on that information.

You should also be skeptical of a poll for which you cannot quickly and easily determine a sponsor. While being unable to determine who paid for a poll is not always an intentional obfuscation on behalf of the sponsor, it should always be a red flag for you. While it may not be the case that the sponsor is trying to hide, it also very well may be the case. Another possibility is that the sponsor (or analyst, reporter, etc.) accidentally neglected to include the sponsor's identity. That raises the question in my mind, "If they aren't paying attention to the little details like identifying the sponsor, what else are they not paying attention to?" Whether the sponsor is intentionally hiding or simply forgetting to include their identification, it should make your alarm bells go off.

Pollster

To put it bluntly, there are good pollsters and there are bad pollsters. I spent more time deciding whether to even include this criterion than I did writing this section because if you're reading a poll in the media, chances are pretty good that you are not having to determine whether the pollster is good or bad. Instead, the media has already determined the poll was run by a good pollster rather than a bad one. The bad ones don't get press. (And if they do, it's not coverage of their polls!) You're only trying to understand to what extent they are good. There are several indicators of how good a pollster is.

First, ask yourself how accurate they've been in the past. But try not to get caught up *too* much on how the pollster performed "last cycle," meaning in the last election. Yes, it's important to know their track record of accuracy, but we all have bad years or even bad polls. One of the most high-profile bad polls in recent years was Ann Selzer's 2024 Iowa Poll, where she showed a Harris victory over Trump in Iowa that was a total miss. (More on the 2024 Iowa Poll miss in the conclusion of this chapter.) Look at how a particular pollster has performed over the years and whether they are getting more accurate.

Second, see if you can determine a pollster's "house effect." This is what we call their partisan bias. Some pollsters, like Rasmussen Reports (which, despite still bearing his name, is no longer Scott Rasmussen's company) has a Republican bias, while others, like PPP, have a Democratic bias. This means their polls, on average, will overestimate the level of support for the pollster's preferred party. Once you determine a pollster's house effect, you would be wise to adjust the poll's reported results slightly to account for that effect.

Third, you can look at pollster ratings. While ABC News shuttered 538, which was its pollster rating feature, in early 2025 (without releasing a ranking of pollsters for 2024), 538's founder, Nate Silver, continues to provide the most cited pollster ratings through his Silver Bulletin. ActiVote also has a ranking with a methodology different than Silver's, but it's worth noting that they reach very similar conclusions. That tells me, regardless of which rater you choose to look at, you're going to get a good idea of how good a pollster is.

Finally, there are professional markers you can look to as an indicator of a pollster's legitimacy. Several professional organizations exist for market research professionals, such as the American Association for Public Opinion Research (AAPOR) and the Insights Association. Membership in a professional association, especially AAPOR, is usually an indicator of a pollster's reputation because we commit to professional ethics as a requirement of membership. Unfortunately, AAPOR membership is restricted to individuals rather than to polling companies or organizations, so you would have to dig a bit deeper. For example, while the Center for Excellence in Polling is not an AAPOR member (because it's an organization), you would have to see who the individual pollster is (it's me!) and determine whether that person is an AAPOR member (I am!). One exception to the no-companies rule at AAPOR is in the transparency initiative. These are the companies and university survey research centers that are among the biggest names in polling and have gone through rigorous processes to show AAPOR that they "pledge to practice transparency in their reporting of survey-based research findings."[21]

Question Wording

The sixth thing you want to look at is how the questions are worded. Some questions are fairly standard, such as, "If the election for governor were held today, for which of the following candidates would you vote?" Some questions, on the other hand, are not as easy to ask. And it is those more difficult questions where bias creeps in to how a question is written. It is important to understand the term bias as I use it here. "Bias" is not shorthand that means "something I don't like." You may dislike the result of a poll, even strongly, but that doesn't mean it is biased. "Bias" is something that leads or could lead respondents to answer the question in a specific direction and in a systematic way.

Sometimes the bias is easy to spot. As political scientist Herbert Asher writes, "Some problems with the wording of questions are obvious, and may even be intentional, particularly [when] sponsors are seeking specific results."[22] If you ever saw a headline that read, "New poll: A majority of Americans oppose abortion," and you looked at the poll question and it read, "Would you support or oppose killing unborn children in the womb?" you'd know immediately the question is biased. The question wording would lead many respondents to state they oppose this policy (that's the specific direction), irrespective of their true feelings about abortion. But this question would not lead very many people to say they support the policy; most people who are swayed by the question wording are moving in one direction and not the other (that's the systematic way). Other times, the bias is harder to identify. Let's consider a real-world example.

In January 2024, *Florida Politics*, a left-leaning blog covering (you guessed it) politics in the Sunshine State, published an article written about a poll that included questions about a bill that was then being considered by the Florida legislature.[23] Here is how the question was worded: "House Bill 49, currently being considered by the Florida Legislature, proposes to change child labor law by allowing employers to schedule 16- and 17-year-old workers past 11 pm on a school night and more than 30 hours in a school week. Do you support or oppose this bill?" Now, there are several technical problems with this question, but the most glaring (and the most relevant for the current discussion) is its introduction of bias. Read the question again and see if you can spot the bias.

It is not as glaring an introduction of bias as the hypothetical abortion question above. The bias comes from the use of the phrase "child labor laws." This phrase is problematic in that it introduces bias in two ways. First, understandably, voters want to protect kids from exploitation. Nobody wants eleven-year-olds working in coal mines (I hear they have a lot of those in Florida!) or eight-year-olds chopping meat with a cleaver in a butcher shop. When you use the phrase "child labor laws," those are likely the images that people unconsciously think about. The use of that phrase likely biased respondents systematically to oppose the question, regardless of what words followed the phrase in the question.

The second way it introduces bias is more contextual. The proposed policy was to give older teens more freedom to set a job schedule that works for them. Using the "child labor law" phrase parroted the overwhelmingly negative framing of the bill preferred by the media and liberals who opposed the bill. For those respondents who were familiar (even slightly familiar) with the bill through media coverage, they had been primed to oppose it. This phrase activated that priming, leading to overwhelming opposition. If the plumbing in your kitchen sink has been primed with water, when you turn on the faucet, you're going to get water. In this case, the media had primed the faucet with a specific and preferred message, so when the pollster opened the faucet for voters, that message was what came out of the tap.

Survey Mode

The seventh and final piece of information you should consider is the mode of data collection. Mode is simply how the respondents were selected and answered the questions. A poll's mode is less critical than some of the other issues we've covered, but knowing it can provide some key insights into the poll. Let's start with how data can be collected.

Pollsters collect survey responses in several ways. Some use live calls, where someone from a call center dials (or their computer dials for them) a phone number to reach a specific voter. The caller then asks the respondent questions and enters their answers into a computer program. Other polling firms use a technology called interactive voice response (IVR). These calls are placed by a computer, the questions are read to the respondent via computer, and the respondent presses buttons that correspond to the answers they want to provide. Still others use online surveys and recruit respondents via an opt-in online panel, from an in-house panel, by text message, or through ads placed online in places like social media or other websites.

Each of these modes has benefits and drawbacks. For that reason, the ideal way to collect data is using a mixed-mode approach, which combines multiple data collection processes, such as IVR mixed with text-to-web. The reason mixed-mode sampling is ideal is that the benefits of one mode can balance out the pitfalls of the other. For example, IVR can only be used to contact landlines because federal regulations will not allow automated dialing of cell phones unless the person receiving the call has previously and specifically agreed to receive automated calls from the caller. That's why your doctor's office can use autodialing to remind you about your appointment, but pollsters cannot autodial your cell phone. Also, certain states, like California and Minnesota, prohibit totally the use of IVR, meaning pollsters must do live dials only in those states. That means a poll conducted with IVR is going to reach a very (*very*) narrow subset of the population—those with a landline phone. Guess who that is. If you guessed older people and people in rural areas without reliable cell service, you'd be correct. That's why all-IVR polling is effectively dead, although some pollsters still use it because it is inexpensive compared to live calling. To balance that IVR sample, you'd need another mode of data collection to reach younger, urban voters. That's where something like text-to-web comes in handy.

To help you understand your analysis of a poll's mode, here are some of the most popular data collection methods and their major drawbacks:

- **Live calls:** People, as I discuss more in the next section, are social creatures. Part of our social nature is the desire to be liked and to please others. Therefore, when a respondent talks to a live person on the other end of the phone, they are more likely (compared to interviews completed electronically, either through IVR or online) to give answers they think the interviewer wants to hear. Rather than giving their honest answer, they'll provide the "right" answer—the one they think is socially acceptable. This is called social desirability bias and is the primary disadvantage of live calls.
- **Interactive voice response (IVR):** This is also known as robo-polling or autodialing. The major flaw with IVR is that it can only be used to contact landlines, meaning it reaches a segment of the population that is older and more rural or is otherwise likely unrepresentative of the whole population.
- **In-house panels:** These are lists of respondents maintained by (and often heavily incentivized by) research organizations. When the organization wants to field a poll or other survey research project, they contact these respondents, who then take the survey. While in-house panels can be recruited and

maintained to provide excellent representativeness, as Pew Research Center's American Trends Panel does, the major flaw with them is that the respondents are repeat or "professional" survey takers. Academic research has shown that repeat survey takers pose myriad threats to data quality and "have consistently lower levels of political interest and engagement."[24]

- **Opt-in online panels:** These panels are lists of respondents who sign up to take surveys through various companies, and researchers pay to have their surveys sent to these panelists. Opt-in panels present the same "professional" respondent problem discussed above. Additionally, these panels may not be representative of the population in important, non-demographic ways. They also require researchers to rely on self-reported behavior (which is often unreliable) on things like whether they are registered to vote and how frequently they have voted in the past.
- **Text and text-to-web:** Many researchers are moving to this mode in which respondents receive a text message from the survey center inviting them to participate in a survey. The respondent then completes the survey in one of two ways, depending on the research organization. Some will continue asking the respondent the questions via text, and their answers are recorded that way. This is good for fairly short surveys. The other possibility is that the respondent is provided with a link and must click the link to complete the survey online. A major drawback of these modes is that older voters (those who are more likely to vote than younger people) may be uncomfortable clicking through a link from an unknown number, meaning the sample is missing a critical demographic.

As you can see, each of the major modes of polling has a critical flaw, which is why mixed-mode polling is ideal—far from perfect, mind you, but still preferable to single-mode surveys. But, as I said earlier, a poll's mode is good to know, but modality is rarely fatal. Indeed, the good news is that a lot of research lately has shown that results are not significantly affected by mode.[25]

Those are the seven things you should look for when evaluating a public poll: margin of error, sample, field dates, sponsor, pollster, question wording, and mode. If a poll doesn't provide these seven things, whoever releases the poll is being insufficiently transparent, and it would be wise to ignore the poll or treat it with deep skepticism. And if in your evaluation of these seven criteria, something seems off—it doesn't pass the sniff test—you should treat the poll with extreme caution.[26] In fact, the more you can ignore single polls and focus on trends, themes, and averages, the better.

Common Criticisms of Polls

On the day after Valentine's Day 2023, I testified on a bill that was being heard in committee in the Indiana House of Representatives. Before I go any further, yes, my wife made the trip with me, so we were together on Valentine's Day. And no, I did not count the committee hearing as our Valentine's date.

In my testimony before that House committee, I told the members of the committee that "a recent survey of likely voters in Indiana found that three-quarters—76 percent—of voters said they support requiring voters to provide a photo ID in order to cast an absentee ballot," and later that "more than two-thirds of Indiana voters oppose sending unsolicited absentee ballot applications. The same poll I referenced earlier reported that 68 percent of voters—including large Republican and independent majorities and a strong plurality of Democrats—oppose this confusing practice."

In response to my testimony, one legislator who opposed the bill in question asked me, "That poll had only 500 responses. Why do you think that can tell me what more than a million Hoosiers think?" This is a common criticism of polls—that the sample size is too small to accurately represent the voice of a population that is magnitudes larger.

Polling (and survey research more broadly) is built on the foundation of an entire scientific literature in mathematics and statistics that supports drawing conclusions about a population based on a small sample. I won't go into the details on that vast literature, but Pew Research Center's Survey Research Director, Courtney Kennedy, has an excellent YouTube video on sampling that you should check out if you are craving more details.[27]

Although I won't go into detail on sampling here, perhaps an example will help explain the concept. When you go to the doctor's office, they can draw a small vial of your blood and tell you a lot about your health—everything from cholesterol levels to blood sugar. They don't need to take the entire gallon and a half of blood out of your body to test it all. In the same way, pollsters take a small sample of the population, test it, and tell us that 95 out of 100 times, the results will be within a few percentage points of that poll's results. A poll with a sample size of 500 (meaning 500 people completed the survey), for example, has a margin of sampling error of 4.38 percentage points in each direction.

Consider this real-life example. In September 2024, the Center for Excellence in Polling, the organization where I lead polling, released a report showing that 87 percent of voters say that an individual should have to be a US citizen to vote in American elections.[28] The survey's sample size was 975, giving it a margin of sampling error of 3.14 percentage points. That means that if we were to repeat this poll 100 times, in 95 or more of those polls, the percentage of voters who support a citizenship requirement for voting in American elections would be within 3.14 percentage points of this result, or between about 84 percent and 90 percent.

As we covered earlier, several factors influence the margin of sampling error I've just illustrated. As these two examples—the hypothetical and the real-world—demonstrate, sample size is the primary driver of the margin of error. As the sample size increases, the margin of sampling error declines. The more people you ask, the less error you will have.

Other factors exert much less mathematical influence on the margin of error. One is the confidence level. I discussed the 95 percent confidence level above—that if I rerun a poll, the results will be close to the first result 95 times out of 100. If I decrease my confidence level to 90 (results will fall within the margin of error 90 times out of 100), my margin of sampling error goes down slightly because I'm giving myself more space to be wrong. Conversely, if I move to the 99 percent confidence level, my margin of error goes up, giving me less space to be wrong. Most pollsters operate at the 95 percent confidence level.

The other primary mathematical driver of the margin of error is the proportion. I can be slightly more confident when the result is 87 percent than when it is 52 percent. Again, the decrease in the margin of error created by an increased proportion is smaller than the decrease created by an increase in sample size. Most pollsters set their proportion to 50 percent because it creates the highest margin of error, making it the most conservative estimate, leaving more room to be wrong.

I alluded to a second common critique of polls earlier: "I've never been called to take a poll, and neither has anyone I know." As I said earlier, maybe you have, and you refused to participate. However, there are a lot of reasons that you might not have received a call. As an example, you might be on the do-not-call registry, which is an opt-in list of phone numbers marketers are prohibited from calling. The list is managed and enforced by the Federal Trade Commission, an agency of the federal government tasked with ensuring fair business practices, including how businesses interact with consumers. While political polling and other legitimate market research surveys are not covered by the do-not-call restrictions, many abide by them out of respect for the individual's wishes or to avoid having to fight a protracted battle defending why they called individuals on the registry.

Another reason you might not be called is that you might be outside the population as the pollster defines it. For example, if a pollster is surveying only voters who have voted in three or more of the past four elections, but you've only been registered to vote for the last two elections, you wouldn't show up on their list.

However, the most likely reason that one individual has never been contacted is that pollsters contact only a small number of participants for each poll. According to Statista, a website that reports statistics on tens of thousands of topics, America is home to 161 million registered voters,[29] and as we saw in chapter 1, nowhere near that many vote regularly. So, let's take the simple number of 161 million, and say that the pollster has defined the population as registered voters. A typical nationwide public opinion poll will sample only about 1,000 of those registered voters. So, as long as you are registered to vote, your probability of being contacted is small—about 0.000006—but that's exactly the same as everyone else's in the population. Those are still better odds than winning the lottery, and it costs you nothing to respond to a survey!

A third common criticism of polling goes something like this: *I don't know anyone who thinks like that/supports that policy/is voting for that candidate, so there's no way that poll is right.* As I said earlier in this chapter, people are social creatures. We are designed and often nurtured to be around other people. People shape our thinking, alter our behavior, laugh with us in good times, and support us in bad times. We are meant to be around other people. And when we get to choose who we are around, we tend to surround ourselves with people like us—those who look like us, think like us, and vote like us. We put ourselves into an insular, largely homogeneous community. We put ourselves in a bubble.

But there is a whole wide world outside of our bubble. Beyond the bounds of our homogeneous community, people think differently than we do. They have different values and worldviews, different lived experiences. And (gasp!) they vote differently than we do. Sadly, we rarely talk to others who are different from us, especially those who are politically different. In fact, deep relationships with people of the other party have become anathema in America today. Consider the following statistics. In a 2014 survey, Pew Research Center found that 15 percent of Democrats and 17 percent of Republicans would be unhappy "if a member of [their] immediate family . . . were going to marry" someone of the opposite party,[30] and in 2016, Pew reported that only eight percent of Democrats and nine percent of Republicans were married to someone from the opposite party.[31]

But it's not just the marriage relationship that is marked by a partisan divide. Friendships are even more homogeneous. According to a series of surveys conducted by YouGov, friendships with people who hold "very different political opinions" are on the decline. In 2016, 10 percent each of Democrats and Republicans said they had no friends with "very different political opinions." By 2020, that number was up slightly to 12 percent among Republicans, and it had more than doubled among Democrats, with 24 percent of Democrats saying they had no friends with differing political views.[32]

The fact is that people are social creatures, and we increasingly sort ourselves into like-minded groups. So, it is becoming increasingly likely that we truly don't know anyone who thinks, believes, acts, or votes differently than we do. Unlike people, however, polls are not social creatures. Polls aren't conducted in bubbles. Public opinion polls are constructed and executed to ask questions of a more widely representative sample, not just those people in our own bubbles. So, if you see a poll and you think, "I don't know anyone who supports that!" don't make a snap judgment that the poll is wrong. Perhaps take the opportunity to reflect on your own friend group and consider expanding it to people who don't necessarily think like you do but will love and respect you just the same.

These criticisms, while common, are simply misguided and reflect a deep misunderstanding of polling. I believe, however, that these critiques are actually proxy arguments. I think people are wary or distrustful of polls, but they lack the technical knowledge and language to articulate their true concerns.[33] This, I believe, points to a larger, more pernicious problem. People mistrust polls because polls are, at times, misused or abused.

The Misuse and Abuse of Polling

Of course, there are ways that polls can be wrong unintentionally. We've covered some of the sources of error above, and those errors can lead to fatal flaws. That's one reason you might see a polling firm be one of the best in the country during one election and fly completely off the rails the next. Polls can go bad because they are inherently fickle, and they can go bad because we pollsters sometimes make mistakes. But that's not what this section is about. There are also bad actors out there who intentionally lead people astray. And when they do, they ruin polling for the rest of us.

Some of those bad actors use flawed polling to advance an agenda that does not align with the true wishes of voters. Take the earlier poll we discussed about teen work in Florida. Despite that poll being deeply flawed, a liberal blog published it in an effort to undermine the legislation then being considered by the Florida legislature. While my organization, the Center for Excellence in Polling, did not poll that issue in Florida around the same time, we have polled it and other teen work policies elsewhere and found bipartisan support for allowing older teenagers to work without unduly restrictive regulations.[34]

Organizations also occasionally engage in this type of behavior. These organizations have pet policies they want legislatures to enact into law, so they commission or conduct a bad poll, put the results in front of legislators without full transparency, and try to use the elected official's sense of duty to accurately represent his or her constituents as a battering ram for their agenda.

Sometimes the media are to blame for sowing distrust in polls. One way they can do this is by reporting on low-quality polls from questionable pollsters. Some media outlets, especially the national ones, have high standards for which polls they report. Others are not as trustworthy. Another way media outlets can misrepresent the polls is by cherry-picking the data they want to share. As an example, a cable news channel with a certain partisan bent might breathlessly report on a poll showing their preferred candidate leading in a race while failing to cover other polls that show their preferred candidate behind or ignoring a trendline showing their candidate in freefall (but still in the narrowest of leads). Their reporting of *that poll* may be technically accurate, but their coverage of *the race* is deeply flawed and misleading to their audience. Fake news, indeed.

Another misuse of survey research is push polling. Let me be as clear as possible to start this section: Push polls are not legitimate survey research. At all. They are abusive calls disguised as polling. Push polls differ from legitimate survey research in at least two primary ways. First, there is the issue of how many people are contacted. Authentic polling has a scientifically collected sample of around 500 or 1,000 respondents. Push polls contact many, many times that number of people.

Second, rather than attempting to measure public opinion (which is the goal of legitimate polling), push polls instead seek to persuade people, usually with universally negative statements about a candidate, party, or policy.[35] Some legitimate polls test negative messages, but push polls take the negativity to the extreme. A negative message seeks to understand how voters respond to new information with a question such as, "Would you be more or less likely to support this candidate if you knew he supports requiring a photo ID to vote?" A push poll would take that "hit" against the candidate to the brink with something along the lines of, "Would you support this candidate if you knew he was a raging white supremacist racist who supports voter ID, which is the modern equivalent of Jim Crow laws keeping Black, Indigenous, transgender people of color from voting and threatens to lynch them on site if they even try?" As a real-world example, here is what would be considered a push poll had it been disguised as a legitimate survey and not an X post of some random social media "influencer":

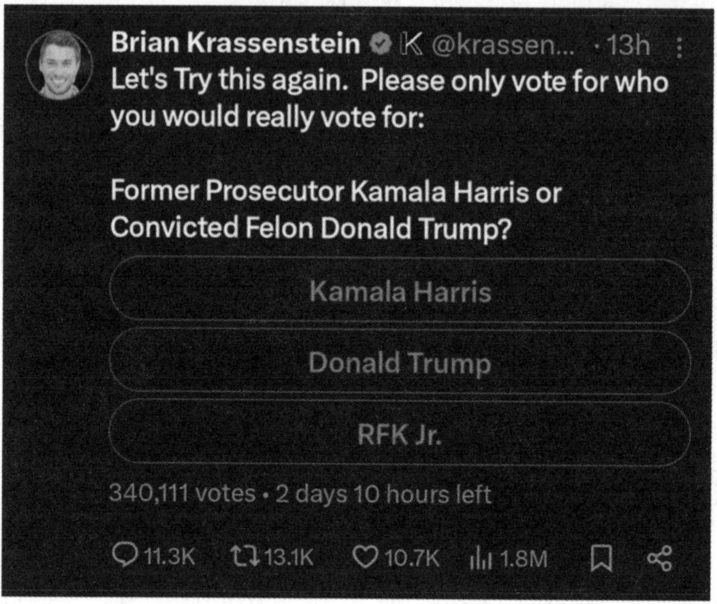

Source: https://x.com/krassenstein/status/1816477014519390323 And, for the record, of the nearly half million votes cast, Trump "won" this push poll, 79% to 16%. Talk about a major backfire!

You can see how push polling is a wolf in sheep's clothing, disguising itself as valid survey research and undermining the public's confidence in legitimate polling. It's a major reason why the American Association for Public Opinion Research strongly condemns the use of push polling because of its misleading effect on the public[36] and requires its members to abide by a code of ethics forbidding the practice.[37]

Before you think I'm going to let pollsters off the hook, don't worry. I'm not. Sometimes pollsters act poorly and unprofessionally. One example is when pollsters withhold unfavorable data. Of course, we aren't the only ones who can be guilty of this—media organizations, politicians, our clients, and others can all choose not to release important information from a poll. This is especially problematic in policy polling when polls are used to convince elected officials to create public policy. When elected officials seek to make decisions that their voters support and avoid ones that their voters oppose, they need the relevant information. Withholding unfavorable results deprives representatives of the ability to represent their people.

Despite this misuse, polls are important. Unfortunately, to get good polls, we must understand that some bad ones will also be released. Fortunately, we can simply ignore the bad ones. In chapter 5, we'll learn about Blackstone's Ratio, a legal concept that I'll alter here to fit the current topic: It's better to suffer through ten bad polls than miss one good one. However, to get the good ones, citizens must be willing to participate in polls when the opportunities arise.

Why Participation in Polls Matters

Polls are an important feature of the American political landscape. As I discussed earlier, they are the best way for policymakers to hear the voice of the people. When elected officials review the polls, as the George Gallup quote that opened this chapter makes clear, they are listening to the people. And, as we've seen, they are doing so in a way that is more systematic and reliable than other methods of collecting public opinion. Participating in a poll is a low-cost, low-stakes way of getting your voice heard in the halls of power. Sure, you could write a letter or call your elected official (and the next chapter encourages you to do so!), but very few people take the time to do so (again, see the next chapter). Thus, participating in a poll adds your voice to a chorus of others, and that chorus gets the attention of the men and women who will be asking for your vote again soon.

Aside from getting your voice heard, there are other reasons to participate in polling. Polls rely on representative samples, allowing analysts to make claims about the population's preferences. When you take part in a poll, you are filling a slot in a grid that, when filled, makes the poll's sample look like the whole target population.

Let's consider a poll of 1,000 respondents with a target of likely voters. In that sample, there will be about 520 women, 280 independent or unaffiliated voters, 380 voters aged 18 to 44, and 390 voters with a college degree. So, if you are a young, independent, and educated woman, you're playing an important role in helping fill out the sample. Just like if you're an older, working-class, Republican man. Perhaps you're a middle-aged, educated, Democratic woman; pollsters need to hear your voice, too. When this chorus of Americans comes together nicely, elected officials tune in to the melody.

Conversely, when a sample is not representative, whether that's in a demographic way or in some other sense that can't be quantified, a poll is flawed and paints an inaccurate portrait of the public's views. In those instances, if elected leaders were to follow the polls, they run the risk of enacting unrepresentative policy. You've surely heard the adage, "garbage in, garbage out." That's what happens when policymakers follow bad polls. They get garbage information about public sentiment and produce garbage policy as a result.

Smoky Bear, the US Forest Service's advertising mascot, reminds us that "only you can prevent forest fires." Well, I'm here to tell you that you can prevent policy dumpster fires, too. When you participate in polls, lending your voice to the quality data that is shared with policymakers, you help prevent garbage policy from being enacted.

In short, participating in polls is important because polls are important, and polls are important because elected officials use them to make important decisions that impact the lives of everyone in their city, county, state, or country. Of course, polls are not meant to "replace more active modes of participation,"[38] like those discussed in the other chapters, but lending your voice to a poll is important just the same. Let's turn now to the Democracy InAction Survey and see why our fellow Americans don't participate in polls.

Democracy InAction Survey

As we saw earlier in the chapter, response rates to political polls are typically around 1 to 2 percent. However, in the Democracy InAction

Survey, 43 percent of respondents say they have participated in a political poll. Perhaps many of them are counting the seemingly political poll they were currently taking when they answered that question. Or maybe because they belong to an opt-in online panel, they have a greater opportunity to be selected to take political polls.[39] Regardless, I am thankful for a sample in which nearly half of the respondents had taken polls because it provides what survey researchers call an over-sample, meaning we get more people from a particular group. Often, we do this so that we have a larger sample size from a group (and a resulting smaller margin of sampling error) in order to make more confident predictions about that group. In this survey, it was just luck! Sometimes that happens to us pollsters.

So, with our healthy sample of participants and even more robust sample of non-participants, let's dive into the data. For those of you who just cringed, don't worry. Just like in the first two chapters (and the two that follow this one), I will briefly summarize the findings, so you can skip ahead to the conclusion.

Apathy plays no role in avoiding polls, but it does decrease feelings of personal responsibility to take them. Alienation, on the other hand, increases polling avoidance and, surprisingly, increases feelings of personal responsibility for taking polls. I'll offer some thoughts on some of these surprising findings in the conclusion.

Now, for those interested in the technical aspects of the results, read on. All others, feel free to skip to the conclusion.

Polling Avoidance

In this chapter, my first dependent variable is Polling Avoidance. This is, again, an additive index variable composed of two undemocratic behaviors related to responding to political polls. Participants who said they have refused to take a poll and/or hung up on a political poll-taker were coded as having engaged in undemocratic polling behavior—avoiding lending their voice to the chorus of citizens whose views help shape a representative government. The higher the number, the more undemocratic polling behaviors in which the respondent admits to having engaged.

Unlike the voting and campaigning behaviors we explored in the previous two chapters, where apathy significantly increased undemocratic actions, we see here that apathy does not play a role in whether respondents avoid taking polls. The coefficient for the Apathy variable, while positive as expected, fails to reach statistical significance.

Alienation, on the other hand, continues to play a positive and significant role in undemocratic behavior. The more alienated an individual feels, the more he feels like he does not belong in the system, the more undemocratic acts he undertakes. This is, indeed, what we saw in the first two chapters—*alienation increases civic avoidance.*

Figure 3.1: Polling Avoidance

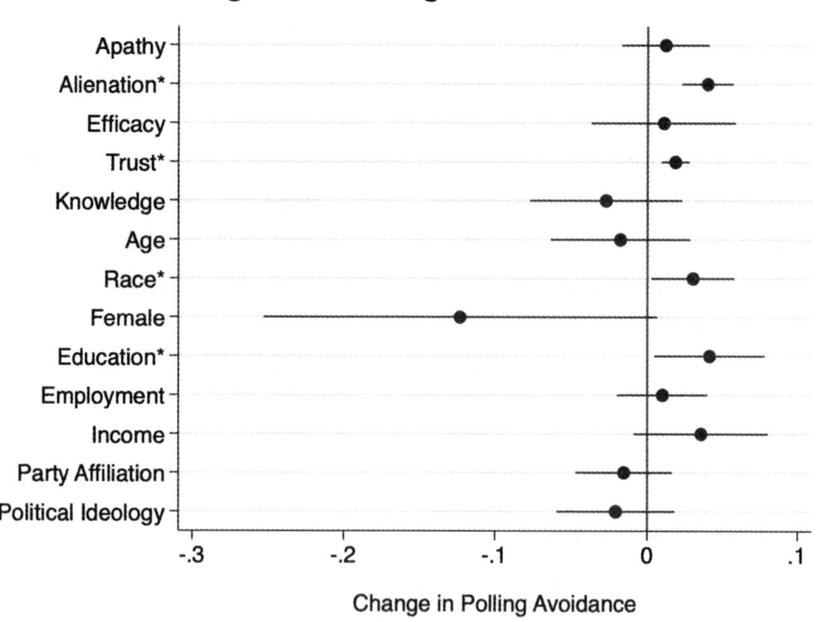

Apathy does not impact an individual's avoidance of polling, but Alienation increases avoidance. See Appendix D for methodological and modeling information.

Of the control variables included in the regression model, only three reach statistical significance: Trust, Race, and Education. More trusting individuals are more likely to avoid taking polls. Perhaps this is because they trust other people to take the polls, so they themselves do not have to; or maybe they simply have greater trust in the institutions to represent the will of the people and thus do not bother contributing their voice to the poll.

Recall from the introduction that Race is a categorical variable, so while each category is assigned a number, there is no logical increase or decrease in the values. Thus, to explain why Race is significant in this model, I explored how respondents of various races avoided polls relative to respondents from other races. Using multiple points of reference, I found two significant comparisons. First, Asians are coded as 1 in the dataset, so they are the natural point of comparison because the positive relationship we see in the results indicates movement upward from 1, the Asian respondents. Compared to Asian respondents, two other races stand out. Hispanic respondents and White respondents are both significantly more likely than Asians to avoid taking polls. Second, when Whites are treated as the baseline, only Asians are significantly less likely to avoid polls. No other races (including Hispanics) are statistically different from Whites in their polling participation or avoidance.

To explain the significant result on Education, I undertook a similar analysis. A major difference, however, is that the Education variable, while categorical, has a natural value—higher numbers are associated with more formal education. Still, to understand the significant relationship revealed in the results, I compared respondents using a baseline of "less than high school," coded 1 in the data. This exploration revealed that respondents with a four-year college degree are significantly more likely than the least educated respondents to avoid participating in polls. No other group was significantly different.

Feelings of Personal Responsibility to Take Polls

Turning again from behavior to beliefs, we see that Apathy plays a negative and significant role in respondents' personal responsibility toward participating in political surveys. As anticipated, the more apathetic one feels—the less they care about civic life—the less responsibility they feel to take a poll.

Alienation, however, exhibits a countervailing effect on feelings of poll-taking responsibility. The more alienated participants are significantly *more* likely to say that they feel a personal responsibility to take a poll. While alienation did not play a role in civic attitudes toward voting (chapter 1), we saw that it did increase personal responsibility to volunteer for a campaign (chapter 2). So far, contrary to expectations, apathy and alienation are not reinforcing one another. Instead, when it comes to civic attitudes, they are playing opposite roles. However, apathy's negative pull is much greater in its effect than any positive impact of alienation.

Trust, Political Knowledge, and Employment are the only control variables to reach statistical significance. Trust performs exactly as expected. Higher levels of trust are associated with a greater personal responsibility to complete political surveys when asked.

Results on the Political Knowledge variable are at odds with expectations: Higher levels of political knowledge are associated with *lower* feelings of personal responsibility to take polls. Perhaps this reflects cynicism—that people who know more about the system believe elected officials do not follow the polls, so they do not feel a responsibility to participate. Maybe it reflects—even adds more evidence for—the (misguided) rational approach to civic participation we discussed in chapter 2. Regardless of the explanation, Political Knowledge continues to play an interesting and puzzling role by decreasing feelings of civic responsibility.

Figure 3.2: Personal Responsibility to Take Polls

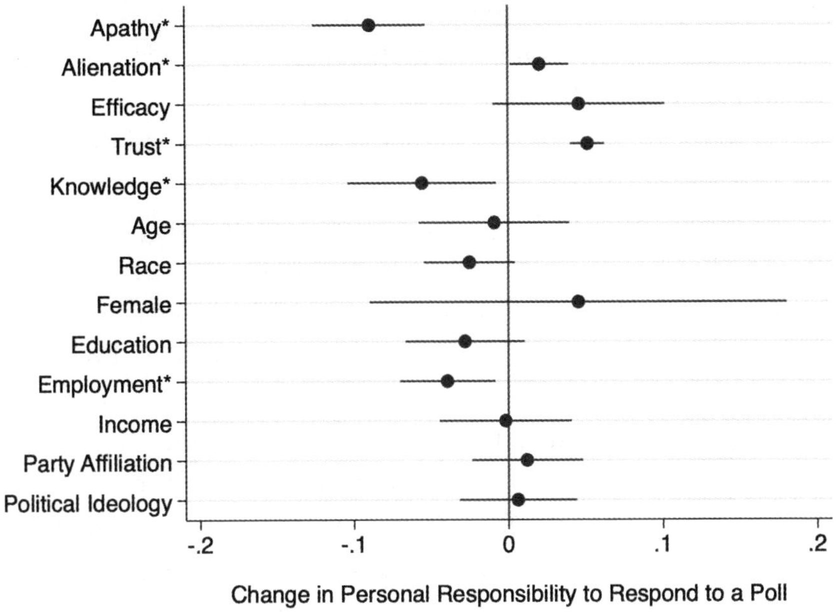

Apathy and Alienation play countervailing roles in an individual's feelings of personal responsibility to respond to a poll. Apathy decreases such feelings, while Alienation increases them. See Appendix D for methodological and modeling information.

Employment, like Race (as discussed above), is a categorical variable with no natural pattern of progression, so its significant result in this model requires a bit of extrapolation. "Employed full-time" is coded 1 in the data, so I began by using it as the baseline for comparison and uncovered only one significant difference between that and another category. Compared to full-time workers, respondents who are disabled or retired feel significantly less responsible for taking polls. No other category of employment was significantly different from full-time work. I also created and tested two additional variables, one comparing full-time workers to everyone else and a second comparing full-time and part-time workers to everyone else. Neither approach yielded statistically significant results.

Conclusion

Polls are important. I get that you may read that and think, *Of course the pollster says polls are important.* But let me assure you: I don't believe polls are important because I am a pollster; I am a pollster because I believe polls are important. Elected officials pay attention to the polls because polls are the voice of the people who elect those officials. It is my honor, my privilege, to bring your voice into the policymaking process. If I did not believe the voice of the people—*your voice*—was important, I would not do what I do. So, I'll say it again: Polls are important.

Polls are important because, as I have said throughout this chapter, they are your voice. Too often, the voice of the voter is relegated to Election Day and not heard in the policy process. Where the voters' voice is absent, the void is filled by special interests. Elected officials do not get elected by NARAL or the NRA. Neither Maggie's List nor EMILY's List gets a single vote in elections. But when you don't share your opinions with your representatives, whether through polls or direct contact (more on that in the next chapter), rest assured, those organizations and dozens, if not hundreds, of others just like them will not hesitate to share theirs.

As pollsters, we do our level best to accurately represent your voice. But ours is an imperfect science. There are many mistakes we can make—everything from drawing a bad sample to writing a question in a way that accidentally introduces bias. And sometimes we get it just plain wrong. Take the 2024 Iowa Poll, for example. On the weekend before the 2024 presidential election, legendary (more on that choice of adjective in a moment) pollster Ann Selzer released the final poll of the Iowa electorate, showing Democratic candidate Kamala Harris leading Republican nominee Donald Trump by three percentage points in the Hawkeye State.[40] It caused quite a stir for two reasons: The Democratic presidential candidate hadn't won Iowa in 12 years, and it had been much longer than that since Ann Selzer made the wrong call.[41]

By the time she released that 2024 report, Selzer had been conducting the Iowa Poll for nearly four decades. For almost 40 years, she had been an impeccable pollster with an unimpeachable record, earning an A+ rating from Nate Silver, who is not a pollster himself but is one of the industry's leading prognosticators and scorers.[42] She had released a final Iowa Poll the weekend before the presidential election for decades, always performing better than the average of other pollsters, even in the hard-to-poll elections during which Donald Trump was on the ballot. Selzer is, indeed, a legend. But she got that one wrong. It happens to all of us. As Selzer herself put it, sometimes "science has a way of . . . humbling the scientist."[43]

But don't let the bad polls (or even the bad pollsters) keep you from speaking up. We cannot do what we do without you.

I get that you may not care about polls. But let me remind you that there is something you care about. Remember when I asked you to think about what that something is? Because polls are a vital part of a functioning democracy, when you participate in them—even when they have nothing to do with that thing you care about—you are contributing to democratic health. And keeping our republic intact remains your best shot at advancing whatever it is you care about.

I also know that it may not be your apathy that keeps you from participating in polls. Because of our sampling methods, you don't get to choose when you participate in polls, even if you're in a panel. As a result, apathy may not impact participation in the same way that it does other behaviors. This may be the reason the results of the analysis in this chapter showed that apathy's relationship with polling avoidance does not reach statistical significance. Still yet, my encouragement to you is this. When the phone rings or you get a text message that invites you to take a political poll, remember what it is you care about and take the poll. And even if you don't care, please don't let not caring stand in the way of you adding your voice to the choir.

Because your voice matters. I have said it throughout this book, and I will say it again (and again in the next chapter, and again in the one after that, and again in the conclusion): You belong in this democracy.

Your voice has a place in our polls. And anyone who tells you otherwise is a damned liar. If you feel alienated from the system, you may even have feelings of personal responsibility to take polls; the results indicate that it is more likely than not that you do. But that alienation decreases participation in polls, and it might lead you to consider hanging up the next time you get a call. But please don't.

Whether you feel apathetic, alienated, neither, or both, your participation in political polls matters. You are helping ensure that the sample we draw is representative of the universe. You are filling an important place in our poll, a vital block in our recruitment grid. More importantly, though, you are letting your elected officials know just how you feel. There are relatively few ways to do that. Polling is one of them, so don't let the chance pass you by. Another way is by contacting your elected officials directly, and that's the democratic activity to which we'll turn in the next chapter.

Three Questions

1. In your view, should politicians pay attention to the polls? Why or why not?
2. What are some reasons you think people don't want to participate in polls?
3. What is your view of why the polls have "gotten it wrong" lately?

Three Actions

1. If you get a call from a pollster, don't hang up. Your voice matters just as much as the next person they are going to

call, so share your opinions with the pollster. And be honest with them. Most of them are professional researchers; you aren't going to hurt their feelings. They genuinely want to know what you think, and you're the only person who can tell them honestly.

2. Many pollsters are using non-probability online samples to conduct their polling projects. Join an online survey panel and hope for the opportunity to answer questions about politics and policy. And when it comes along, take it.
3. Even if you never get the opportunity to participate in a poll, you can still be a wise consumer of them. Learn more about polling by doing a deep dive into one. Find a news story or other article about a poll. Then find the poll and run it through the evaluative process I covered in this chapter. You never know what kind of biases or mistakes you might uncover!

Additional Resources

1. https://www.pewresearch.org/course/public-opinion-polling-basics/
2. https://www.sciline.org/elections/surveys-polling/
3. https://aapor.org/election-polling-resources/
4. Political scientists Barbara Norrander and Clyde Wilcox provide an excellent, more detailed primer on statistics and public opinion in their textbook, *Understanding Public Opinion*.[44]

CHAPTER 4

PETITIONING THE GOVERNMENT

"Remember, write to your Congressman. Even if he can't read, write to him."

WILL ROGERS

In what year were you born? That's a question pollsters like me ask regularly. It's one of the easy ones, and we ask it to get a sample that is representative. But I'm asking you here for a different reason. Those born before 1980 came into a world with a much different policy environment for driving under the influence. That's because in 1980, one woman in California called her state legislature and started the ball rolling on a series of policy reforms that would reshape America's criminal justice system for decades to come.

I have told you repeatedly throughout the previous chapters that you should find a reason to get involved in politics and civic affairs. You need to find something you care enough about that will spur you to action. That's what happened to Candace Lightner. She found her something to care about when, one day in 1980, thirteen-year-old Cari Lightner was walking to a church event and was struck and killed by an intoxicated driver.

Did you know that before the 1980s, each state was permitted to set its own minimum legal drinking age and maximum level of blood alcohol content (BAC) for impaired driving? After Cari's death at the hands of a drunk driver, Candace founded MADD, which stands for Mothers Against Drunk Driving, to work to change the laws in California, where Cari lived and died. Candace's something (in this case, *someone*) to care about and her action in petitioning the government changed the course of American public policy.

Candace's organization took off. Just four years after Cari's death, in 1984, Candace and dozens of other moms stood alongside President Ronald Reagan as he signed a law setting a national minimum drinking age—21. Sixteen years passed before Candace and the moms were back at the White House, this time in an Oval Office signing with President Bill Clinton, who set a national BAC limit of .08 for drunk driving.

MADD's policy advocacy continues to this day, nearly fifty years after Cari was killed and Candace started the organization.[1] But what's important for you to keep in mind is that Candace and countless other moms (and later dads and their kids—think SADD, Students Against Drunk Driving) found something they cared enough about. Candace started as a one-woman, elected-official-contacting machine. And she shaped the course of American law because of it. The other thing to note is that Candace and MADD were patient. They didn't get big policy wins right away. It took years and decades to accomplish the policy that we take for granted today.

Candace Lightner was a Mama Bear. You've heard of Mama Bears? Yeah, them. They're scary as hell when you mess with their cubs. Four decades after Cari's death unleashed Mama Bear Candace, another storm was brewing that woke up Mama Bears around the country. During the COVID-19 pandemic, remote learning shone a bright light on the classroom because the classroom came to the dining room, and parents did not like what they saw. It turns out schools have been messing with cubs for decades, but the Mama Bears didn't know it. The pandemic changed that. And boy, did they roar.

In addition to forming organizations like Moms for Liberty, they contacted local school boards and state legislatures to oppose some of the radical curriculum that was being taught in taxpayer-funded, public schools. And they showed up at meetings and hearings en masse. Their efforts paid off as school boards changed policies and legislatures passed laws designed to protect students and empower parents.

The show of force at government meetings is remarkable. Indeed, it's become incredibly rare for citizens to make their voices heard at public meetings. Citizens seldom bother to show up at City Hall for the council meeting or at the high school auditorium for a school board meeting. It is also rare for everyday Americans to write letters to or call their elected officials to express an opinion.

It is accepted wisdom among political scientists that the primary goal of an elected official is to get reelected. That is not necessarily a bad thing. Politicians believe in a cause enough to put their name on the ballot, ask for money and votes, and seek to change policy for the better. They cannot do the latter without being in office. And as long as work remains to be done, why not keep running for reelection?

What that means for democracy, though, is that elected officials face a choice when it comes to their behavior in office. One option is to fly under the radar, do what seems right in their own eyes, and hope their votes either reflect the will of the people who elected them or, if not, that the voters never find out. Option two is to listen to the people. That is usually the safer bet for politicians who want to keep their jobs the next time Election Day rolls around. Retrospective voting is indeed a double-edged sword.

One way that elected officials can listen to the people is through public opinion polls. As a pollster, I firmly believe that polls are the best way for politicians to hear the voices of constituents. We covered that in the previous chapter. However, participating in a public opinion poll is largely a passive act of participation—voters have to wait for their phone to ring (either literally or figuratively, depending on the poll's mode) so they can make their voices heard. And, as we saw, the chances of any one individual being selected to participate in a poll are incredibly small.

In this chapter, I will address another, much more active way for you to make your voice heard and your opinions known to those in power. In what is likely one of the most overlooked clauses in the First Amendment, Americans have a guaranteed protection of their right to "petition the government for redress of grievances." In other words, if the government does something citizens dislike, the people have a constitutional safeguard to let the government know. They can call, write letters or emails, or simply show up and express their dissatisfaction. But they don't, and that is a threat to democracy because it undermines the ability of elected officials to adequately represent the views of everyday Americans they have been elected to serve.

Some Anecdotal Evidence

When I worked as a legislative correspondent in the office of a member of Congress, my primary responsibility was to listen to the folks "back home" who took the time to share their thoughts on policy with my boss. I answered phone calls, read letters, and sorted through messages sent through the website. Then, I would write a letter or email in reply that addressed the constituent's concerns on pending legislation. And I would keep the boss apprised of what letters and calls were coming in so that he could make decisions that reflected the will of his constituents as closely as possible. It was a job that kept me quite busy.

It may sound like a contradiction to say that many citizens do not contact their elected officials, and that responding to such contacts kept me busy for forty hours per week. But it's not, for three reasons. First, Congress deals with many issues over the course of months and years. So there were a lot of bills and debates on which citizens had the opportunity to contact our office and share their thoughts. The sheer number of issues naturally increases the opportunities for contact.

Second, on any one issue, there were not many contacts. We might get twenty or thirty calls and messages on a bill, and when we did, that was a lot. That's at most thirty contacts from a district of nearly 700,000 people. Flipping that around, there were 699,970 people who didn't bother to contact us on any given issue. (Even removing children from the population, the percentage of people who contacted our office was minuscule.)

Third, many of our contacts across issues came from the same people. Much like travelers who are loyal to a given airline, we had our frequent flyers. Because some advocacy organizations that work on multiple issues make it simple for their followers to contact legislators, we might receive correspondence from the same constituent on a whole host and range of issues. This fact keeps the percentage of constituents reaching out to congressional offices relatively small.

The bottom line is this: Very few people bother to contact their congressional representatives. And if they are not contacting the most high-profile legislators who represent them, the odds are that much smaller that they are petitioning their state legislators, city councilors, or county commissioners.

Indeed, that was my experience working in a Louisiana state senator's office after graduating from college. As the only full-time staff member in the senator's district office, I fielded requests that fell into one of two general categories. First, I handled speaking requests. The senator I worked for was quite the character, and he knew how to charm an audience. As a result, a lot of groups wanted him to speak at functions or events they were hosting. He spoke to as many of them as he could. (The rest usually got stuck with me speaking on his behalf, and I always made sure they knew he sent his apologies for that.)

Second, I received requests for assistance in dealing with a state agency. Usually, that meant asking the state police to "take care of a ticket" the constituent had just been issued, and most definitely, they assured me, did not deserve. But sometimes, people needed real help on a real issue, and the bureaucrats at some state agencies were not fulfilling their duty to the senator's constituents. We'd step in and light a fire under the bureaucrats. Things usually got done with a phone call from me to the agency, but sometimes the senator would need to send a strongly worded letter to an agency head, and that would really grease the skids.

While these kinds of constituent services are important, sometimes fun, and nearly always meaningful, those aren't (or, at least, shouldn't be) the primary function of legislators. Whether they are city councilors, state senators, or members of the United States Congress, a legislator's job is to legislate—to make law. And they should be doing so in a way that represents their constituents. That, of course, requires their constituents to tell them *how* to best represent the folks back home.

Advances in technology have made petitioning the government for redress of grievances much easier and more accessible. At one point in time, contacting an elected official meant meeting them face-to-face or sending a letter. In-person meetings could happen by chance—running into them in a bar or on the street—or more intentionally by attending a town-hall event or meeting them at the Capitol building. All of those modes of contacting elected officials—both in-person and through postal mail—are, of course, still available to anyone who wants to use them to express their opinion to their representatives.

Then came the telephone—just one for the whole Congress at first, followed years later by one in each office. When Alexander Graham Bell's invention made its first appearance in the halls of Congress, there was one telephone, just off the floor where Members cast their votes, and it was answered by the doorman. Later on, Congress added a switchboard with operators, and constituents who wanted to reach their member of Congress would have to call the main number, and the operator would have to connect their call to their representative's office. That is still a possibility.[2] Now, the number for each Member is listed on their website, and you can call their office directly.

As technology advances, the ways you can contact elected officials grow in number. In the 1990s, you could start sending email to members of Congress, and at some point, they added contact forms to their websites. Now, you can even reach out to your elected representatives through social media apps, although since elected officials represent people in a specific geographic area, and it is difficult to verify a social media user's residence, this is a less effective way to share your opinions.

With the ever-expanding technology that allows us to communicate with one another, getting in touch with a legislator or other public official is easier than ever. But so few people do. Unfortunately, there is no universal database of every contact made by a constituent to some elected official, so we can't know how truly rare it is. But we can look at some numbers and conclude that the number of people who contact legislators or elected executives about an issue is probably very small.

A Look at the Numbers

Writing for *The New Yorker* magazine in 2017, journalist Kathryn Schulz explored the history of congressional contact.[3] She writes that congressional staff keep under wraps how many calls from constituents are taken each year, leaving an estimate of phone contacts elusive. However, the amount of mail received, she says, is public record, and the US Senate received about 6.4 million letters in 2016. Political scientist Matt Glassman, writing more than a decade ago, demonstrated that the amount of congressional mail received each year between 1996 and 2011 was fairly constant, hovering between about 25 million and 40 million pieces annually.[4] Glassman adds to that 300 million emails, and the Congressional Management Foundation reports that social media is becoming a more prevalent tool for congressional communication.[5]

Not all of those letters, emails, and social media messages are from constituents about pending legislation or congressional action. Let's make some assumptions and do some back-of-the-napkin math. Let's assume: (1) Schulz's Senate mail number is about right for an average year and that the House receives the same number of constituent letters, that means 12 million out of 40 million (30 percent) pieces of mail are constituent letters; (2) an equal share of the emails are from constituents, meaning

90 million emails fit the bill; (3) there are no duplicates—each letter and email comes from a different person (this is an absurd assumption, but let's roll with it for now just to get an absolute high-water mark for participation); and (4) that all of those communications are equally distributed among voting members of Congress. That means, not counting phone calls or social media messages, 102 million Americans contact Congress each year. We could whittle it down even further since many of those contacts are not related to petitioning the government but requesting things like help with a federal agency, setting up a Capitol or White House tour, a nomination to a US Service Academy (like West Point or the Air Force Academy), or any number of other services unrelated to legislation. So, in a country of roughly 335 million people, 102 million, or again, about 30 percent, of them make contact with Congress each year. Of course, the numbers are probably nowhere near that high. Contact with elected officials most likely comes from a much smaller, highly politically engaged subset of Americans.

So, with that high-water mark—a very generous estimate that 30 percent of Americans contact their elected officials each year—let's look at some of the previous survey research on this topic. Turning once again to the 2003 work on political mobilization by political scientists Steven Rosenstone and John Mark Hansen, we see that on average, 15 percent of Americans report having written to a member of Congress between 1973 and 1990.[6] Those contact rates, of course, are from a generation ago. Perhaps things have changed. Maybe people are more engaged with their elected officials now.

Spoiler: They're not. In six iterations of the American National Election Study (ANES) between 1992 (the first ANES wave after the end of the Rosenstone and Hansen study) and 2020, respondents were asked in various ways about contacting their federal elected officials.[7] While contact ticked up in 1992 to about 45 percent, it dropped precipitously after that. Looking at figure 4.1, which shows the percentage of respondents in the ANES who said they have not contacted their federal elected officials, we see that non-participation has risen nearly every time the question has been asked. Not contacting elected officials peaked in 2016, when more than 88 percent of ANES respondents told researchers they had not contacted their federal elected officials in the twelve months prior to the survey; that number fell to 86 percent in 2020.

Things are no better when it comes to contacting state and local elected officials, who make decisions much closer to the people than do federal officials. In the last two available presidential iterations of the ANES, 2016 and 2020, researchers also asked respondents if they had contacted a local or state elected official.[8] Results were as dismal as the federal question. In 2016, when 88 percent of respondents said they had not contacted a federal elected official, an equal number—88 percent—said they had not contacted a state or local official either.[9] In 2020, when 86 percent of respondents said they had not reached out to their federal officials, a full 95 percent said they had not attempted to contact state or local officials in the prior year.[10]

Contacting elected officials, as I discussed earlier in the chapter, is relatively easy to do and can run the gamut from a quick phone call to say, "Hey, vote no on that bill," to a carefully crafted email or letter laying out a thoughtful argument about why the official should do what you're asking. Either way, it's a pretty low bar to contact an elected official. It takes place on your schedule, when you have the time.

A higher burden is placed on those who would seek out meetings to attend to voice their concerns. Those meetings take planning. They happen on someone else's schedule, not yours. If you're going to go, you go whether or not you have the time. Elected officials may not necessarily attend these events; the event could be an informal planning meeting among members of the community. But often, these meetings do feature elected officials, so let's consider them. Fortunately, ANES researchers also asked respondents whether they had attended a meeting about an issue in their community or school, which I plot in figure 4.2.[11]

Figure 4.1: Percent of Americans Not Contacting Elected Federal Officials

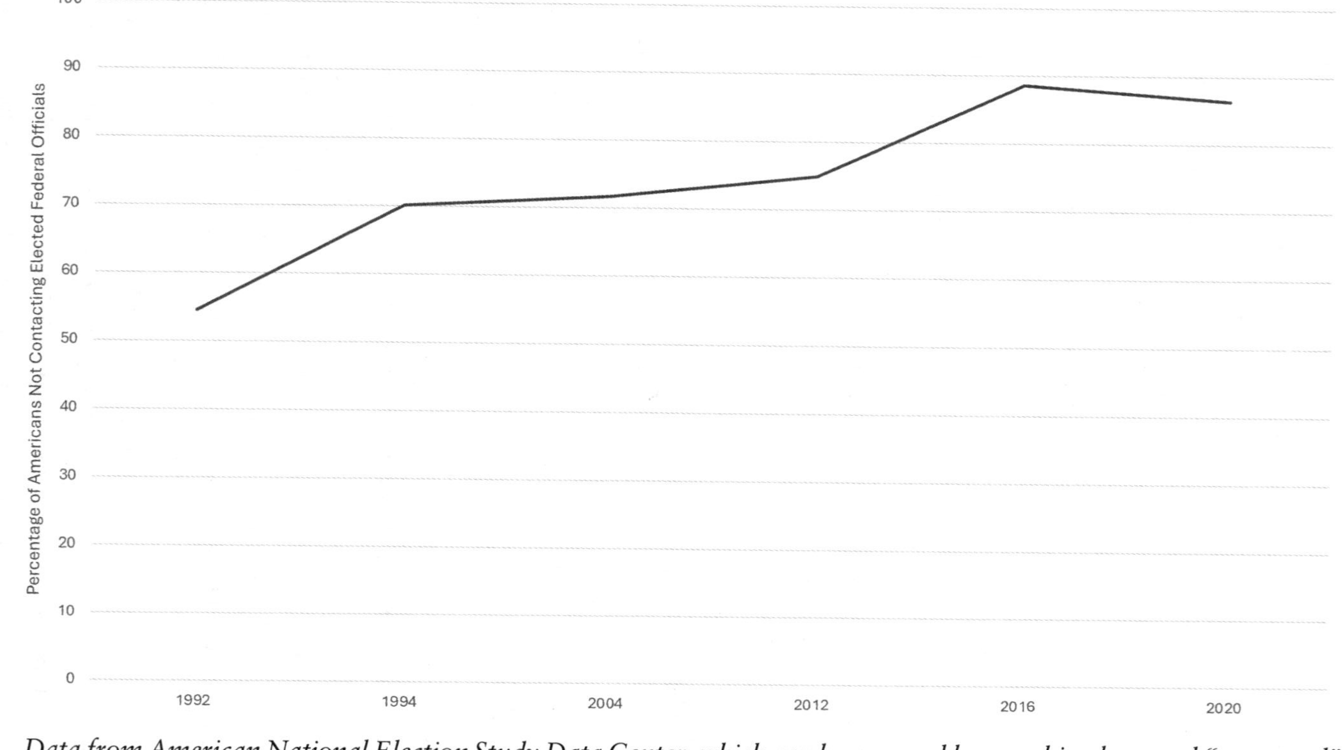

Data from American National Election Study Data Center, which can be accessed by searching keyword "contacted" at https://electionstudies.org/data-tools/anes-question-search/.

Looking at this figure, we see that non-participation in community meetings tracks at roughly the same average level as non-participation in contacting elected officials. Whereas there is more movement in the contact rates from year to year, the people who attend community events is relatively stable. However, there is a spike in non-participation during 2020, the year that COVID shut down many community events. So, even though many events went virtual, meeting via Zoom or similar platforms, thus making "attendance" easier, more people opted not to participate. I suspect non-participation rates plummeted in 2021 as angry parents flooded school board meetings that fall, but the ANES data do not answer that question for us.

Democracy InAction Survey

Turning now to the Democracy InAction Survey, we can see how well our results align with the ANES. The ANES questions restrict respondents to a constrained time frame in which they are asked to consider their prior activity. This is typically sound survey research practice to ensure respondents do not misremember issues the survey researcher is asking about, and I take no issue with the way the ANES asks these questions. However, I asked the respondents in my survey to recall their prior civic activity without the constraints of time. I asked two questions: "Have you ever called or written an elected official?" and "Have you ever attended a meeting with an elected official?" Given that so few people engage in these activities year over year, if we are to believe the ANES data (and I do), if someone had *ever* engaged in contacting an elected official or attending a meeting with one, it surely would stand out in their mind. Thus, I am not concerned about respondents misremembering this prior engagement.

The results show that at a high level, the data are not that far outside what we would expect after exploring the ANES data. We see that 66 percent of respondents say they have never called or written to an elected

Figure 4.2: Percent of Americans Not Attending Community Meetings

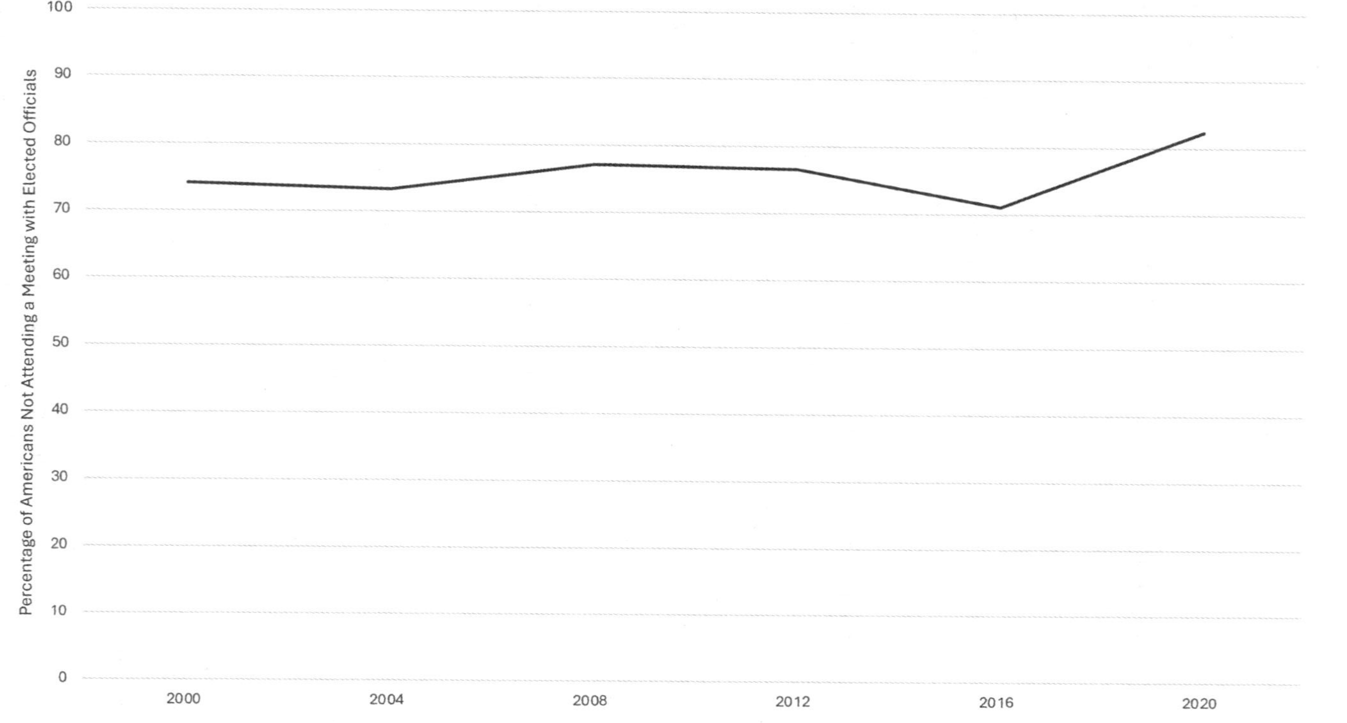

Data from American National Election Study Data Center, available at https://electionstudies.org/data-tools/anes-guide/anes-guide.html?chart=attend_meeting_about_community_issues.

official. The average percentage of respondents answering no in the ANES from 1992 to 2020, with all their different question wordings, was 74 percent. The way I interpret that data is to say in a given year only one in four Americans contact their elected officials, but over the entirety of their lives, one in three do. The pattern for attending meetings is similar, with 65 percent of my survey respondents saying they have never attended a meeting with an elected official, while the average from 2000 to 2020 in the ANES is 76 percent.

But the question I ask in this book isn't *How many do or don't?* My question is *What is the role of apathy and alienation in who does or does not?* For that answer, let's turn back to the regression models. Before we dive into the technical details, here's your key takeaway: Apathy increases avoidance of contacting elected officials and decreases personal feelings of responsibility to contact elected representatives about an issue. Alienation continues to play a countervailing role, decreasing avoidance and increasing feelings of personal responsibility.

Next up? Regression models! If you want to avoid them, now's your chance to skip ahead to the conclusion. For the rest of you, buckle up, and let's go.

Contact Avoidance

To construct the dependent variable for this model, I created an additive index variable combining the two questions discussed above—avoiding writing or calling an elected official and avoiding meetings with elected officials. I then regressed Apathy and Alienation indices and the now-familiar control variables on that dependent variable. The results are presented in figure 4.3.

Beginning with Apathy, we see that it plays a positive and significant role in avoiding contact with elected officials. The more apathetic one is, the more likely they are to avoid exercising that First Amendment right to petition their government for a redress of grievances. This is as we expected. For every point increase in the Apathy scale, respondents avoid

0.06 activities. That increase in avoidance is nearly twice as devastating as the benefit of Alienation, which decreases avoidance by 0.03 activities for every increase in the Alienation scale. These results track with what we saw in chapter 2 with Campaign Avoidance, providing another critical piece of information to show that Apathy and Alienation have countervailing effects on our democratic behaviors.

Figure 4.3: Avoidance of Contacting Elected Officials

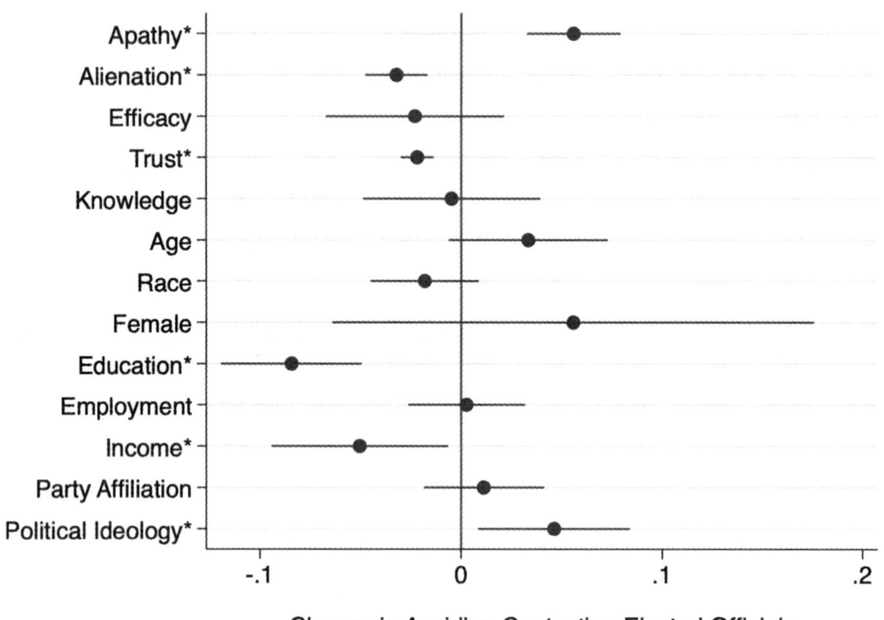

Apathy increases avoidance of contacting elected officials, while Alienation decreases avoidance. See Appendix D for methodological and modeling information.

Turning to the control variables, everything that is significant performs as expected. Higher levels of Trust, more formal Education, and higher Income levels are all associated with decreased Contact Avoidance.

Put another way, the more trusting, educated, or wealthy a person is, the more likely they are to contact their elected officials, even controlling for other factors, with Education exerting the greatest effect of any variable in the model. Education is clearly vital to Americans' willingness to express their views to their elected representatives.

Political ideology is also significantly related to avoidance. The more conservative one is, the more they avoid contacting their elected officials. Conservatives, as we saw in chapter 1, are more likely to vote but are less likely to work on campaigns (chapter 2), and now we see that they are less likely to contact their elected officials. Conservatives are, more than liberals, relying on their vote to make their voices heard, while liberal Americans rely more on active and ongoing engagement. When you consider the organizing capabilities of left-leaning organizations in the US, such as labor unions, environmental and anti-gun groups, Code Pink, and many others, perhaps these results are not so surprising. After all, it was the Democrats who nominated a former community organizer, Barack Obama, as their party's candidate for president in 2008 and 2012.

Personal Responsibility to Contact Elected Officials

Turning once again from behaviors to attitudes, let's explore the effect of Apathy and Alienation on Americans' feelings of personal responsibility to contact elected officials. The results of the regression model are in figure 4.4.

First, we see that Apathy is negative and statistically significant, telling us that the more apathetic one is, the less they feel personally responsible to contact their elected officials. It is also, by far, the largest predictor of feelings of personal responsibility. The negative impact of Apathy on personal responsibility is two times larger than the positive effect of Efficacy, three times larger than the positive effect of Trust, and four times larger than the positive effect of Alienation. Apathy's detrimental effect on personal responsibility to contact elected officials is also larger than its negative impact on any of the other attitudes explored in this book.

Alienation continues its countervailing effect here. The more alienated one feels, the more they believe they have a personal responsibility to contact their elected officials. The alienated among us may feel like they don't belong in our system, but they feel like they owe it to themselves and their fellow citizens to at least try. Good for them!

The only significant control variables are Efficacy and Trust. Both are positive, as expected. The more one feels like they can make a difference, and the more trusting one is, the more likely they are to feel a responsibility to put their democratic skills to use, believing the government will listen and get things done.

Figure 4.4: Personal Responsibility to Contact Elected Officials

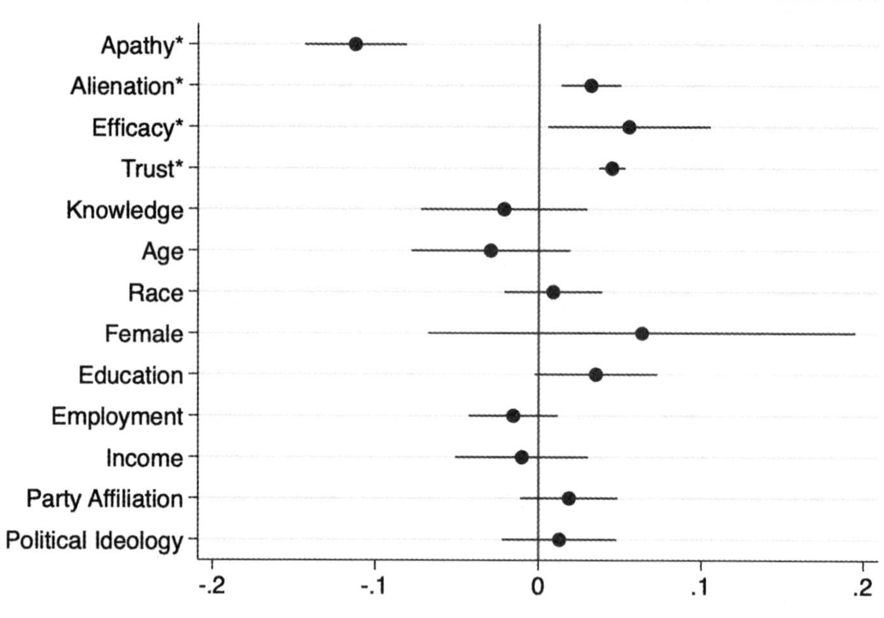

Apathy decreases feelings of personal responsibility to contact elected officials, while Alienation increases feelings of personal responsibility. See Appendix D for methodological and modeling information.

Conclusion

As I said extensively in the previous chapter, polling is the most scientifically valid and reliable way to tell representatives what the masses are thinking. But there is only one way to tell elected officials what you are thinking, and that's to tell them yourself. When I moderate focus groups, I tell participants something along the lines of, "There is only one person in the world who knows exactly what you think, how you think, and why you think that way, and that person is you." And every time I say that, I mean it wholeheartedly. So, that's what I'll tell you as well. You are the only person on the planet who can share your thoughts perfectly with your representatives. While I am immensely thankful that participants in my focus groups share their thoughts and opinions with me and trust me to fairly and accurately represent those to policymakers, I would also be thrilled if they cut me out of the middle and told their elected representative themselves.

But as we've seen in this chapter (and in the ones before it), apathy is a roadblock for Americans' pursuit of the democratic ideal. Americans who don't care simply are not spurred to action. But, as I've done in the previous chapters, let me say this. If that's you, if you don't care about what's on the government's agenda, find something you do care about and then contact your elected officials. Trust me, they want to hear from you. And (again, trust me), when you and enough people like you make your voices heard, policymakers pay attention.

Don't believe me? Remember MADD, the organization I introduced to you at the beginning of this chapter? Drunk driving laws are different—drastically different—than they were in the 1970s and before. All because one mom called her elected representatives. And hundreds of public schools across the country are free from radical, politically motivated curriculum because parents showed up to demand change from elected school board members and legislators.

You may be thinking, *But I have no idea how to even begin.* First, despite the examples I have provided, you don't have to be a parent! It's just easy for parents to see threats to their children and take action. But what you have to do is what I have told you all along—find your something. As someone who has been on the receiving end of constituent contacts, let me give you some tips. Before I do, I'll preview the Additional Resources section of this chapter, which provides an excellent website for you to find out who your elected officials are. Contacting them requires knowing who they are, which brings me to my first tip.

Only contact your representative. Each elected official is responsible for representing their own constituents—the people who live in the geographic area (district or state) from which they are elected. (The best way for them to verify you've contacted the right office is to share your home address with them.) And those constituents keep them busy; they don't have the time, or the obligation, to respond to people from outside their district or state. Let me give you a fun example. When I worked on Capitol Hill, I worked for a member of Congress who represented a district in my home state, but not the district I grew up in, where a lot of my family lived. One day, I received a contact form from the congressman's website. The contact was from one of my cousins. But he lived in my hometown, which my boss did not represent. Even though the person was my relative, I didn't respond to him. I didn't reply to his contact, didn't call him. Nothing. All I did was forward his information and message along to *his* congressman, the person elected from that district to represent him. To this day, I don't think he knows that story. Maybe he'll read it for the first time here!

Aside from the fact that that they represent you, try to make some kind of personal connection with them. Maybe you're from the same hometown. Or perhaps you've met that official somewhere before. Remind them of that. Maybe your cousin works in their office. They should know that! Remember the story about MADD above? Maybe you didn't immediately put it together, but Candace Lightner, the founder of MADD, achieved her first major federal policy win with President Reagan signing the federal minimum drinking age into law. Both Lightner and

Reagan were Californians. Without a doubt, that gave them an important connection.

Third, have a specific request. You are less likely to make an impact if you call or write your US senator and say, "Fix the immigration problem!" than if you call and tell them you want them to vote for or against a specific bill. I saw this firsthand recently in a city council meeting.

The library board was seeking a zoning variance (a fancy way of saying they wanted to change the type of development that could be on the land they own) for a proposed new construction. The current library building is as old as I am and was built to serve a population that was a fraction of our city's current size. The library's architect designed a mixed-use building with a new library (that would be double the current building's size) on the ground floor and several floors of apartments above the library (that my five-year-old asked, on the way to the city council meeting with me, if we could move into once they were built). The change in use required the city council's approval.

Listening to the screeching at the city council meeting, you would have thought the library wanted to build a satanic temple and open-air sacrificial altar in the middle of Main Street. There were lots of hyperbolic claims, grounded in nothing but emotion and hysteria. To say the speakers had a problem would be an understatement. What they didn't have, though, was a solution. They had nothing to offer but unfounded claims and insults to councilmembers. The were Rayburn's jackasses. You probably guessed that they didn't get their way, and the council approved the variance. As of this writing, the library is now closed, and they have relocated the collection to a temporary home across town, demolished the old building, and started the construction of a brand-new mixed-use building with a library that is better suited to serve our community.

Finally—and I'll be blunt here—don't be a jerk. Maybe you already know how they're going to vote on a bill. Or maybe you're upset about a vote they've already cast. Share your opinion candidly and, if relevant, ask them to vote the way you would prefer. Be firm but polite. Don't make threats. Keep in mind that, when you contact your elected official's office, the vast majority of correspondence will not be read by the official but by a staffer—usually an intern in their late teens or early twenties, or a junior staffer in their mid-twenties. They're there to help you and serve you, so be kind to them.

Your elected officials want to hear from you. You now have the tools to do just that and hopefully to make a real impact. But you have to put in the work to crafting your outreach. Grassroots expert Christopher Kush writes, "Most legislative offices tend to ascribe a level of value to grassroots communications depending on how much effort they take."[12] In other words, if you don't put in enough effort for your representative to know you care, they probably won't either. Find something you're passionate about—whether it's something they're already working on or something you want to put on their radar—and put those tools to work. You never know how you might shape your representatives' views on an issue. And who knows? You might change the landscape of American law for decades to come. All because you picked up the phone.

Three Questions

1. Have you ever contacted an elected official—either by writing, calling, emailing, etc., or attending a meeting with them? If so, what was the topic of that contact? What was the outcome? If you haven't, what are some of the reasons for that?
2. You read about MADD and their fight against drunk driving in this chapter. What's something you are passionate enough about to start an organization to fight for that issue?
3. What advice would you give someone else who is thinking about contacting their elected official about an issue?

Three Actions

1. Write a letter to the editor of your local newspaper, encouraging your elected officials to take action on some issue. Letters to the editor are usually fairly short (around 300 words), so don't feel like you have to write the final book in the Iliad, Odyssey trilogy.
2. Contact—by phone, email, or website form—your elected representative to share your thoughts on an issue. This is most impactful when you (A) contact them regarding an item currently on their agenda, such as pending legislation, and (B) offer a unique, novel, or personal argument rather than simply echoing talking points from the public domain.
3. Attend a local government meeting, such as a city council or school board meeting. You can go simply to observe or, if you're feeling adventurous, sign up to speak during the public comments time. Most boards will limit what you can speak about to a topic on that meeting's agenda, so have an idea of what's on the agenda and what you might want to say about it.

Additional Resources

1. To be able to contact your elected officials, you need to know who they are! Rather than having to wade through multiple websites to track down who represents you, Ballotpedia has a great one-stop resource at: https://ballotpedia.org/Who_represents_m2.
2. While I provided some basic tips in the conclusion about how to contact your representatives, this guide is more in-depth and worth checking out as a resource: https://guides.lib.berkeley.edu/contactingofficials/tips.

CHAPTER 5

JURY SERVICE

"Trial by jury is only tolerable because no better way of approximating the truth of guilt, or innocence, has been invented."

THE NEW YORK TIMES, 1856

In the summer of 1985, Larry Joe Powers was drinking in a house with some acquaintances, a woman and two other men, when the woman noticed that Powers had a gun. After being confronted about the weapon, Powers shot and killed the two men, while the woman escaped without being shot.

Powers was subsequently indicted in Franklin County, Ohio, on charges of aggravated murder, attempted aggravated murder, and possession of a firearm during the commission of a felony. When the State of Ohio put him on trial, Powers claimed self-defense. The jury wasn't buying that, though. The jury convicted Powers and sentenced him to a lengthy prison sentence for his crimes.

Through a series of appeals in both the state and federal court systems, Powers's case reached the US Supreme Court. In his appeals, Powers questioned the constitutionality of jury selection in his case. He alleged that the prosecutor unlawfully eliminated Black citizens from the jury pool, a practice that had been forbidden by the Supreme Court in a case the year before Powers's trial.[1] The primary question Powers raised on appeal was whether the exclusion of Blacks from the jury was unconstitutional, even though Powers was White.[2]

While the justices decided that primary question (spoiler: yes, it is unconstitutional), the Court went a step further on the issue of jury service in a way that is important to *you*, even if you are never charged with a crime, never sue anyone, or are never accused of wrongdoing in a lawsuit.

• • •

Justice is essential to a fully functioning democracy.

When most people think about jury service, they don't think about democracy. Perhaps that's because jury service in the US, unlike voting in the US, is compulsory. Don't want to vote? No big deal, right? (Wrong. Go back and re-read chapter 1.) You cannot be thrown in jail for not voting. There is no crime on the books under which you can be charged with contempt of the election board. Your voter registration card is for informational purposes only. Not so with a jury summons. If you receive a jury summons in the mail, you had better present yourself to the court at the appointed date and time. Or else.

But there is something inherently democratic about the American jury system. Indeed, the *New York Times* quote about jury trials that opened this chapter bears a striking similarity to Winston Churchill's much more famous quip about democracy itself: "Democracy is the worst form of Government except for all those other forms that have been tried."

Think about the parallels between jury service and other forms of democratic engagement. In most places, the qualifications for voting and jury duty are identical or, at least, very similar. Indeed, registering to vote gets you a fast pass to the jury list in 43 out of 50 states.[3]

In both political campaigns and trials, you have two sides competing with one another, trying to get you to believe their story and not that of their opponent, and they're asking for your vote. And in both trials and campaigns, given the high number of lawyers who run for political office, the odds are that it is two attorneys bickering with one another.

Elections and jury trials are both decided by a vote. One side wins, the other side doesn't. The voter and the juror both have an important role to play in saying what the law is. Voters decide who gets to make the law, while jurors decide how the law is applied to a specific set of facts.

The bottom line is this: Voters and jurors alike are just normal, everyday folks going about their lives until the government intervenes, forces them to come together (often reluctantly so), to consider arguments and make a collective decision. In other words, the jury system is democratic, and a refusal to participate is an antisocial and undemocratic act.

What Exactly Is a Jury Anyway?

A jury is a group of individuals drawn from the community who resolve legal disputes in a courtroom. They do so by listening to evidence presented during a trial, privately discussing the case with one another, and issuing a verdict—a decision about who wins and who loses—in the case. While more than a million Americans serve on a jury every year, most people are familiar with the jury system through popular media, such as courtroom dramas, news reports, and books. Most of these portrayals focus on only one type of jury—the trial jury. In fact, there are two types of juries: grand juries and petit, or trial, juries.

Grand juries are vastly underrepresented in both media portrayals and reality. The federal government is required to use grand juries in criminal cases, and some, but far from all, states employ them.

Here's how a grand jury works: Prosecutors convene grand juries to review evidence in a case and determine whether enough of it exists for the prosecutor to proceed to trial against a criminal defendant. When a grand jury finds that enough evidence has been presented to them to proceed with criminal charges against the defendant, they issue what is called an indictment or a true bill; conversely, when they find an insufficient basis for charges, they issue what is called a no true bill, meaning the prosecutor cannot take the defendant to trial at that time.

That's it. No guilty or not guilty. No fines or jail time. Just, is there enough evidence or not? Pretty boring. Maybe that's why there are no "grand jury room dramas" on television. They probably wouldn't get the kind of ratings courtroom dramas do. But, as we will see later in the chapter, grand juries serve an important function in checking the power of a potentially out-of-control government official, the prosecutor.

A second type of jury is called the petit jury or trial jury. This group of citizens sits in the courtroom during a trial and evaluates the evidence presented. Evidence can take the form of witness testimony; video or photographs; phone, medical, or financial records; DNA test results; and so on. A trial jury's task is to use the evidence to determine the facts of a case and apply the law to those facts. This task is accomplished through discussing the evidence and law with one another—called deliberating—and coming to a group decision, called the verdict, about which party wins and which one loses.

Grand juries and trial juries are distinct from one another in a number of ways. First, grand juries are typically larger. They usually have around eighteen jurors, sometimes more, while a trial jury has between six and twelve. Second, grand jurors hear only one side of the case—the prosecution. Defense lawyers are not permitted to respond to the prosecution's case to the grand jury, to present evidence, or even be present in the room. This is why it has been said that prosecutors can indict a ham sandwich, a colloquial (and delicious) way of saying that prosecutors almost always get their way in front of a grand jury. Third, grand jurors typically serve for much longer periods of time than trial jurors. This occurs because petit jurors sit for a single case, which usually lasts for only a few continuous days, while grand jurors are called in intermittently to hear the prosecutor present several cases and then released until the next time they are called to hear a new batch of cases. This grand jury call and release can go on for months at a time before the jurors are dismissed and a new group is summoned and seated.[4]

Trial juries hear two types of cases—criminal and civil—while grand juries are convened only in criminal matters. If you've ever watched a courtroom drama series, like *Law & Order*, you are likely most familiar with criminal trials. Or, to be more precise, you are likely most familiar with the TV portrayal of criminal trials. Criminal cases involve the government charging a person,[5] called the defendant, with committing a crime, such as theft, embezzlement, fraud, driving under the influence (DUI), assault, murder, and so on. In a criminal trial, the prosecutor presents evidence of the defendant's guilt, while the defense works to undermine the evidence. To convict a criminal defendant, the criminal jury must find that the defendant is guilty beyond a reasonable doubt. The US Supreme Court recently ruled that the criminal verdict must be unanimous, meaning every juror must agree to convict.[6] If even one juror holds out, the defendant cannot be found guilty. This results in what is called a "hung jury," and the prosecutors must decide whether to try the defendant again with a different jury. (You may have heard about double jeopardy, the Fifth Amendment's protection against facing the same charges more than once, but that only applies when the jury unanimously acquits the defendant, finding them not guilty.)

Trial juries are also selected in civil cases. Civil cases are disputes between two parties that involve non-criminal matters, any case in which one person sues another. If you've ever seen a billboard with a grim-faced, cross-armed man in a suit next to the words "INJURED? CALL NOW!", you have been introduced to one aspect of civil law. The attorneys adorning billboards and bus stops—usually called personal injury lawyers, plaintiffs' lawyers, or trial lawyers—represent people who claim to have been injured through the fault of someone else, for example, in a vehicle crash or slipping and falling on someone else's property. Personal injuries are only one type of civil case, however. Civil disputes range from simple contract breaches, where one person says the other person broke their contract, to complex multi-jurisdiction tort cases involving a range of issues such as bad pharmaceutical products or, famously, the tobacco litigation of the 1990s. (*Tort* is the legal term for any civil action that is not related to a contract between two parties.)[7]

Civil juries must overcome much lower hurdles in deciding the cases before them. In criminal cases, guilt must be established beyond a reasonable doubt, whereas civil juries typically use a burden of proof called the preponderance of the evidence, meaning that the allegations are more likely to be true than not true. That is a much lower burden. Criminal juries must be unanimous, but many states allow civil juries to return a verdict even if not every juror agrees.

Interestingly, and perhaps confusingly, the same incident with the same set of facts can lead to both civil and criminal cases. Let's consider an example. Two cars are involved in a crash in which one of the drivers is killed. The police arrive to investigate the crash and discover that the driver who survived was driving while high on marijuana, ran a red light at a high rate of speed, and T-boned the other car as it was crossing through the intersection (with a green light). That impaired driver would likely face criminal prosecution for DUI and some variation of vehicular homicide for killing the other driver, and possibly a litany of other charges. The family of the deceased driver could also sue the surviving driver for wrongful death and other torts, such as intentional infliction of emotional distress, in civil court. Even more confusing is that sometimes the outcome of the criminal trial and the outcome of the civil trial are at odds with one another.

This is what happened with football legend O.J. Simpson. In 1995, Simpson was found not guilty in a criminal trial of killing his ex-wife, Nicole Brown Simpson, and her friend, Ron Goldman, the year prior. The families of Nicole and Goldman sued Simpson for wrongful death, and in 1997, a civil jury found him liable for their deaths and awarded the families more than $30 million in damages. These disparate outcomes are likely due, to a great extent, to the different burdens of proof—beyond a reasonable doubt for criminal trials and preponderance of the evidence in civil trials.

Jury Duty Is Important Because the *Jury* Is Important

I am certainly not the first author to claim that jury service is a democratic act. For decades, scholars have claimed, explored, and demonstrated a link between serving on a jury and other activities traditionally associated with democracy and civic health. Their research makes clear that they believe jury service is a democratic act, right down to titles like *We, the Jury*,[8] an obvious play on the first three words of the Preamble to the US Constitution, and the more on-the-nose, *The Jury and Democracy*.[9]

Because serving on a jury and democracy are intertwined, exploring some reasons for the importance of jury service is worthwhile. One of the oldest justifications for requiring juries is that they give a voice to the citizens. In this way, juries have a direct semblance to electoral participation. Law professor Andrew Guthrie Ferguson calls this the conscience of the community.[10]

The jury represents the voice of the people in their community. If the average group of citizens in a local area believes a criminal statute is unfair, they can acquit a defendant charged with that crime. If they think plaintiffs are only out to make a buck, they can find for the defendant in a civil case. The catch is that if they release a criminal defendant or find for a civil defendant, and those parties offend again, it is the jury's community that suffers. Regardless of their reasons for issuing a given verdict or the consequences of that verdict, the fact is that the jury provides a voice to the community.

Just as elections have consequences, so too do verdicts.

The Representative Jury

For the jury's decision truly to be the voice of the people, the jury must be drawn from a representative cross-section of the community.

Achieving a jury that is a fair cross-section has long been the legal standard against which jury selection procedures have been measured. This means that the jury pool must reflect the community's diversity, and the US Supreme Court has repeatedly said that such representation is a legal requirement, that it is "fundamental to the jury trial guaranteed by the Sixth Amendment."[11]

In chapter 1, I discussed the expansion of voting rights throughout American history. Jury composition has similarly shifted over the years, so today's juries—or at least the jury pools—look and think much like the average citizen. But that has not always been the case.

Juries in early American courts were made up of white, land-owning men. Even as recently as the middle of the twentieth century, jury pools were not selected from the community at large. Instead, the courthouse regulars—judges, attorneys, clerks, and so on—selected "key-man" or "blue ribbon" juries. These panels were made up of community members deemed to have a good reputation. Because they were known by the courthouse elite, they tended not to represent the whole community but rather only one segment of it.

Now, we live in a country where the jury is more representative, thanks to a line of Supreme Court jurisprudence that has demanded a fair cross-section. For example, in 1975, the Court issued its ruling in *Taylor*[12] *v. Louisiana*, in which it held that systematically excluding women from juries or granting them automatic exemptions violates the constitutional requirement for a fair cross-section.[13] The Court later built upon its ruling in *Taylor* when it held that it is also unconstitutional to exclude men from a jury simply because they are men.[14] Indeed, how can any panel be representative when it excludes roughly half the population?

Similarly, a decade later, in *Batson v. Kentucky*, the Court ruled that prospective jurors could not be excluded from service simply because of their race.[15] The Court held that prosecutors, when challenged by the defense for excluding prospective jurors of a particular race, must provide the judge with a good reason for doing so. The Court was clear, however, that not just any old excuse would do. Writing for the Court's majority, Justice Lewis F. Powell instructed, "The State cannot meet this burden on mere general assertions that its officials did not discriminate, or that they properly performed their official duties . . . Rather, the State must demonstrate that 'permissible racially neutral selection criteria and procedures have produced the monochromatic result.'"[16] In other words, Justice Powell said that prosecutors cannot simply say "race wasn't the reason"; they must give a reason that has nothing to do with race. The Court's logic in *Batson* was expanded, as we've already seen, in *Powers* to preclude the exclusion of Black jurors even when the defendant is White,[17] to forbid race-based strikes made by criminal defendants[18] and in civil cases,[19] and to prohibit strikes based on ethnic origins.[20]

As I said earlier, the jury is the voice of the people, which requires the jury to represent a fair cross-section of the community. However, these are idealistic and legal justifications, respectively. This raises the question of why these features of the American jury system are important. In other words, what is the practical reason for having a representative cross-section? The answer lies not in the process of selecting a jury that *looks* like the community, but instead, one that *thinks* like the community. That's because the real work of the jury happens in deliberations.

The Deliberative Jury

Deliberation is when the jury discusses the case as a group. They have heard all the testimony, viewed all the physical evidence, and been instructed on the law by the judge. Now the case is theirs to decide. And this is where the cross-section becomes critically important. It is here, in deliberations, that the perspectives and experiences of various community elements are aired, that each person on the jury provides everyone else with a fresh perspective, a different way of looking at and thinking about the case. You see, it's not that diversity on a jury is important for diversity's sake. Demographic diversity is critical because it produces diversity of thought, and that leads to richer deliberations and, likely, to a more correct outcome of the case.

Put another way, the jury system, because of diversity and deliberation, leads to better decision-making. If ever an instance existed where making the right decision—getting the verdict right—is absolutely essential, trials are it. In criminal trials, a defendant's liberty and perhaps even life are at stake. In civil trials, where money is at stake, getting it wrong means one party pays damages they should not have had to pay, or someone is deprived of an award they should have been entitled to receive. That's a lot of pressure to put on an outcome. Fortunately, the collective wisdom of juries helps get it right because even judges sometimes get it wrong.

Take, for instance, a study of cases where judges issued what is called a summary judgment. Summary judgment means that a judge rules in favor of one party or the other without ever holding a trial, deciding that the evidence is so one-sided that no reasonable jury could find for the other side. But how can one judge decide what is reasonable? A long line of research shows that judges exhibit some of the same biases that every other human has. It's no wonder because judges are, after all, human too. Back to the summary judgment study. The researcher identified 263 cases where the trial judge issued a summary judgment, an appeals court reversed the trial judge's decision, and a jury ultimately heard the case. In 25 percent of the cases, the jury's verdict was *for* the party the judge ruled *against* in summary judgment.[21] Put bluntly, judges got it wrong in one out of four cases.

The one-in-four statistic tracks with other studies as well. In a classic study of the American jury system, researchers from the University of Chicago surveyed judges in over 3,500 criminal cases, and the judge disagreed with the jury's verdict 22 percent of the time, while in more than 4,000 civil cases, the judge also disagreed with the jury's damages award 22 percent of the time.[22] More recent studies have found that judges disagree with juries between 29 and 37 percent of the time.[23]

The fact is that sometimes judges can get it wrong. Certainly, juries can as well, but the features we've discussed above go a long way in making sure they don't. On the one hand, juries are (supposed to be) representative of the community. Bringing different perspectives and experiences to the table enhances discussion and decision-making.[24] Judges simply don't have that capability. A judge is one person with one personality (I hope), one perspective, and one lived experience. Sure, a judge may discuss a case with colleagues, but at the end of the day, the judge gets to make his or her own decision without having to consider anyone else's point of view. Not so with a jury.

Jurors don't decide cases; juries do. It is a group decision brought about by deliberation—discussion, debate, argument, shouting matches. Before the foreperson (the jury's informal leader and scribe) can sign the verdict form, all jurors must agree with the verdict. Judges don't have to deliberate. They don't have to convince anyone else of their position. They don't have shouting matches with themselves (I hope). Judges can sign an order without even consulting anyone else. Deliberation is the keystone of the jury system, and it is how juries come closer to getting it right in many cases (about one in four of them) than a judge acting alone can.

The Checking and Balancing Jury

Because the representative and deliberative natures of juries make them more capable of reaching the correct outcome, they can also correct the errors of other actors. In this way, juries serve as a sort of checks-and-balances system. First, grand juries can correct the mistakes of other grand juries. Even though prosecutors stand an excellent chance of obtaining an indictment when they seek one, there are rare instances in which they fail to do so. Sometimes, prosecutors jump the gun and try to indict too early before they have amassed enough evidence, and the grand jury returns a no true bill, even though the accused is factually guilty. The prosecutor can then obtain additional information and seek the indictment a second time (or third or fourth, etc.). When the grand jury returns an indictment of a factually guilty defendant when previous grand juries have failed to do so, they are checking one another.

Second, trial juries can correct mistakes made by grand juries. Recall that only the prosecutor gets to present his or her case to the grand jury, meaning the State runs the risk of indicting an individual who is factually and completely innocent, or one who committed a crime for a justifiable reason, such as self-defense. Remember the ham sandwich? The indictment of an innocent (or at least a legally not guilty) person is a mistake. Fortunately, the trial jury serves as a check on the grand jury and can acquit the wrongly indicted.

Finally, trial juries can also check other trial juries. If the jury reaches the wrong outcome and a new trial is ordered, the second jury could correct the mistake of the first one.

Getting the right outcome is important. In fact, justice demands that our system get it right. English jurist William Blackstone once wrote that it is "better that ten guilty persons escape than that one innocent suffer." Taking what has become known as Blackstone's Ratio magnitudes further, Benjamin Franklin argued that "it is better a hundred guilty persons should escape than one innocent person should suffer." But justice is about more than the outcome of an individual case. Getting cases right is about faith in the system.

When juries get it right, it provides legitimacy for the outcome as well as the system. Jurors get to see the system work from the inside, leading to greater support for the traditional actors in the court system. Political scientist John Gastil and his colleagues write that "jury service often makes citizens more supportive of not only the jury system, but also of local judges and even the Supreme Court."[25]

Support for the courts is critical because they rely on legitimacy for their survival. In Federalist 78, Alexander Hamilton said that, when compared to the executive and legislative branches of government, "the judiciary, from the nature of its functions, will always be the least dangerous to . . . political rights."[26] Judges cannot enforce their own decisions, so they have to rely on the executive branch to do so. They also cannot raise taxes to fund their operations; for that, they must rely on the legislature. Because judges have "no influence over either the sword or the purse," as Hamilton continued in Federalist 78, they are effectively toothless compared to the political branches. To operate, courts rely on legitimacy, the support of the people, to gain acquiescence from elected officials.[27] Juries serve a critical role in providing legitimacy to the courts.

Juries also provide protection from government overreach. The State has seemingly endless resources to devote to "getting their man." Police have healthy budgets, the power of arrest, and in many instances, legal immunity for their actions. Prosecutors have nearly boundless authority in bringing charges, especially when they are unchecked by grand juries, and typically have an intimate working relationship with the police. Judges also have power that is largely unchecked, except through the appellate process and to some extent the ballot box. Moreover, because prosecutors appear before judges on a regular basis, their relationship is likely to be highly cordial, potentially putting the opposing party at a disadvantage. In fact, there is some evidence that attorneys who appear before the same judge frequently enjoy high levels of success.[28] This leaves the jury as the only meaningful decision-maker standing between the people and the government.

Finally, serving on a jury builds other civic skills. For example, research has found that, under certain conditions, individuals who serve on a jury are more likely to vote than they were before having performed jury duty.[29] Talk about a strong democratic link! The effect of jury service on increasing voter participation is roughly equivalent to taking a semester-long civics course or nonpartisan face-to-face get-out-the-vote efforts.[30] Beyond increasing the likelihood of voting, serving on a jury increases the frequency with which people talk to their friends and families about public issues, and when they personally contribute to the conversation during deliberations, they are more likely to participate in civic groups.[31] In addition, jurors develop a greater understanding of and appreciation for legal processes.[32]

For all these reasons, jury service is critically important to our democratic health. In fact, the ability to have a jury of our peers hear and decide our cases has long been recognized as important in the United States. Our founders recognized this and were willing to fight a war against England, in part, over the right to a trial by jury. But don't take my word for it. Remember the Declaration of Independence? That piece of political hate mail the colonists sent to King George, declaring America's freedom from England? It included a list of grievances, a (quite lengthy) list of reasons the colonists were peeved with the Crown. Here's the portion relevant to this discussion of the American jury:

> But when a long train of abuses and usurpations, pursuing invariably the same Object evinces a design to reduce them under absolute Despotism, it is their [the people's] right, it is their duty, to throw off such Government, and to provide new Guards for their future security.—Such has been the patient sufferance of these Colonies; and such is now the necessity which constrains them to alter their former Systems of Government. The history of the present King of Great Britain is a history of repeated injuries and usurpations, all having in direct object the establishment of an absolute Tyranny over these States. To prove this, let Facts be submitted to a candid world . . . For depriving us in many cases, of the benefits of Trial by Jury . . . In every stage of these Oppressions We have Petitioned for Redress in the most humble terms: Our repeated Petitions have been answered only by repeated injury. A Prince whose character is thus marked by every act which may define a Tyrant, is unfit to be the ruler of a free people.[33]

The men who signed their names at the bottom of that list of grievances weren't establishing the first Festivus. They were making bold, world-shifting, history-changing assertions. They claimed the right—the "duty"—of the people to get rid of an unrepresentative government. They called the King of England a tyrant for depriving them of certain rights and liberties. They knew they were declaring not only independence but also a war to secure that freedom.

And they put the right to trial by jury among a list of critically important issues—matters like disbanding legislatures, military occupation, and inciting insurrections—issues that they deemed important enough to declare independence and war.

Following America's victory over England in the Revolutionary War, the nascent United States operated for a few years under the Articles of Confederation—what might be called our first constitution. However, it didn't take the early Americans long to figure out that the Articles were an insufficient document for governing a nation, so they began to explore and debate the idea of a new constitution for the growing country.

The proposed constitution included the guarantee of a jury trial. Article III of the Constitution establishes the Judicial branch of the new federal government. Section 2 of that Article begins to correct that grievance listed in the Declaration of Independence. Rather than "being depriv[ed] . . . in many cases, of the benefits of Trial by Jury,"[34] the Constitution promises Americans that "The Trial of all Crimes, except in Cases of Impeachment; shall be by Jury."[35]

But that wasn't enough. A group of Americans called the anti-Federalists wrote essays opposing the proposed constitution because it did not contain more stringent protections for jury trials, including, for example, the right to a trial by jury in civil cases.[36] To secure ratification (legal acceptance) of the Constitution, the Federalists (those Americans who supported the Constitution and wrote essays, now called the Federalist Papers, in support of it) promised that the new legislature would pass a bill of rights further protecting the freedoms of people and the States.

When the Bill of Rights (the first ten amendments to the Constitution) was ratified, it included several new provisions directly protecting the right to trial by jury. These include the requirement that criminal charges be approved by a grand jury (Fifth Amendment), that criminal charges must be tried by a jury (Sixth Amendment), and that civil cases with a disputed amount of $20 or more must be heard by a jury (Seventh Amendment).[37]

Over the years, the Courts have decided many cases that have shifted the reality of jury service in America—not just the ones that have shaped representativeness as we saw earlier, but ones that have altered the power of juries. For example, in early America, juries were permitted to decide both the facts of the case and the law. Today, the ability of juries to decide the law has been largely removed, and in most courtrooms, judges instruct juries on the law *and* that they must follow the law as the judge instructed them in it. Legal scholar Suja A. Thomas contends that the Court's jurisprudence has served to strip away power from the jury in favor of what she calls the "traditional branches" of government—the legislative, executive, and judiciary—and the states.[38] However, the most relevant case for our purposes is the by-now-familiar *Powers v. Ohio*, which I introduced at the beginning of the chapter.[39]

As we saw earlier, Larry Joe Powers's case reached the US Supreme Court, which decided that excusing Black people from the jury pool simply because they are Black is unconstitutional, even if the defendant is White. The Court's decision was a logical extension of its ruling in *Batson*, declaring it unconstitutional for the prosecution to exclude Blacks from jury service when the defendant is Black, depriving the defendant of the constitutional right to "a jury drawn from a cross-section of the community."[40]

But Justice Anthony Kennedy wasn't quite satisfied to settle the question of the *defendant's* rights, so he took his argument a step further. Writing for the majority in *Powers*, Justice Kennedy wrote, "An individual juror does not have a right to sit on any particular [trial] jury, but he or she does possess the right not to be excluded from one on account of race."[41]

In other words, the right to have a jury trial belongs to the defendant (or to the parties in a civil case). But the citizens—*you*—have a right, too. That's right, none other than the United States Supreme Court has said that *you* have the right to sit on a jury. Not any specific jury, mind you, but the right to not be excluded for discriminatory reasons nonetheless.

The defendant's constitutional right to a jury requires the citizen also to possess the right to sit on a jury. But it's not just a right. Rights can be relinquished. You have the *right* to practice any religion you desire, but you can choose to abstain. You have the *right* to remain silent when being questioned by police, but you can waive that right and make a statement anyway. So, while you have the right to sit on a jury, you also have the responsibility to serve when called.

After all, if you were ever the defendant or a civil litigant, wouldn't you want your fellow citizens to make themselves available to hear your case? Most Americans would, as surveys have shown that a large plurality of Americans would prefer to have their case decided by a jury rather than a judge.[42] In fact, most *judges* say they would rather face a jury than have a case in which they were a party decided by their fellow judges.[43]

Running Away from Jury Duty

In his 1996 legal thriller, *The Runaway Jury*, bestselling author John Grisham tells the story of Nicholas Easter, a man who goes to extraordinary lengths to serve on a jury. A 2003 film adaptation by the same name, sans the article adjective, brought the story to the big screen. Unlike Grisham's Easter, many Americans will go to extraordinary lengths to *avoid* jury duty. Rather than trying to serve on a runaway jury, Americans try to run away from serving on any jury.

If jury duty is important (as I have contended throughout this chapter that it is) and required (as the law contends that it is), then how pervasive is the refusal to serve on a jury? How can one refuse service that is, as we have already seen, compelled by the threat of fines and potentially jail time? Let's consider both a reduction in jury service alongside a reticence to serve and how both threaten America's democracy as it manifests itself in a box of twelve seats tucked along the side wall of an ornate room on Main Street, USA.

Unfortunately, a single source of data on jury skipping does not exist, so I rely on survey data and anecdotes. The primary takeaways for you are (1) skipping jury service is more pervasive than you might think, and (2) people will take surprising actions to get out of jury duty.

Perhaps we should not be surprised that legal compulsion is insufficient motivation for people to show up for jury duty. Consider other, more serious offenses. Murder is punishable by prison time and is illegal in all fifty states, yet nearly 25,000 people were victims of homicide in 2022.[44] There were also more than one million burglaries in the US in 2019, even though burglary is also prohibited by law.[45] And those are the serious crimes that can land someone in jail. More run-of-the-mill offenses are more widespread. For example, more than forty million traffic citations were issued in 2018 to one out of every five licensed drivers.[46] In fact, even in countries where voting is required by law, turnout is not 100 percent,[47] indicating that some people are willing to face the threat of punishment to abstain from civic activities.[48]

The same is true of jury service in the US. A survey of sitting judges is particularly illuminating. Across the country, judges say they have noted an increase in people ignoring jury summonses, with some judges saying that response rates are below 50 percent.[49]

The judges' perceptions are backed up by anecdotal evidence. Consider the following. News media reported that in one Florida judicial district, 20 percent of people called for jury duty failed to show up,[50] while in Houston, Texas, a full one-quarter of people failed to report to jury duty when called to serve.[51] A recent study of the jury system in Philadelphia found that one out of every three residents summoned for jury duty skipped out.[52] The story is even worse in San Diego. According to a local news station there, a recent jury sitting saw only forty-four appearances out of 900 summonses issued.[53] Indeed, as FOX5 San Diego reported following that abysmal appearance rate, "Courts in Hartford, Connecticut, San Diego and Norfolk, Virginia, have had to delay jury selection for trials because too few people responded to jury duty summonses."[54] South Carolina Courts are seeing similar problems, even delaying a murder trial because only thirty-nine out of one hundred and fifty people summoned appeared for duty.[55]

While these anecdotal stories are intriguing, the question is whether they point to a larger problem. In other words, these accounts are smoke, but is there fire? One analysis by 538, an elections, polling, and statistics blog, previously a feature of ABC News, seems to indicate that there is a fire we need to be concerned about. According to 538's analysis of a 2012 National Center for State Courts report, approximately three million Americans fail to appear for jury duty when summoned. That is twice as many people as actually serve on a jury in a given year.[56] And the problem appears to be getting worse. According to a 2007 report from the National Center for State Courts, courts across the country have been increasingly challenged by citizens who fail to return their qualification questionnaires or who fail to appear (FTA) for jury service. Twenty percent of one-step courts reported non-response/FTA rates of 15 percent or higher. Even more remarkable, 10 percent of two-step courts, which had already located and qualified the prospective juror, reported FTA rates of 16 percent or higher. Twenty percent of courts reported non-response/FTA rates of 15 percent or higher.[57]

Even those individuals who do appear to answer their jury summons will attempt to find ways to avoid serving. Many will avail themselves of legitimate excuses, such as age, ongoing medical treatments, or intimate knowledge of the case or one of the parties. In these instances, the court will release the prospective juror. However, not every excuse is deemed acceptable to the courts. Prospective jurors will seek to avoid service for myriad reasons, such as believing they are too busy, they have objections to sitting in judgment of other people, or they may even fear the repercussions they or their families will be forced to endure in some high-profile case. Still others will push the bounds even further. Based on survey data, somewhere between 7 and 10 percent of Americans admit to having lied to get out of jury service.[58] And given that admitting to having lied is a socially undesirable answer (and, conversely, denying having lied is socially desirable), the 7 to 10 percent likely underestimates the true number of people who have lied—or are at least willing to lie—to get out of serving on a jury.

Democracy InAction Survey

The Democracy InAction Survey shows similar results. Of the respondents who are jury eligible[59] and say they have received a jury summons, more than 10 percent say they have lied to get out of jury service.

But my concern is not only lying to avoid jury service. Any attempt to skirt this important civic responsibility threatens the institution of the jury. Yes, some people often have valid reasons to delay jury service until the next term. I'm not talking about those folks. And yes, sometimes the ability to remain impartial means someone is removed from service by the attorneys during jury selection. I am also not concerned about them. The threat to the American jury comes from people who have the impartiality and ability to serve but try their hardest to avoid service.

Before we get into all the technical stuff, let me give you the key takeaways from this chapter's regression analyses. First, alienation leads to more jury avoidance. People who feel like they don't belong in the system try the hardest to get out of serving. But Apathy doesn't play a role here. (I will explain why I think that is in the conclusion of the chapter.) Second, Apathy reduces feelings of personal responsibility for jury service. While apathetic Americans don't appear to avoid jury service, they don't exactly feel like they should have to serve.

Okay, there you have it. That's the short version. If you want to avoid the technical details of regressions and control variables and numbers, feel free to skip ahead to the chapter conclusion.

Jury Avoidance

In the Democracy InAction Survey, I asked several questions that uncover behaviors that indicate jury avoidance. I then created a variable that counts how many of those jury avoidance behaviors a respondent has engaged in. The three jury avoidance behaviors are: (1) having ignored a jury summons, (2) having lied to get out of serving on a jury, and (3) having attempted to get out of jury service by doing something other than lying. A respondent who has done none of these three things would be scored a 0, and someone who has done all three would be scored a 3. So, the higher a respondent's score, the more actions they've taken to avoid jury service.

To analyze Jury Avoidance (and the subsequent analyses in this chapter), I restricted the data to include only respondents who are eligible to serve on a jury and who said they have received a jury summons. Being ineligible for jury service means someone likely would not be called to serve on a jury, so including their data would make the analysis less reliable, as would including data on people who have never received a jury summons. You can't avoid serving if you've never been asked to serve.

That brings us to the important question of this chapter: What role, if any, do Apathy and Alienation play in Jury Avoidance? We have seen in the preceding chapters that Apathy and Alienation are significant predictors of undemocratic behavior, from not voting to not making one's voice heard through polls or direct contact with elected officials. But what about jury service? Let's look at figure 5.1.

First, consider Apathy. The coefficient for Apathy is positive, which indicates that respondents who score higher on the Apathy scale engage in more Jury Avoidance. And while this is the relationship we would expect, the coefficient is not statistically significant, meaning we cannot say for certain that Apathy plays a role in Jury Avoidance. That's the good news.

But then we must consider Alienation. And that's the bad news. The coefficient for Alienation is positive and statistically significant. The more alienated an individual feels from government, the more jury avoidance they will engage in. However, the magnitude of change is small enough to give us hope that efforts to engage citizens in civic life will have a meaningful impact. The size of the change is only three percent, which means that moving from completely unalienated to feeling completely alienated will increase jury avoidance by only one item (for example, from zero avoidance behaviors to one, or from one to two, and so on).

As Age increases, Americans engage in fewer Jury Avoidance behaviors, and women avoid jury service less than men. Both findings make sense considering non-voting political behavior is so highly correlated with voting behavior, and women and older people vote more than men and younger people, respectively. Whether or not you consider jury duty to be political behavior, the civic nature of it apparently leads people to behave similarly to voting and other political behaviors.

Higher levels of Trust are associated with more Jury Avoidance, although the magnitude of change is very small (smaller even than alienation's effect). One possible, even likely, explanation for this requires thinking about this finding in its reverse—that people with lower levels of trust are less likely to avoid jury service. People who don't trust the system may see jury service as a way to change what they don't like. Thus, less trusting individuals are more likely to attempt to engage with the system in a way that gives them the opportunity to bring about a direct and immediate change. Jury verdicts give them such an opportunity. Moreover, jury service provides a greater likelihood of their voice making a difference—being one voice out of 12 is much more impactful than when you have one voice in thousands or even tens or hundreds of thousands.

Figure 5.1: Jury Avoidance

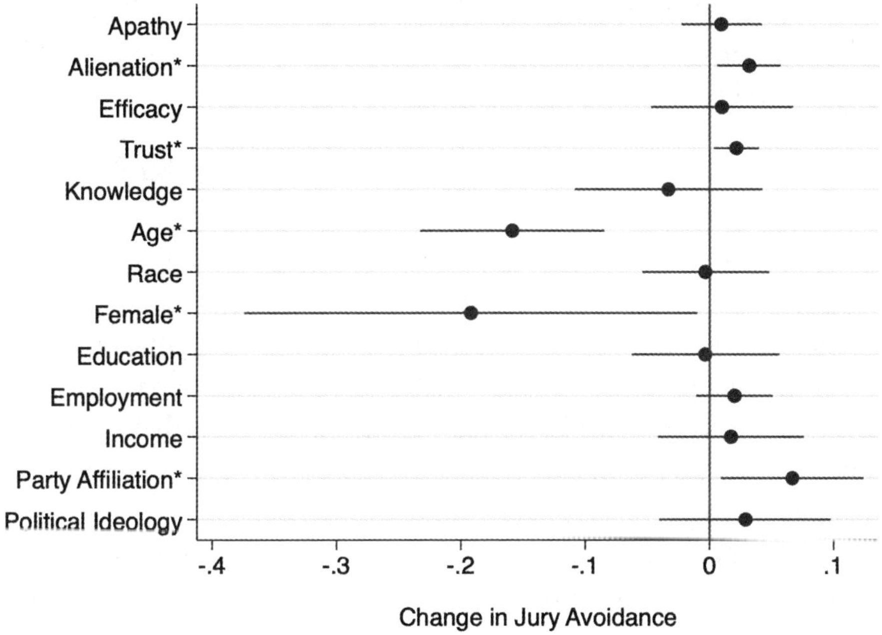

Alienation increases an individual's Jury Avoidance behavior, while Apathy plays no role. See Appendix D for methodological and modeling information.

Partisanship is also significantly associated with Jury Avoidance. The more one moves toward the Democratic Party in their partisan affiliation, the more jury-avoiding behaviors they engage in. I believe the likeliest explanation is that the finding may be a temporal fluke related to the coronavirus pandemic. During the pandemic, many Democrats sought to avoid jury service because of the fear associated with contracting the virus. For example, law professor Melanie Wilson writes, "Jury pools [are] dominated by Republicans and young people . . . these are the groups who may be most willing to serve because they generally feel less concerned about COVID-19 and more comfortable gathering in groups."[60] Some of these jurors sought legitimate deferrals of service, so it stands to reason that more Democrats than Republicans would have also attempted—through less legitimate means—to avoid jury service during the pandemic. I believe this is the most likely explanation for this finding.

Feelings of Personal Responsibility for Jury Service

Next, let's look at how respondents view their personal responsibility for jury service. In figure 5.2, we see now that Apathy has a negative and significant relationship, as we would expect. The more apathetic an individual is, the less they feel personally responsible for serving on a jury. Conversely, the less apathetic one is, the more personal responsibility they express for serving on a jury. And, while the sign on the Alienation coefficient is negative as expected, it has no significant relationship with feelings of personal responsibility toward jury service.

What does the Apathy finding mean for personal responsibility? Let's consider what this regression model tells us. When all the included variables are held at their mean, the average respondent would answer, roughly, that they somewhat disagree with the statement, "I feel a personal responsibility to serve on a jury" (the constant is 1.9; "Somewhat disagree" is coded 2). Among jury-eligible respondents who have received a summons, the average Apathy level is 11.76 (on a scale from 5 to 20, with 20 being more apathetic). If we increase Apathy from its mean to the maximum (an increase of 8.24), that decreases a respondent's feelings of personal responsibility by 0.40, taking them down from the constant of 1.9 to 1.5, about halfway between somewhat disagree and strongly disagree.

Only two control variables are statistically significant. Trust is significant, and, unlike with Jury Avoidance, the sign here is positive. More trusting individuals feel a greater personal responsibility for jury service than individuals with lower trust. This is as we would expect. Political Ideology also has a significant relationship. More conservative respondents express greater levels of personal responsibility for serving on a jury.

Figure 5.2: Personal Responsibility to Serve on a Jury

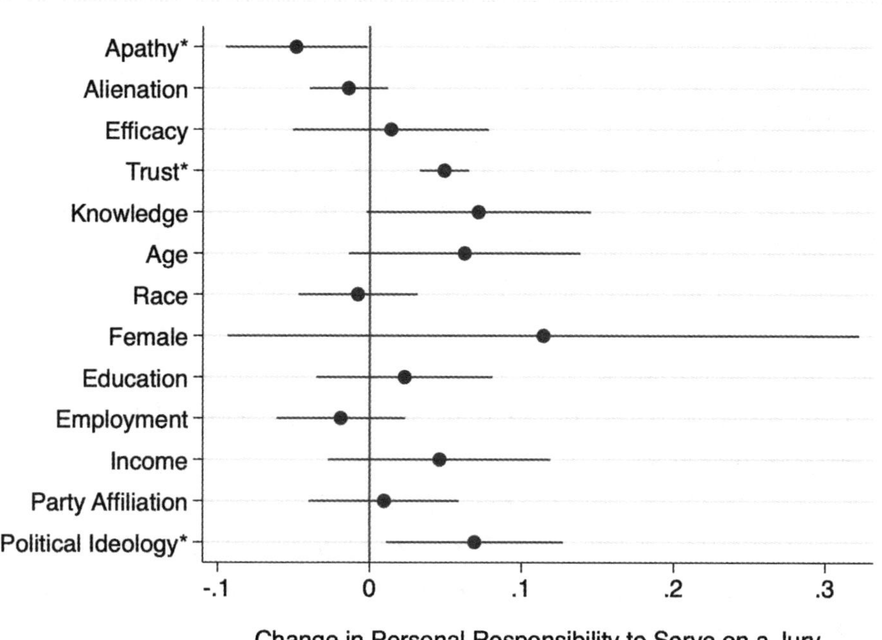

Apathy decreases an individual's feelings of personal responsibility for serving on a jury, while Alienation plays no role. See Appendix D for methodological and modeling information.

Conclusion

America's jury system is tied inextricably to our sense of democratic self-governance. When jurors are drawn from a representative cross-section of the community, as the law requires them to be, juries represent the voice of the people. They get a say in how our government enforces the law. Jury service is important and critical to democracy because the *jury* is important and critical to democracy.

Despite the importance of jury service, Apathy and Alienation play significant but unique roles in the minds and behaviors of jury-eligible Americans. In fact, they play different roles—one in the mind, the other in the behaviors. Apathy affects how Americans view their role in jury service, while Alienation predicts how they will behave in relation to the jury system.

As we've seen in this chapter, people who feel alienated from the system engage in more jury avoidance than people with a strong sense of belonging. If that's you, let me encourage you. If you feel like you don't belong, take my word for it: You do! As I explained earlier in this chapter, a good jury is a representative jury. In fact, the United States Supreme Court has said a *legal* jury *must be* a representative jury. And a representative jury means everyone matters. Everyone belongs. And, because you are part of everyone, *you* belong.

I know what you may be thinking. *Yeah, Dr. Taylor, that sounds nice. I hope it helps you sell a lot of books. But I just don't buy it.* Well, let me encourage you further. Try it before you buy it. Check out the Three Actions section at the conclusion of this chapter. There are a couple of great suggestions for you to see what jury service means for your community and why the system really does need you.

And for the apathetic reader—the one who simply doesn't care about the system or participating in it—let me encourage you. You may not feel a personal responsibility to serve, but the system needs your perspective. Again, the only good (and legal) jury is a representative jury. And, I will say this: Thank you. Even though you don't feel a responsibility to serve, the data tell me that you show up and serve anyway. Perhaps that's because of the compulsory nature of jury service. Sitting in a jury box probably sounds better than sitting in a jail cell. But, regardless of whether you serve happily or grudgingly, willfully or under compulsion, thanks for doing your part.

Research other than mine gives us one more reason to consider serving. You may not want to, you may not feel a responsibility to, and you may have even actively avoided it in the past. But give it a shot. According to

John Gastil and his colleagues, 75 to 90 percent of jurors who served say they had a good experience.[61] If you don't serve on a jury for the system, do it for the experience. Chances are good that you won't regret it.

Three Questions

1. I, along with scholars before me, have attempted to make the case that jury service is a democratic act, even though it is compulsory, unlike the other democratic behaviors covered in this book. Do you view jury service as vital to democracy, or is it something else?
2. Aside from apathy (not caring) and alienation (not belonging), what are some reasons you think people might try to avoid jury service?
3. What do you think would happen to the jury system, to the courts, and to American democracy if legal compulsion were removed and jury service became strictly voluntary? Who would serve? Would that system be representative? (Okay, that's technically three questions in one, but I get to number them, so I'm counting it as one!)

Three Actions

1. Don't try to get out of serving on a jury when summoned. Do I really need to explain this one to you? If so, go back and reread this chapter!
2. Go watch a jury trial. Most court proceedings are open to the public, and judges (most of whom are elected) and prosecutors (most of whom are elected), along with other trial

attorneys, like performing in front of an audience (especially an audience of voters). It may feel awkward to be the one person in the gallery of the courtroom (that's where spectators sit), but trust me, it's not.

3. Talk to your local jury coordinator about jury service. These public servants take their jobs seriously and genuinely care about the quality of the jury pool and about treating jurors fairly. Most of them would be greatly impressed (and appreciative) that you took the time to try and understand their world a little better.

Additional Resources

1. The National Center for State Courts is an excellent organization that serves as an important source of information, data, training, and more for state courts and judges across the nation. The Center runs a project called the Center for Jury Studies, which provides resources for judges and jury administrators for dealing with jurors. In many ways, they are an advocate for jurors and try to help courts make jury service more tolerable, if not enjoyable. Check out their Jurors Outreach page for more information. https://www.ncsc-jurystudies.org/what-we-do/jurors-and-new-media2
2. The American Bar Association, a leading organization of lawyers and judges across the country, also has a project called the Commission on the American Jury, which provides research and other resources on the jury system while also advocating for juries. https://www.americanbar.org/groups/judicial/american_jury/
3. Many local courts have webpages dedicated to providing jury information. Look up yours to find information like how the

jury pool is created, when jury trials are scheduled, and who the jury administrator is, plus much more. The more you know about the system and process now, the less daunting the jury summons will seem when it shows up in your mailbox.

CONCLUSION

"By participating in democratic processes, we come to appreciate their value."

US SUPREME COURT JUSTICE NEIL GORSUCH[1]

Your vote matters. Your campaigning matters. Your poll response matters. Your letter matters. Your deliberation matters. Your voice matters. *You* matter.

Because you and your voice matter in the US, you should get involved. As I said in the introduction, I'm not asking you to become a political activist. We have plenty of those, and if I'm being completely honest, that's part of the problem. You know the old saying: The squeaky wheel gets the grease. The activists are plenty squeaky. What they aren't is representative. They are loud, but being loud does not equate to being right. Or popular. I don't want you to be an activist. I want you to be you. And I want you to do your small part while everyone else does theirs to keep our democracy on track. In doing so, the voice of the people drowns out the squeals of the activists. The will of the people thwarts the desires of the connected.

Major Themes

As we enter the home stretch of this book and our time together, it seems appropriate to reflect on the journey we've taken in the past couple of hundred pages. It is also a good opportunity to take a thirty-thousand-foot view of the empirical results and identify some key themes we saw emerge in the research. I have four overarching key takeaways from the survey analysis.

There exists in game theory a concept known as the first mover advantage. This concept holds that in a repeated game, the first mover enjoys a strategic advantage, often forcing the second mover to make a suboptimal decision. We see that advantage in the empirical results in this book. When citizens are the second mover, their apathy is overcome, and they make choices they otherwise likely would not make. In responding to polls and answering the call to jury duty, apathy is not a predictive barrier to participation. When the pollster calls, citizens are equally likely to answer the poll, regardless of how little they care about politics and government. When the jury summons arrives, apathy does not predict whether the citizen will appear as instructed or not.

Apathy is, however, predictive of how we act—rather, how we *fail* to act—when we are the first movers. The impetus is on us to register to vote, show up at the polls, volunteer for campaigns, and contact our elected officials. The less we care about politics and government, the more likely we are to avoid engaging in activity that requires us to act apart from any external motivation.

A second key theme is that apathy plays a greater role in our attitudes than our behaviors. It shapes our views of personal responsibility in the democratic system, but not always our civic behavior. Across all five chapters, we see that apathy decreases feelings of personal responsibility toward civic behavior. The less one cares, the less they believe civic engagement is incumbent upon them. While apathy plays a more sporadic role in predicting our behaviors, it is a powerful and consistent predictor of our civic attitudes.

Third, alienation is a strange creature. Perhaps, given its name, we should have expected that. I anticipated that alienation—feelings of not belonging in the system—would redouble the effects of apathy. Sometimes it does; in predicting electoral avoidance and personal responsibility to serve on a jury, apathy and alienation act to amplify one another. But, sometimes, the two traits work against one another, for example, as we saw in chapter 4, apathy decreases feelings of personal responsibility to contact elected officials, while alienation significantly increases those same feelings. And in other instances, alienation has no impact at all.

In addition to its contradiction of apathy, alienation almost always moves our attitudes of personal responsibility in the same direction (positively), but not always significantly so. In four of the five chapters (with jury service the sole exception), the more alienated feel a greater responsibility to engage in the activity explored in that chapter. Those who feel like they don't belong in the system, ironically, feel the greatest responsibility to participate in it. This finding was so counterintuitive, I thought the likeliest explanation was that I had reversed the coding of the alienation questions, in effect miscoding the alienated as connected and those who feel like they belong as alienated. However, as I reviewed the data, I confirmed that the coding was correct, and the mixed findings in the behavioral models provide further evidence that it is not a coding issue. It is just one of those mysteries that we will have to leave unexplored for now.

Finally, the other major predictors of political attitudes and behaviors found in previous political science research are not as potent when apathy and alienation are added to the mix. Efficacy and trust matter, but not nearly as much as apathy. In most of the models throughout the book, the coefficient for apathy is larger (sometimes double) than the coefficient for efficacy and trust, meaning apathy plays a much bigger role in shaping our attitudes and behaviors than either efficacy or trust.

Political knowledge, however, is still an important predictor of our civic beliefs and actions, but not always in the way we would expect.

When knowledge proves to predict our behaviors, it is in a more democratic direction, decreasing our avoidance of civic activity. However, the more we know about politics and government, the less personal responsibility we feel to participate in the system. I will talk more about this in the solutions section later in the conclusion.

Chapter Recap

With that high-level overview out of the way, let's review the purpose and findings of each chapter. Remembering where we've been helps set the stage for the rest of this conclusion and where we go from here.

Chapter 1 was the logical starting place for a book about democracy. In it, we traced the history of voting rights in the United States, exploring the times, laws, and constitutional amendments that expanded the franchise to an increasingly wider swath of Americans. We also traced this history of voting participation and voter registration, showing lackluster performance on both metrics through the years. We concluded chapter 1 by exploring the results of the Democracy InAction Survey and saw that apathy plays a strong role in keeping Americans away from the voting booth. The more apathetic a person is, the more likely they are to avoid electoral civic behavior and feel like they do not have a personal responsibility to engage.

In chapter 2, we moved away from voting to non-voting political participation, specifically related to volunteering for political campaigns. We saw from previous data that relatively few Americans give freely of their time for campaigns. I also covered how important volunteers are for campaigns by discussing all the traditional roles that volunteers play on a campaign, from keeping lists updated to knocking on doors in the blazing summer sun. *Fun*! In the end, we saw that, as with voting, apathy drives Americans away from campaign volunteerism and reduces the personal responsibility we feel to help candidates and their campaigns.

We took a break, in chapter 3, from activities that require you to act first and discussed polling. Although polling response rates are abysmal, as we discussed in the chapter, I was fortunate that so many people responded to the Democracy InAction Survey. The educational part of chapter 3 was to help the reader—you—be a wiser consumer of public polls. We walked through what makes a poll good or bad (but never perfect, so don't expect that!) and what you can look for when you see a poll covered in the media. However, the results of the survey analysis took a bit of a twist here and gave us our first glimpse at how apathy doesn't always affect us in the same ways. We saw that apathy decreases our feelings of personal responsibility for taking a poll, but not whether we respond to them.

Chapter 4 shifts the first-mover position back onto the individual, as we covered contacting elected officials. We looked at the scant data available on the topic and pieced together some other anecdotal evidence, but reached the same conclusion as we did with the first three civic activities—relatively few Americans bother with it. I also walked through how you can contact your elected officials with confidence. Once again, we saw that apathy leads us to avoid contacting elected officials and to feeling like we do not have a personal responsibility to do so.

Our final chapter, chapter 5, explored jury service. We discussed why the jury is an important feature of American democracy and traced its history from colonial times, through the Declaration of Independence and Constitution, and hit some of the legal highlights that protected and expanded participation in jury service. Serving on a jury requires another actor to move first, so, as we saw with polling, apathy does not affect our participation in jury duty, but it does make us feel like we do not have a personal responsibility to serve.

Disengagement is Downstream from Disconnectedness

Apathy clearly drives up disengagement in many aspects of civic life. I firmly believe the apathy many Americans feel toward politics, government, and civics in general is mostly a result of the general trend in disconnectedness among Americans, trends documented extensively in 2000 by political scientist Robert Putnam in his groundbreaking and bestselling book, *Bowling Alone*. Putnam's research shows that over the last third of the twentieth century, Americans disengaged from all forms of civic life. No longer did relatively large swaths of Americans participate in community organizations, bowling leagues, and churches; large numbers simply checked out of any activities that put them in contact with their fellow citizens. In the forward to the twenty-year anniversary edition of *Bowling Alone*, Putnam makes clear that things have not gotten any better.

The impact of that disconnect on politics and government has been severe. Americans are more polarized than ever and, as we covered in the introduction, more likely to see people on the other side not merely as wrong but evil or stupid. Such toxic attitudes and increasing violence toward fellow Americans surely increase feelings of not caring and not belonging in the system, which in turn diminish our civic behavior.

Moreover, as we have withdrawn from other people, we have lost our sense of community. Throughout this book, I have used community as a reason to heed my advice. Civic engagement makes better communities. Perhaps this was an unconvincing argument for you because you do not feel a sense of community where you live. Maybe your apathy extends to the community: *I don't care what happens to the rest of this place; I'll be okay, though.* You are almost certainly not alone. But if you feel disconnected or apathetic toward your community, getting plugged back in (or getting plugged in for the first time) to the people and places that make your neighborhood, town, city, or state great is an excellent way to decrease those feelings of apathy and alienation.

But doing so requires getting out of the house. Literally. In *Bowling Alone*, Putnam identified technology as the primary driver of our disconnectedness. As people become more immersed in isolating technology, the more antisocial behavior becomes their norm. One of my favorite findings from *Bowling Alone* is that people who watch more TV are also more likely to flip the middle finger at another driver in traffic. (Seriously, that's a real finding!) More recently, the social psychologist Jonathan Haidt documented the role of technology in destroying our ability to be social.[2]

Solutions

Recall I told you earlier in the book that I don't want to document a problem without offering solutions? Now is the time for that. Apathy is detrimental to civic engagement, as we have seen throughout the book. But what is the fix for that? How do we get Americans to care about the politics that govern their country and their community? I believe the solutions come from both individuals and institutions. It begins with individual Americans who are committed to building a meaningful civic life—one in which they participate in our experiment of self-governance. But institutions, and the people who run them, have a vital role to play as well to encourage civic engagement, especially in the five areas we have covered in this book. So, for each solution that follows, I will discuss the role of both the individual (that's you) and the institutions that guide us.

Destigmatize Politics

Talking about a problem is the key to solving it. However, I, like many in my generation and the one before me, was taught that you never discuss politics or religion in "polite company," whatever that means. That so-called life lesson created an inner turmoil for me. Such an edict was in tension with the things I found fascinating. As a student, I was always more fascinated by the social studies than by biology or English. I enjoyed learning about American history, and Coach King's Street Law class was engaging and entertaining. Outside school, I was probably the only kid watching CNN. I was fascinated by politics, something I wasn't allowed to discuss with others. Politics was taboo.

For too many Americans today, it still is. And a prohibition against discussing politics in "polite company" is a fact of life for many, even though we are inundated by political discussion. From the 24-hour cable news networks (which make political discussion more extreme, more polarizing, more volatile; in other words, infinitely worse[3]) to social media algorithms (which make political discussion more extreme, more polarizing, more volatile; in other words, infinitely worse[4]), Americans are offered an unrestricted diet of political talk. The problem is that it's not good political talk. But to get to a place where Americans can consume and engage in healthy political dialogue, we must remove the stigma associated with talking about politics.

The way we do this, as individuals, is to find someone with whom to talk about politics. My friend and fellow political scientist, Dr. Lindsey Cormack, wrote a book on how to talk to our children about politics and government. I'll talk more about Lindsey's exceptional book in a bit, but for now, I have to tell a story about how she helped promote the book. To get people engaged, she would wear a shirt that read, "Let's Talk Politics." And at least once that I know about, she set up a table on a sidewalk in her New York City neighborhood with a sign inviting passersby: "Will you chat with me about politics for 3 minutes?"

Granted, Dr. Cormack is a political scientist. She is trained to talk about politics, and when she teaches, she talks about politics for much longer than three minutes at a time. She's a professional. But *you* don't have to be. You just need to find a friend or family member with whom you can talk about what's going on in your community and your country at any given time. And take it slow at first. Again, someone can't (or at least shouldn't) get off their couch on Tuesday, having never run a step, and decide to compete in a marathon on Saturday. You don't need to run a marathon. Just take the first step and talk about politics and government for a few minutes once a week with someone you know and trust. You'll be surprised at how quickly you develop your political legs.

A word of caution. These conversations should, ideally, be held face-to-face. In-person communication allows each of you to read facial expressions and body language, to evaluate fluctuations in voice tone. We use these communication skills to fully understand the person with whom we are communicating. And they are especially critical for civic dialogue because they drastically reduce the potential for misunderstandings that can destroy trust and credibility. Meaningful civic talk should not take place online with people we don't know or don't know well. You should be seeking to build a community. While online environments have some hallmarks of traditional community,[5] they are poor substitutes for real, interpersonal connections.[6]

What do I mean by *meaningful conversations about politics and civic affairs*? First, as I have already stated, they're meaningful because they are in person with someone you know and trust. Second, they aren't debates; someone doesn't have to win. The goal is to discuss the important issues of the community—be it the school district, city, state, or nation—in a polite way. Your goal should be to learn from your friend. My grandma used to say that God gave us two ears and one mouth because we should listen twice as much as we talk. That's good advice in life, but especially in conversations about politics. There are two possible scenarios when talking about civic affairs. Either you and your conversation partner agree, or you disagree. If you disagree, try to find common ground or simply agree to disagree. It's cliché but true: You can disagree without being disagreeable. If the two of you agree, and you see a problem, work together to find a solution. Meaningful conversations do not end friendships. They strengthen friendships, and strong relationships are the foundation of a stronger society and civic life.

While having meaningful conversations about politics and government is a great step for individuals to destigmatize politics, institutions have a role to play as well. The most impactful reform our institutions can implement is to prioritize civics education. Ted McConnell, the executive director of the Campaign for the Civic Mission of Schools, points out in a 2019 study that the United States spends five cents per student on civics education, while we spend more than a thousand times that much—$54 per student—on science, technology, engineering, and math (STEM) courses.[7] Now, I have nothing against STEM; those fields of study can provide students with excellent opportunities for professional success and personal enrichment. But the truth of the matter is that none of those fields, important as they may be, appropriately prepare students to be good democratic citizens.

Civics education does. It provides students with a baseline of requisite knowledge to engage in public life. Where STEM curriculum might teach students how to code new computer programs, civics teaches them to decode how government programs work, so they can engage with their elected officials to ensure those programs appropriately represent the will of the American people. Civics education teaches students the importance of engagement, voting in elections, jury service, and so on. And when students are instructed in the machinations of government in the same environment in which they learn proper sentence structures, the order of operations, and that the cell is the basic unit of life, it teaches them that civics, government, and politics are important matters to learn, and those topics are not taboo. Put another way, civics education would go a long way to destigmatizing politics.

Unfortunately, as we've seen, the US deprioritizes civics education. In fact, *deprioritizes* is maybe too weak of a word; *ignores* is perhaps a more accurate verb. That's why Lindsey Cormack wrote her book. If *public* schools fail or refuse to prepare students for *public* life (some deep irony there, huh?), then it is up to us to teach and train the next generation of voters, poll respondents, and jurors about the importance of their participation and the value of their voice. You are at the tail end of this book, which is somewhere around Political Science 201. So, if you skipped ahead in the coursework and you need an accessible, fun refresher on government at a Political Science 101 level, Lindsey Cormack's book *How to Raise a Citizen* is an excellent place to start.

But, I have digressed into individual-level solutions. Let's get back to the institutional. Public schools must prioritize civics education. This should be a nonnegotiable. But, of course, they should be required to do so in a strictly nonpartisan way. What does civics education look like? When I interviewed Lindsey for *The Politics Guys* podcast,[8] she talked to me about scaffolding—the fancy pedagogical way of saying that early coursework should lay a foundation for later coursework in the subject. You don't start mathematics curricula in Algebra 1 learning that y=mx+b is the equation for the slope of a line; you first have to learn the concrete concepts of addition and subtraction, then, later on, the much more abstract idea that letters can represent unknown numbers. Likewise, you don't start learning the basics of 1+1=2 in eleventh grade. These same principles are true with civics education—it must start early and build upon itself.

The way I see it, a robust civics curriculum must include some essential elements, including:

- Facts about American government, including its constitutional basis and basic structures and institutions;
- Practical knowledge about some of the topics covered in this book, such as registration and voting, contacting elected officials, and jury service;
- Philosophical arguments surrounding democracy, republicanism, constitutionalism, truthfulness, the proper role of government, etc.;
- Critical thinking, including media consumption (e.g., identifying and resisting disinformation and misinformation), spotting logical fallacies, and developing statistical literacy

You'll notice that some of these essential elements of civics education revolve around factual knowledge—knowing the branches of government and how to register to vote. These are important, indeed essential. But, if the results presented throughout this book are any indication, they are insufficient. Reflecting on the effect of knowledge on the topics covered herein, we see that factual knowledge increases civic behavior, but it decreases our attitudes about personal responsibility. Being able to recite basic facts is wholly insufficient. Factual knowledge is, in the language of social science, necessary but not sufficient to turn the democratic ship.

For that, we need civics education that moves beyond the basics (1+1=2) to the advanced (y=mx+b). The rest of the elements I have listed above should be designed to address the psychological conditions that have been the focus of this book—apathy and alienation. Understanding not just *how* to vote but *why* we vote, not just that we *have* a president but why we *don't have* a king, helps us find our place in this historic democratic experiment. It teaches us that we are part of the system, that we belong to the system, that our voice is how we make change. Civics education, then, needs to focus as much (if not more) on reducing apathy and alienation as it does on producing factual knowledge. Civics education—like language arts, math, science, and other subjects—needs to scaffold the advanced upon the basic.

In doing so, it will teach students not only about politics and government but also about their role in those institutions. Importantly, it will serve to destigmatize politics—to show the next generation of American citizens that matters of public life are acceptable topics of conversation, even in "polite company."

Make the Private Public

Having destigmatized politics, we should then make the private public. By that, I mean we shouldn't keep politics to ourselves. Politics, government, civics, and current affairs are topics best suited for discussion among citizens as equals. Civic dialogue is part of the democratic ideal. It's how good ideas flourish and bad ideas die. (The latter does not happen through cancel culture.) As Supreme Court Justice Lewis Brandeis once alluded to in a concurring opinion, the remedy for bad speech is "more speech."[9] How do we make the private public when it comes to American civics?

In his 1989 book, *The Great Good Place*, sociologist Ray Oldenburg developed a theory of "the third place."[10] The third place is a place for conversation and community building besides the home (the first place) and work (the second place). Oldenburg argues that third places are vital for individuals, communities, and democracy. It is in these third places that deep community connections and bonds are forged, and, as the research discussed earlier in this book shows, strong communities are places with vibrant democratic action.

To help individuals make their private public and move toward replacing apathy with concern for the community, people should find their third place. Remember the old sitcom, *Cheers*, about an eponymous bar, the place where everyone knew everyone else by name? That's the kind of place I (and Oldenburg before me) am talking about. Find a place where you can have casual, respectful conversations about life and, more to the point, about politics. Remember, social media is not a community, it's not a place. TikTok and Reddit cannot be your third place.

There's a donut shop near my home where, every morning, a group of older men and women sit together eating their donuts and drinking their black coffee before starting their days. Some are farmers, one a truck driver for the state highway department, others, surely, retired. But they are there, every morning, often decked out in some kind of apparel adorned with the local high school mascot. The donut shop employees, including several teenagers, know them by name. The donut shop is their (quite delicious) third place.

Maybe the neighborhood pub or donut shop is not your thing. Maybe it's a local coffee shop. And by "local," I don't mean the chain place that happens to be on the nearest corner; I mean a truly local place, run by local people who care about the local community. (And I certainly don't mean the place with only a drive-through.) Or a community center. Or a church. The Brookings Institution scholar Jonathan Rauch (an atheist, no less) holds up the church as an integral part of American democracy,[11] and economist Arthur Brooks shows that religious people tend to volunteer (even in non-church-related activities) more than nonreligious people.[12] Religious communities are an important feature of civic life, especially in America, and Putnam highlights their decline as part of the problem of America's civic decline.[13]

Regardless of where it is, you should find a third place—somewhere you can be part of a community, to talk about current affairs, and shed your apathy. But you (and others like you) need the support of institutions. Places must do their part to be a third place. But, too often, they don't.

As I was working on this book, I wanted to talk to people about their civic experiences and share with them what I was working on. *What better place*, I thought, *than the local branch of the public library?* Think about it. They're a place that's all about books; I was writing a book. They are part of the knowledge economy; I was both seeking and generating knowledge. They are the local library; I am a local author. Seems like a great place, right? I thought so. So, I talked to the branch manager about hosting a listening session where I could share what I'm working on, maybe read some of the early version of the introduction, and let people share their experiences. Boy, was I wrong! She told me, "We don't really do political events."

Political event? I am not a candidate running for office. I was not trying to hold a political rally or protest. All I wanted to do was host an event, free and open to the public, to talk about democracy and civic life. To give the people in my community a third place to have an open, honest, and respectful dialogue. But that was considered a "political event." And that's a shame, especially since Putnam and Felstein specifically identified branch libraries as an exemplar of the third place.[14]

Institutions need to host civic events, especially when those institutions (such as libraries, community centers, parks, and others) are funded with taxpayer dollars. I'm not saying that community centers should necessarily allow political rallies, but they absolutely should not only *allow* but also *host and promote* civic events like debates and forums.

Libraries should invite scholars and authors in to talk about public policy, current affairs, and urban planning (and books about democracy!) without labeling them "political events." Public parks could host Election Day parties with games and food trucks, where everyone with an "I voted!" sticker gets a free bag of kettle corn.

Of course, making the private public in this way requires institutions to break out of their fear of "politics." I'm not talking here about destigmatizing politics, the previous solution offered. Here, I mean, they need to stop conflating civic and democracy-boosting events with political ones. That will take some educating and convincing of leaders in those institutions. I will be making sure the leaders in my local institutions get a copy of this book (maybe with this section flagged and highlighted). Once you've made the decision to get involved at an individual level, you can make sure your institutions follow suit.

Give and Take

Individuals, like you, and institutions must work together to create a thriving democracy, one in which citizens are involved, and institutions create opportunities for involvement. We've seen that theme throughout this solutions section. Rich democratic involvement truly is a give and take, with both sides giving and taking.

As we discussed in the chapter on voter participation, boosting turnout is possible when campaigns spend the time and resources to engage citizens. Thus, campaigns have a role to play in increasing participation in elections through their mobilization efforts, and that increase must run through less frequent voters. Campaigns can increase participation by reaching voters who don't always participate. Fellow pollster and political scientist Michael Cohen puts it bluntly: "Fight for every vote."[15] But this requires volunteers to knock on doors and make phone calls. That means ordinary people like you need to give of your time, while campaigns take your volunteer hours. But you get the enrichment that comes with a more engaged community and vibrant democracy.

Pollsters must find a way to reach citizens. That might mean charging clients more or operating on thinner margins in order to pay for incentives for research participants. Incentives boost participation in surveys, so what the pollster gives in the way of higher costs, we get from higher participation and more representative samples. Participants give of their time and take the incentives. But, as an increasing share of survey research moves online, individuals have to take the initiative by signing up to participate in research panels.

Elected officials must lead the way to engage disaffected and disengaged citizens. I know the time constraints placed on elected officials, especially members of Congress and state legislators, during the legislative sessions. But that's where staff comes in. Staffers must identify issues that will engage the disengaged and host events around those issues. But for those efforts to work, not only do staff and elected officials need to get the word out about those events, but people who would be interested also need to show up. Give and take.

Despite the criminal penalties associated with ignoring a jury summons, people still do it. As failure-to-appear rates increase, jury coordinators must find ways to improve efficiency, communication, and experience. My first (and so far, only) experience as a juror was when I was 18. I was summoned and showed up at the courthouse at the appointed time on the appointed date. And I sat around, waiting. And waiting. And waiting. Fortunately, my waiting was not in vain; I was selected to sit on a jury. Many others were not as lucky; their time spent was in vain, waiting around only to be sent home. My wife, on the other hand, has been summoned twice in recent years. And in both instances, she only had to call the courthouse the night before to find out whether she needed to appear. In both instances, they kept her on the hook for several days but never required her to actually make the trip to the courthouse. These kinds of efficiencies and communications enhance the experience for prospective jurors. The National Center for State Courts provides excellent resources for jury coordinators to improve the experience for their communities.

And, of course, community members must give of themselves and their time, by not ignoring summons and finding enjoyment in the experience, despite its frustrations. No pain, no gain. Give and take.

The Role of Business

Admittedly, a lot of the burden of sustaining democracy falls on us as individuals. After all, democracy is rule by the people, and ruling is hard work. As we have seen, governing and political institutions also have a role to play. But businesses also benefit from democracy. A free-market economy is a hallmark of democracy, and as we have seen, a thriving democracy is associated with beneficial economic outcomes. Businesses have a stake in democracy's survival and thus have a responsibility to encourage participation among their employees. Here are a few ways they can accomplish that.

Owners could close their businesses on Election Day. This would provide employees with not only the time to vote but also the time to serve as campaign volunteers or as poll workers. (We haven't discussed poll workers in this book, but they are vital to elections. These are the people who give up their entire day from before the polls open until well after they are closed to ensure people can vote and that those who do vote are abiding by the required laws.) As an alternative to closing on Election Day, businesses could ensure employees have time to vote without losing wages and encourage them to vote early or provide enough coverage on Election Day so employees can leave work for a time to go vote.

Businesses should make clear that jury service is important. Too often, owners guilt-trip their employees who receive summonses (as if they had a choice!), rather than supporting them through this critical civic exercise. At the very least, owners should ensure coverage for those who are summoned to serve.

Companies can also get involved more directly. They could hold a company-wide day of service. Maybe the employees don't volunteer for a campaign, but they could host a candidate forum. Or perhaps the company hosts a voter registration drive. Of course, make sure the employees are registered first, and check with local officials about the logistics and legal requirements of such an undertaking. Or maybe owners encourage employees to contact their elected officials about a policy issue relevant to their business or industry.

Business owners are smart people—they're entrepreneurial and think outside the box. This list is but a small sampling of ideas on how businesses can promote civic engagement among their employees and the larger community. Surely, some business owners will think of other, more novel ideas. The point is they should think about them and make them happen.

Why not compulsory voting?

Some readers might use these results to argue for the use of compulsory voting. But, like me wearing jeggings to Walmart, just because you can doesn't mean you should. I admit, the use of compulsory voting is an appealing argument, especially when you consider the results from chapters 1 and 5—apathy decreases participation in elections but does not impact the avoidance of jury service. Why not, then, simply require voting in the same way we require jury service? That is the argument, equally reasonable and flawed, that Dionne and Rapoport make in their book advocating for what they call "universal voting."[16] Aside from the fact that compulsory voting could potentially limit only the effect of apathy and none of the other determinants of electoral avoidance (even countries with compulsory voting do not have 100 percent voter turnout), there are at least three good reasons why compulsory voting is not a proffered solution here.

Fines for Not Voting Are a Poll Tax in Reverse

Political science research has shown[17] (and compulsory voting advocates tacitly acknowledge[18]) that compulsory voting works to increase voter turnout only when the requirement to vote is coupled with a reasonably harsh, enforceable penalty for abstention. For example, political scientist Costas Panagopoulos writes, "I observe no differences in turnout between voluntary systems and systems with only token sanctions for abstention or no real enforcement mechanisms."[19] Those penalties range from monetary fines to the denial of civil liberties to imprisonment—all for not showing up to vote.

Of course, it is reasonable to argue that the government levies plenty of fees and fines on us already. Adding another fine for merely making a personal choice not to do something seems to me unconscionable. Fining someone for taking a harmful action, such as running a red light, is wholly appropriate. To fine someone for inaction, rather than action, reeks of overreach. But that's not even the most egregious wrong for imposing a fine on someone for not voting.

To impose a fine for not voting is nothing more than a poll tax in reverse. Rather than taxing someone to participate, compulsory voting activists advocate for taxing someone for not voting. Lest you think that I'm conflating taxes and fines, I'll point out that the federal government argued, and the Supreme Court held in the ObamaCare case, that a fine for inaction (in that case, not having health insurance) is indeed a tax. Thus, a monetary cost for voting abstention, regardless of what you call it, is a tax.

And, just like poll taxes of old, this one would disproportionately impact poor and minority communities. Dionne and Rapoport argue for a $20 poll tax for voting abstention in their compulsory voting proposal.[20] They offer an alternative to the tax of "an hour or two of community service."[21] Either way, people with lower incomes will pay more than those of greater means. Who do you think can more easily afford a $20 tax to get out of an activity they don't want to do? Someone making the federal minimum wage of $7.25 or the lawyer who skips Election Day to make her closing argument in a big trial? Whose schedule will be more upended by "an hour or two of community service"? The single mom who has to work three part-time jobs just to make ends meet, or the professional whose employer gives them time off work for community service (or who can tap into their unlimited or otherwise generous and flexible vacation time)?

If we as a country took seriously the abolition of poll taxes during the Jim Crow era, we must ensure they remain forbidden. Since compulsory voting works only with an enforced sanction, like a poll tax (or worse yet, imprisonment), then requiring people to vote seems a bridge too far to boost turnout.

Jury Service is Different From Elections

Serving on a jury is different from voting. Don't misunderstand that last sentence as contradictory to the argument I made in chapter 5. Jury service is important to democracy, and it bears some similarities to voting. But there are also some major differences that do not justify compulsory voting in the way American courts compel jury service.

Seating a jury (or even several juries) requires the participation of a relatively few randomly selected citizens. This raises two differences from voting—selection and scope. With regards to selection, jury pools are randomly selected from the community. Compulsory voting would involve no such selection of a subset of the population; it would, by definition, require everyone to participate, which brings me to the difference of scope. Juries do not require every adult in the county to show up at the courthouse on the same day to sit in judgment of accused lawbreakers, both criminal and civil. Whereas jury service inconveniences only a few dozen to a few hundred people, depending on the size of the jurisdiction and the number of trials on the docket, compulsory voting would inconvenience every adult. Those who don't want to vote would be inconvenienced by having to show up, and those who want to vote would be inconvenienced by the presence of hundreds of other people who don't want to be standing in line with them. It's a lose-lose for everyone.

Jurors are also paid for their time. Granted, it's not much, but they do at least recoup some compensation for doing their duty. Voters are not paid to vote. In fact, federal law clearly prohibits paying people to vote.

So, in order to make the comparison with jury service work, compulsory voting advocates would not only have to change existing federal law with regards to providing incentives for voters but also convince appropriators (those are the lawmakers who write the government's budget) to set aside (likely) billions of dollars every two years to pay people to vote.

Compulsory jury service, moreover, has a rich historical tradition in the United States. State courts and, eventually, the federal courts have long required people to serve on juries. The same cannot be said of compulsory voting. While compulsory voting has been (and continues to be) a tradition in other countries around the world, it has never been attempted in the United States. What works in Belgium or Egypt may not necessarily work in the US because of cultural, political, and institutional differences between other countries and ours.

Most importantly, jury decisions are (usually) final, while election outcomes are not. Yes, we have to live for four years (more or less) with the results of an election. But when the next election rolls around, we have the opportunity to undo the mistakes of the previous election. Rarely is that the case with a jury's verdict. Sure, appellate courts sometimes order new trials for various reasons, but those instances are not a regular or frequent occurrence like elections. Most of the time, when a jury decides a case, that is the final word. Citizens upset by the outcome cannot organize, wait four years, and show up en masse to hold a new trial. They can, however, do that with elections.

The jury and elections are both critical to democracy, but they are also very different institutions. Because of these important differences, any comparison of them to argue that compulsion in one justifies compulsion in the other is an apples to watermelons comparison (bordering on an apples to Mac Truck tires comparison).

Compulsory Voting Violates Our Right to Abstain

Requiring people to vote undermines our fundamental right as Americans to be left alone, (mostly) free to pursue a life we desire without government interference. Don't get me wrong. I want you to participate in elections (and other civic activities). I have spent the better part of my life trying to get people to participate in public life and make their voices heard. I worked on campaigns to convince people to vote and to persuade them to vote for my candidate. I worked in legislative offices, making sure elected officials knew what their constituents were saying. I taught political science to university students in an effort to show them how to engage in public life professionally. I help elected officials understand voters, and attorneys understand juries. Now, I have written a book with tens of thousands of words designed to encourage you to get involved. I am all for civic engagement.

But I'm not for compulsion. I would never force you to engage in the public square, and I would never suggest you should be forced to act. Those who want to compel others to do something often resort to force because they can't persuade you. They give up on trying to convince and turn instead to compulsion. That's not the way to win. You are your own person. You should be the only one who gets to decide what you do on the first Tuesday after the first Monday in November.

Compulsory voting advocates try to make their case by wordsmithing. For example, Dionne and Rapoport argue that voting is not speech but behavior. There is some truth there—voting is a behavior. But the behavior itself is secondary to the speech. Behavior is the delivery device for speech. Showing up to the polls is no more fully democratic than driving by the track is fully athletic. Simply showing up does not help decide an election's outcome. What matters is the selection of a candidate. What matters is your speech.

Advocates of compulsory voting offer blank ballots and "none of the above" options as solutions to the compelled speech issue. *You don't have to vote for any particular candidate, so you're not speaking*, they argue. Then what's the point? What is the difference between not showing up and showing up to cast a blank ballot? I would argue that the difference is an inconvenient infringement of your right to be left alone. In my view, what matters in an election is selecting a candidate. Speech is what matters for democracy. That's why I've said repeatedly throughout this book that the reason I want you to engage in these behaviors is to make your voice heard. Your voice is what matters to democracy. And government cannot compel you to speak.

Government, in my view, exists to protect our rights. I believe firmly in our right to vote (and our right to petition government, to speak freely, and so on). It is the government's job to safeguard those rights. It is not the government's job to force me to exercise those rights. Think of the parallels. Americans (with limited exceptions) have the right to bear arms. We have the right to carry a gun to defend ourselves if necessary. Governments, according to the Second Amendment, must protect that right and not infringe upon it. They cannot, however, require any of us to carry a gun if we don't want to. Don't like guns? Let's apply the analysis to newspapers. The First Amendment guarantees a free press. Government must protect that free press by not passing laws that limit it. What government cannot do is force someone to open a newspaper, open a broadcast station, or start an online news blog. In the same way, government's role in voting is to set the rules and protect our right to vote. It is not their job to force anyone unwilling to exercise that right to do so against their will.

Where Does It End?

If we were to entertain the idea of compulsory voting as a response to my findings of apathy's detrimental impact on electoral participation, where does the compelled behavior end? Let's work through the chapters of this book. Should we force people to volunteer for a campaign when not enough people show up to knock on doors? (Is it even volunteering if it's forced?) Should we threaten Americans with monetary penalties for hanging up on pollsters? (Yes! Just kidding, of course not!) If too few people contact their elected officials, should we pass a law that requires them to call their senator's office once every quarter or face a fine? (But don't worry. The law won't require you to say anything substantive; you can just call and register your name for the sake of compliance, then hang up.) If these requirements sound nonsensical, it's because they are. Anyone lobbying for them would be laughed out of the Capitol building. But, as laughable as they may be, they are the logical extension of using the results in this book to argue for compulsory voting.

Bringing It All Home

My goal in this book has been threefold. First, I have documented the effect apathy plays in driving up civic disengagement. That purpose was mostly academic (trust me, I don't go around talking about regression models all day . . . except at work), but it was essential to lay the foundation for the other purposes of the book. Those are the purposes that mean the most to me because they are about the Americans who would read this book in search of something meaningful.

I went to graduate school and earned a doctoral degree because I love teaching, and I wanted to make a career out of it. But sometimes, things don't shake out the way we plan. So, I seek to teach in ways that do not always involve the four walls of a university classroom. That brings me to the second purpose of this book: to educate. I hope that, along the way, you've learned something new. Possibly it was a better understanding of how public opinion polling works. Or perhaps you didn't know the history of the American jury system. Maybe you just learned a new and catchy way to describe the reasons for your own civic malaise—because you can't, because you don't want to, or because nobody asked. Regardless of what it was, I sincerely hope you learned something new from reading this book.

Finally, and most importantly, I want to encourage you. I have devoted a great deal of space in these pages to spur you to action. I have reminded you that, as the old folk song goes, "this land is your land . . . this land was made for you and me." (I actually briefly considered titling this book "This Land is Your Land," but under wise counsel from a trusted friend who told me it sounded too much like a land acknowledgment, I conceded.) I have given you reasons why your voice matters, why you matter to American civic life. And, for those who just don't know where to begin, I have provided you with small steps you can take to get started. As much as I hope you learned something new, or rather *more* than I hope you learned something new, I hope the time you spent with this book has encouraged you to become more engaged in the civic life of our country.

You may be sick of hearing me say it at this point, but my goal is not to turn you into an activist. This isn't a couch-to-marathon civics text. It's a couch-to-leisurely-stroll-around-the-block civics text. Democracy needs action, but it also needs space to flourish. Live your life largely free from politics and the political. Find space to engage corporately without a focus on politics,[22] but keep an eye on the state of current affairs and when the time comes, step up in a mighty way.

Maybe you've seen your story in these pages. Perhaps you read this book and thought, *Yeah, I definitely haven't cared about politics that much.* Well, whatever brought you here, whatever it was that made you pick up and read a book about a topic you are not interested in, I hope it continues to guide you. And, in case you need reminding, as I close this book, here are three reasons I think you should be involved.

First, our democracy is too important for you to sit on the sidelines. Freedom is at the heart of democracy, and as President Ronald Reagan once said, "Freedom is a fragile thing and it's never more than one generation away from extinction. It is not ours by way of inheritance; *it must be fought for and defended constantly by each generation*" (emphasis mine).[23] When the flame of freedom is threatened, democracy itself is on the verge of extinction. This may sound existential. Let me assure you: It is. So, my question to you is: Will you fight for and defend our freedom for your generation and the ones that come behind you? Will you get involved in our democracy, for "ourselves and our Posterity"?[24]

Second, something you care about—perhaps *everything* you care about—is touched in some way, somehow, by politics and government.

So, my question to you is: Are you going to fight for and defend what you care about?

Third, if you don't, someone else will. Maybe that sounds like a good thing to you. Perhaps it is even the reason you've abstained for so long—"Eh, someone else will do it, so why should I?" Because someone else is not *you*. I'm not you, your neighbor is not you. Heck, even your husband or wife is not you. I have my voice, your neighbor has his, and your wife has hers. Only one person has the exact combination of your voice, your views, your lived experiences, your values, and so on. And that person is you. When you sit on the sidelines while other people are in the game, you're letting them do it their way. And you may not always agree with their way. You have to do your part to try to make sure things are done the way you agree with. So, my question for you is: Are you going to let other people have *their* way in *your* country?

I hope not.

ACKNOWLEDGMENTS

In the acknowledgements of both my master's thesis and my doctoral dissertation, I thanked God for his provision in my life, especially the intellectual capacity and the endurance to finish both those works of original research. I echo that here with one addition. This project was truly inspired by God. I am a nocturnal person, so I often have trouble sleeping when I'm "supposed" to. Even as I sit here writing that sentence, it's 1:44 in the morning. As I lay awake one night, I suddenly felt an urge to write a book. It was a clear and unmistakable call from God. But, like Jacob, I decided I'd wrestle with God. "I've tried that multiple times, and I keep getting stuck," I told God. Then, he laid it all out for me: the title, what each topic would be, and how I would go about the research. Finally, I gave in, got up, and went to my desk. During that 2 a.m. work session, I put all that God had given me down on paper. What you now hold in your hands is the result of God's call and my response. I pray what I've done is pleasing to him.

I also owe a huge debt of gratitude to my family. My wife, Stephanie, is the type of person this book was written for. Before she married a political scientist, née political consultant, she was the least political person in America. Over the years, I've gotten her more engaged in the process. We have been married thirteen years as of this writing. I hope you, dear reader, don't take that long to heed my advice. Stephanie also read the manuscript and offered keen editorial advice. Being married to a woman with an English degree does have perks for a writer! My sons are also a source of inspiration. I want this country to be better for them than it is now. I want America to be prosperous, blessed, safe, and free. To keep it that way, we all need to do our part. Etched in the façade of City Hall in Stockton, California, are the words, "Let that which the fathers have builded inspire their sons to civic patriotism." As much as I pray that this book is a faithful response to God's call, that is my prayer for this book. Thank you, boys, for the love, laughter, and support!

Dr. Lindsey Cormack is an engaging scholar and supportive friend. She provided valuable guidance on the publication process and so much other excellent advice. As if that weren't enough (it truly was *more* than enough), she read and provided amazing feedback on chapter 5. Thanks, Lindsey; I don't know how I could have gotten this done without you.

I am also part of an amazing team at the Foundation for Government Accountability, including Adam Gibbs, Mikayla Hall, Piper Alfonso, Steven Stafford, and a former teammate, Andrew Welhouse, who provided me the intellectual stimulation and conversations that have made this book possible. Sarah Coffey, who is also on our team, deserves extra recognition because she read the entire manuscript and provided not only excellent copyediting, fixing all my mistakes as she does on a daily basis, but also tightening up the language and making it more accessible to the non-academic reader when I tended to fall back into the safety of my scholarly writing style. Thanks for all your help on this project and every day, Sarah.

Beyond my immediate team, I am blessed to work for an organization with an amazing group of leaders, starting with my vice president, Nick Stehle, who read every word of the manuscript and made valuable improvements. Our CEO, Tarren Bragdon, and COO, Jonathan Bechtle, have created a collegial, intellectual, and simply incredible place to work. Having a job that I love at an organization I love has meant I still had the energy and brainpower at the end of (most) days (except those two weeks in May 2025!) to spend time working on this book. Thank you all for your leadership. And to the entire FGA team, thank you for being such amazing colleagues. It is an honor and a blessing to get to work with you all on a daily basis to help our fellow citizens live the American Dream.

Over the course of earning four degrees, I have learned a tremendous amount from countless professors and advisors. Almost all of them shaped this work in some way. But several deserve special recognition for the role they've played not only in my academic work but in my life. Dr. Rick Swanson, who had the good sense to talk me out of law school circa 2009. And while he may still be upset that I didn't name a kid after him, he still holds a special place in my heart, and I hope this mention earns me all the metaphysical bonus points I never seemed to quite pull down in the classroom. I also wish him all the best in retirement. During my first master's program, my thesis committee was the David Show: Dr. David Rehr, who remains a friend and source of great encouragement to this day, and Dr. David Ettinger, who was one of the earliest people to teach me what it means to do true academic research.

In my doctoral work at the University of Kentucky, my advisor, Dr. Mark Peffley, and I butted heads more than we probably should have. That's what happens when you have two stubborn men who are set in their ways trying to collaborate and get things done. Still yet, I knew he had my interests on his mind in all he said and did. In addition to Mark, Drs. Steve Voss, Justin Wedeking, Mike Zilis, Abby Córdova, and Janet Stamatel were incredible professors and committee members who always pushed me to be better, think deeper, and keep my .do files clean. Dr. Dan

Morey, a fellow veteran, had absolutely no reason to take an interest in my success, but he did, and I am eternally thankful that he did. Despite having taught me regression, which clearly still plays a prominent role in my research, the most valuable lesson Dan taught me applies to research as well as every other aspect of life: When things get tough, Dan always said to "embrace the suck." Dr. Clayton Thyne was the director of graduate studies who recruited me to Kentucky and later served as the department chair. He told me in my first semester than I had an only 40 percent chance of finishing my Ph.D., and proving him wrong remains one of my greatest professional accomplishments. Now, as a Dean, Clayton has moved out of the nosebleed section of the sixteenth floor to the much nicer seats on the second floor, and it's a much-deserved move.

Finally, Dr. Ryan and Tonya Teten. Doc and Tonya, and their two incredible kids, Aiden and Seth, were my family in college. From tailgating to dogsitting, I have so many amazing memories. I have so much to say about these incredible people that would fill exponentially more space than I have here, so I'll just say two things. First, unlike Rick Swanson, I *did* name a kid after them, so that tells you how truly special they are. And second, I love you guys and appreciate you more than you'll ever know.

I owe a great deal of gratitude to graduate school friends, who were (and often still are) a source of intellectual stimulation and intrigue. Dr. Gargi Vyas, I hope you never stop wondering or wandering. Drs. Chip O'Connell and Baylee Harrell, thank you both for all the laughs! Dr. Jaclyn Johnson, I hope you one day end up on the IR group chat, but in the meantime, you can always be on the Americanist chat with me. Dr. Sherrelle Roberts, I don't know what I would do without you. Your unrelenting faith and unparalleled sense of humor are truly life-sustaining. And you were always great to share campaign war stories with. Thanks for being my friend. Dr. Greg Saxton was an incredible office-suite neighbor. I'll never forget your kindness and encouragement. You were right about two things: I was never as smart as I was during comps, and correlation does not equal causation . . . except when it does. Drs. Jennifer

"J-Fli" Flinchum, Erik Fay, Katie Angell, Helen Kras, Abbie Wood, Audrey Baricovich, EmiLee Smart (yes, that's her real name, and it's incredibly fitting!), and Trey Wood, thank you all for your friendship over the years. My friend and mentor, Alex Denison, never got to hang the Ph.D. behind his name because this world lost him entirely too soon. I'll never forget the impact he made on my life and my role as a teacher. Chris and Hannah Crumrine made life as a married grad student infinitely better. Chris was and is a remarkable friend, consummate scholar, and unparalleled professional. Hannah is whip-smart, fun to be around, and was a great friend to Stephanie during our time in Lexington. We love you guys!

I am eternally thankful to have amazing mentors, especially Gordon Reese, who is a top-notch political consultant and trained me to be about half as good as he is, and Bari Weinhausen, who taught me almost everything I know about qualitative moderating and made me the researcher I am today. I hope the lack of qualitative work in this book does not disappoint her. I am also thankful for the guidance and continued friendship of former bosses, especially Kristian Magar, Speaker Hunt Downer, Senator Elbert Guillory, Congressman (now Senator) James Lankford, and Congressman Steven Palazzo. Kristian deserves special recognition because, like the Tetens, the Magars were like family to me. Kristian, "Kut Throat" Kyla, Katie, Kaille, Kincade, and Kian will forever be part of my life, and my life and my family are so much better off because of it.

Daniel Copeland, the vice president of research at Barna, is a true friend and source of encouragement. I hope that one of my future books is coauthored with him. Daniel, thank you for your prayers and encouragement over the years.

I also owe a debt of gratitude to the trial consultants I have had the pleasure to work with and learn from during my time in the field. Thank you to Drs. Lee Meihls, Stuart Miles, Dan Wolfe, Rachel York-Colangelo, and Ryan Malphurs, as well as Sarah Murray and Ryan Liffrig. You all are incredible colleagues, and I am thankful for you. A special debt is owed to Michelle Rey LaRocca, who helps lead the Trust in Justice Project, because she helped me think through why trust might be associated with jury avoidance, a finding from chapter 5.

This work was greatly improved by the insights and feedback from several other professionals who generously shared their time and expertise and who were not afraid to give me candid feedback about what worked, what didn't work, and what could work with some small (or not-so-small) tweaking. They include John Geraci, Dr. Adam Probolsky, Geoff Pallay, and Christopher Kush.

Lastly, I'd like to thank the team at RealClear and Amplify Publishing for their confidence in this book. Evan Valentine is my acquisitions editor, and he took one look and didn't hesitate to move forward. Camma Duhamell and the rest of the publishing team at Amplify made the publication process remarkably easy, and I thank them all.

While working on the survey that provided the original research basis for this project, I worked with an online panel company called Cint. I had two excellent partners at Cint who deserve my thanks. First, Frank Gervasi was my account manager. He was more than a salesman; he was a true partner on this project as well as on many others. Nick Mahler is a tech wizard. Any time I had a problem with the Cint platform, Nick was able to quickly diagnose the issue and work with me to solve it. Thank you, guys, for making this project possible.

Even though this village helped make this book what it is today, all remaining mistakes are mine and mine alone.

APPENDIX A

BOOK CLUB DISCUSSION QUESTIONS

Introduction

1. Taylor argues that politics in America is increasingly negative and exhausting. Do you agree with this assessment? How does this perception affect people's willingness to engage in civic life?
2. This chapter discusses rising negative ad spending and political violence. How do you think these trends impact the health of our democracy?
3. The author cites evidence that a majority of Americans have stopped talking about politics because it is too divisive. Have you personally experienced this phenomenon? How can we encourage respectful dialogue about political issues?
4. The author discusses the trustee and delegate models of representation. Which model do you think best describes

the relationship between elected officials and their constituents today?

5. Do the book's definitions of apathy and alienation align with your view of these words? In what ways are these definitions the same or different from how you view these concepts?
6. Taylor mentions three things he hopes to accomplish with the book. Which of these goals resonates with you the most, and why?
7. What do you hope to gain from reading and discussing *Democracy InAction*? Are there specific questions or concerns about civic engagement that you hope the book will address?

Chapter 1: Registration and Voting

1. The author uses a "voting funnel" analogy to illustrate how the pool of eligible voters shrinks at each stage of the electoral process. Does this funnel accurately reflect your understanding of voter participation? Why or why not? What other illustrations can you think of that reflect voter participation?
2. The chapter discusses the National Voter Registration Act ("Motor Voter Law"). Do you think this law has been effective in increasing voter registration? What are its strengths and limitations?
3. Taylor presents data showing that a substantial portion of Americans are not registered to vote and that this statistic has remained fairly consistent over time. What factors do you think contribute to this persistent problem?

4. The chapter emphasizes the importance of voting as a means of holding elected officials accountable. Do you believe that elections are an effective accountability tool in our current political climate? Why or why not?
5. Results from the Democracy InAction survey show that apathy is a major driver of electoral abstention. What solutions can you think of that would decrease people's apathy and increase their rates of registration and turnout?

Chapter 2: Campaign Activities

1. Taylor emphasizes the importance of volunteers for political campaigns. Why are volunteers so crucial, and what specific roles can they play?
2. The chapter presents data showing that relatively few Americans volunteer for campaigns. What are some of the barriers that prevent people from getting involved in this way?
3. Have you ever volunteered for a political campaign? If so, what was your experience like? If not, what would motivate you to volunteer in the future?
4. The author identifies several types of campaign activities. Which of these activities do you think are most effective in reaching voters and influencing their decisions?
5. The chapter suggests that getting involved in a campaign can be a way to meet new people and develop new skills. Have you found this to be true in your own experience?

Chapter 3: Responding to Polls

1. The author argues that polling is a vital instrument of democracy. Do you agree with this assessment? Why or why not?
2. This chapter discusses the challenges that pollsters face in obtaining accurate and representative data. What are some of these challenges, and how do they impact the reliability of poll results?
3. Have you ever participated in a political poll? If so, what was your experience like? If not, what would make you more likely to participate in the future?
4. The author provides guidance on how to critically evaluate polls. What are some of the key factors to consider when assessing the credibility of a poll?
5. The author notes that apathy toward polls shapes our views of participating in polls but does not directly affect our actual participation. Do you find these conclusions surprising or fitting based on your perception of apathy?

Chapter 4: Petitioning the Government

1. The chapter focuses on the right to petition the government for a redress of grievances—the right to contact our elected officials. How familiar were you with this right before reading this chapter?
2. The author cites statistics showing that relatively few people contact their elected officials. Why do you think this is the case?

3. The author is clear on the importance of making personal connections and having a specific request when contacting representatives. How might you go about contacting your elected official?
4. How could organizations engage and promote direct communication between citizens and political officials?
5. Do you think that elected officials are responsive to constituent concerns? What factors might influence their responsiveness?

Chapter 5: Jury Service

1. The chapter describes the two types of juries: grand juries and trial juries. What are the key differences between these two types of juries, and what role does each play in the justice system?
2. The author emphasizes the importance of representative juries. Why is it so crucial that juries reflect the diversity of the community they serve?
3. Have you ever served on a jury? If so, what was your experience like? Would you be willing to serve on a jury again in the future? Why or why not?
4. What do you think are the biggest challenges facing the jury system today, and how could these challenges be addressed?
5. The author argues that jury service is a vital democratic act. Do you agree with this assessment? Why or why not?

Conclusion

1. One key takeaway from the book is that apathy plays a greater role in our attitudes than our behaviors. Does this finding resonate with you? Why or why not?
2. In the conclusion, Taylor offers solutions at both the individual and institutional levels. Which solutions do you find most compelling, and why?
3. The author suggests individuals must find a way to engage with their community, whether it be by finding a location to be in community with others or finding a group to get involved with. How would a person get started on that search?
4. Taylor argues that, in order to increase engagement and understanding, public schools must offer more education about civics. How effective would public education be?
5. The author stresses three reasons to get involved in politics: It is important to safeguard our democracy, something people care about is touched by government and politics, and if you don't act, someone else will. What do you think about this argument, and would you add anything else to it?
6. Throughout the book, Taylor said people must find the thing they care about that would spur them to action. What is that thing for you? How is it impacted by politics and government?

APPENDIX B

SURVEY METHODOLOGY

Results for this poll were collected using a sampling frame from an online panel collected by Strategic Insights Research, LLC. The national sample is of 1,904 American adults.

The survey was conducted October 15–28, 2024. The margin of sampling error is ± 2.25 percentage points. The margin of sampling error may be higher for subgroups. Results presented may not always appear to total 100 percent due to rounding.

Data were post-stratified using weighted demographic information from the US Census Bureau's Current Population Survey Voting and Registration Supplement and the state election authorities. Demographic information for actual voters in past elections was used to construct sample target weights.

Strategic Insights Research, LLC, paid for all costs associated with this survey.

The national survey was conducted via Alchemer, an online survey platform, among a sample of 1,904 American adults drawn from a non-probability, opt-in online panel from Cint. Respondents were compensated for their participation. The survey was conducted in twelve sections with various behavioral and attitudinal questions dispersed throughout the questionnaire. The survey proceeded according to the following outline:

- **Introduction and Consent.** In this section, I introduced the survey, including the approximate time commitment and number of questions. Respondents were informed that their individual answers would be kept confidential and that all reporting on the survey would be done in the aggregate. Participants were asked to affirmatively consent to participate in the survey.
- **Past Civic Participation.** Respondents were asked whether or not they have, in the past, participated in any of 23 democratic behaviors. This section was fixed in the survey order, while the 23 behaviors were randomized within the section.
- **Distraction 1.** A section of 13 questions used to distract respondents from guessing the purpose of the study. This section was fixed in the flow.
- **Personal Responsibility.** I asked respondents to indicate the extent to which they agree or disagree with eight statements about their personal responsibility to participate in various democratic activities. The section was randomized in the flow, and the eight statements were randomized within the section.
- **Trust.** Respondents were asked to what extent they trust various institutions and people. This section was randomized within the survey order, and the 12 questions were randomized within the section.
- **Knowledge.** Participants responded to a standard battery of political knowledge questions. The questions were randomized within the section, and the section was randomized in the survey flow.

- **Apathy, Alienation, and Efficacy.** This section employed three standard psychological batteries of questions to evaluate respondents' level of apathy, alienation, and political efficacy. In total, respondents answered 16 questions in this section. Some questions evaluated these characteristics in the affirmative (i.e., higher agreement indicates the presence of the trait), while some were evaluated in the negative (i.e., higher agreement indicated the absence of the trait). The section was randomized within the survey flow, and the questions were randomized within the section.
- **Distraction 2.** A section of seven unrelated questions used to distract participants from guessing the purpose of the study. This section was randomized within the survey flow.
- **Distraction 3.** A section of eight unrelated questions used to distract participants and prevent them from guessing the purpose of the study. This section was randomized within the survey flow.
- **Emotional Reaction.** This section asked respondents to indicate on an emotions quadrant the emotion they feel when confronted with a scenario in which various civic behaviors are implicated. The behaviors were randomized in the section, which was fixed in the survey flow. I learned at the completion of collecting the survey data that, unfortunately, Alchemer's reporting system did not provide the kind of data manipulation that would have made analyzing these reactions productive.
- **Unrelated Research Vignette.** This section, fixed in the flow, contained a 157-word vignette with five questions. It was unrelated to the present research.
- **Demographics.** I collected demographic information for both weighting and analytical purposes, including party affiliation, political ideology, sex, gender, race, income, and educational attainment.

Demographics

AGE		
	18 to 24	12.2%
	25 to 34	17.6%
	35 to 44	16.6%
	45 to 54	15.9%
	55 to 64	16.5%
	65 or older	21.2%

RACE		
	Asian or Asian American	5.5%
	Black or African American	11.4%
	Hispanic or Latino	17.3%
	Middle Eastern or Indian	1.1%
	Native American or Alaska Native	1.0%
	Pacific Islander	0.2%
	White or Caucasian	56.8%
	Another race or ethnicity	6.7%

GENDER		
	Male	49.0%
	Female	51.0%

EDUCATION		
	Less than high school	8.9%
	High school or GED	25.9%
	Technical or trade school	1.4%
	Some college, no degree	18.9%
	Associates or two-year degree	8.8%
	Bachelors or four-year degree	21.8%
	Advanced or professional degree	14.3%

INCOME		
	Less than $25,000	15.2%
	$25,000 to $50,000	17.1%
	$50,001 to $80,000	16.1%
	$80,001 to $100,000	12.7%
	$100,001 to $150,000	17.4%
	More than $150,000	21.5%

PARTY AFFILIATION		
	Democratic	48.0%
	Republican	49.0%
	Independent	3.0%

Demographic percentages presented are weighted proportions.

APPENDIX C

SURVEY QUESTIONNAIRE & WEIGHTED TOPLINES

Results presented below may not appear to equal 100% due to rounding.

Past Civic Participation

Q1. Some people are registered to vote, while others are not. Are you registered to vote?	
Yes, I am	74%
No, I am not	22%
Don't know/not sure	4%

Q2. Do you have a current state-issued ID card or a valid driver's license?	
Yes, I do	87%
No, I do not	10%
Don't know/not sure	3%

Q3. Have you ever updated your voter registration after moving?	
Yes, I have	61%
No, I have not	34%
Don't know/not sure	4%

Q4. In the past five years, have you voted in an election?	
Yes, I have	70%
No, I have not	27%
Don't know/not sure	2%

Q5. In the past five years, have you intentionally skipped voting in an election?	
Yes, I have	28%
No, I have not	68%
Don't know/not sure	4%

Q6. In the past five years, have you accidentally missed an election?	
Yes, I have	23%
No, I have not	71%
Don't know/not sure	6%

Q7. Have you ever volunteered for a political campaign?	
Yes, I have	23%
No, I have not	73%
Don't know/not sure	4%

Q8. Have you ever displayed a political yard sign or bumper sticker?	
Yes, I have	33%
No, I have not	65%
Don't know/not sure	3%

Q9. Have you ever donated money to a political campaign?	
Yes, I have	31%
No, I have not	66%
Don't know/not sure	3%

Q10. Have you ever answered a political survey on the phone?	
Yes, I have	41%
No, I have not	55%
Don't know/not sure	5%

Q11. Have you ever hung up on a political survey taker?	
Yes, I have	34%
No, I have not	58%
Don't know/not sure	9%

Q12. Have you ever refused to take a political survey?	
Yes, I have	25%
No, I have not	67%
Don't know/not sure	8%

Q13. Have you ever called or written an elected official?	
Yes, I have	31%
No, I have not	66%
Don't know/not sure	3%

Q14. Have you ever attended a meeting with an elected official?	
Yes, I have	31%
No, I have not	65%
Don't know/not sure	4%

Q15. Have you ever been summoned to jury duty?	
Yes, I have	55%
No, I have not	40%
Don't know/not sure	5%

Q16. Have you ever ignored a summons to jury duty?	
Yes, I have	13%
No, I have not	84%
Don't know/not sure	3%

Q17. Have you ever been selected to serve on a jury?	
Yes, I have	41%
No, I have not	54%
Don't know/not sure	5%

Q18. Have you ever lied to get out of jury duty?	
Yes, I have	14%
No, I have not	84%
Don't know/not sure	3%

Q19. Have you ever tried to get out of jury duty?	
Yes, I have	27%
No, I have not	69%
Don't know/not sure	5%

Personal Responsibility

Q37. I personally feel a responsibility to register to vote.	
Completely agree	54%
Somewhat agree	26%
Somewhat disagree	11%
Completely disagree	9%

Q38. I personally feel a responsibility to vote.	
Completely agree	57%
Somewhat agree	22%
Somewhat disagree	12%
Completely disagree	9%

Q39. I personally feel a responsibility to volunteer for a political campaign.	
Completely agree	16%
Somewhat agree	25%
Somewhat disagree	30%
Completely disagree	29%

Q40. I personally feel a responsibility to respond to political polls.	
Completely agree	22%
Somewhat agree	34%
Somewhat disagree	26%
Completely disagree	18%

Q41. I personally feel a responsibility to contact elected officials about an issue.	
Completely agree	25%
Somewhat agree	35%
Somewhat disagree	23%
Completely disagree	17%

Q42. I personally feel a responsibility to serve on a jury.	
Completely agree	41%
Somewhat agree	31%
Somewhat disagree	16%
Completely disagree	12%

Trust

Q45. How much trust do you have in the federal government?	
Trust completely	14%
Trust a great deal	32%
Hardly any trust	36%
Do not trust at all	17%

Q46. How much trust do you have in your state government?	
Trust completely	14%
Trust a great deal	37%
Hardly any trust	36%
Do not trust at all	14%

Q47. How much trust do you have in the federal courts?	
Trust completely	15%
Trust a great deal	41%
Hardly any trust	31%
Do not trust at all	13%

Q48. How much trust do you have in your state and local courts?	
Trust completely	16%
Trust a great deal	43%
Hardly any trust	30%
Do not trust at all	11%

Q49. How much trust do you have in elections?	
Trust completely	20%
Trust a great deal	40%
Hardly any trust	27%
Do not trust at all	13%

Q50. How much trust do you have in political polls?	
Trust completely	12%
Trust a great deal	31%
Hardly any trust	43%
Do not trust at all	15%

Q51. How much trust do you have in pollsters?	
Trust completely	11%
Trust a great deal	27%
Hardly any trust	46%
Do not trust at all	17%

Q52. How much trust do you have in the jury system?	
Trust completely	18%
Trust a great deal	48%
Hardly any trust	24%
Do not trust at all	10%

Q53. How much trust do you have in people you don't know?

Trust completely	11%
Trust a great deal	24%
Hardly any trust	45%
Do not trust at all	20%

Q54. How much trust do you have in people you know?

Trust completely	23%
Trust a great deal	55%
Hardly any trust	16%
Do not trust at all	7%

Q55. How much trust do you have in churches and other religious institutions?

Trust completely	22%
Trust a great deal	37%
Hardly any trust	25%
Do not trust at all	16%

Q56. How much trust do you have in community organizations?

Trust completely	15%
Trust a great deal	54%
Hardly any trust	23%
Do not trust at all	8%

Knowledge

Q57. Do you happen to know what job or political office is now held by Kamala Harris?

President	9%
Vice President (Correct Answer)	69%
Senator	6%
Representative	4%
Supreme Court Justice	3%
I don't know.	8%

Q58. Whose responsibility is it to determine if a law is constitutional or not?

The president	11%
Congress	18%
Supreme Court (Correct Answer)	55%
I don't know.	16%

Q59. How much of a majority is required for the US Senate and House to override a presidential veto?

50%	12%
67% (Correct Answer)	31%
75%	14%
80%	10%
I don't know.	32%

Q60. Do you happen to know which party has the most members in the House of Representatives in Washington, D.C.?

Democrats	28%
Republicans (Correct Answer)	42%
Another party	5%
I don't know.	25%

Q61. Which of the parties is more politically conservative?

Democrats	20%
Republicans (Correct Answer)	59%
They're about the same.	8%
I don't know.	12%

Apathy

Q62. I am interested in things related to government and politics.

Strongly agree	28%
Somewhat agree	42%
Somewhat disagree	19%
Strongly disagree	11%

Q63. I am interested in learning new things related to government and politics.

Strongly agree	30%
Somewhat agree	42%
Somewhat disagree	17%
Strongly disagree	11%

Q64. I put little effort into anything having to do with government and politics.

Strongly agree	18%
Somewhat agree	33%
Somewhat disagree	32%
Strongly disagree	17%

Q65. I am less concerned about problems with government and politics than I should be.

Strongly agree	16%
Somewhat agree	31%
Somewhat disagree	30%
Strongly disagree	22%

Q66. I have the motivation to get involved in government and politics.

Strongly agree	20%
Somewhat agree	32%
Somewhat disagree	30%
Strongly disagree	18%

Alienation

Q67. I do not trust any information from public institutions.	
Strongly agree	19%
Somewhat agree	35%
Somewhat disagree	35%
Strongly disagree	12%

Q68. I feel betrayed by those in power.	
Strongly agree	26%
Somewhat agree	40%
Somewhat disagree	22%
Strongly disagree	12%

Q69. Society is changing in a direction I do not understand.	
Strongly agree	30%
Somewhat agree	42%
Somewhat disagree	18%
Strongly disagree	9%

Q70. I am discriminated against because of my worldview or politics.	
Strongly agree	16%
Somewhat agree	25%
Somewhat disagree	33%
Strongly disagree	26%

Q71. I feel like I can be part of this society.	
Strongly agree	35%
Somewhat agree	43%
Somewhat disagree	14%
Strongly disagree	8%

Q72. I can be fully myself in this society.	
Strongly agree	29%
Somewhat agree	41%
Somewhat disagree	20%
Strongly disagree	9%

Q73. With my voice, I can make a difference in this society.	
Strongly agree	29%
Somewhat agree	41%
Somewhat disagree	21%
Strongly disagree	10%

Q74. I feel that I am among the losers in this society.	
Strongly agree	15%
Somewhat agree	24%
Somewhat disagree	27%
Strongly disagree	34%

Efficacy

Q75. I feel that I have a pretty good understanding of the important political issues facing this country.	
Strongly agree	39%
Somewhat agree	41%
Somewhat disagree	14%
Strongly disagree	7%

Q76. I consider myself well-qualified to participate in politics and community affairs.	
Strongly agree	27%
Somewhat agree	40%
Somewhat disagree	21%
Strongly disagree	11%

Q77. People like me don't have any say about what the government does.	
Strongly agree	23%
Somewhat agree	34%
Somewhat disagree	27%
Strongly disagree	16%

APPENDIX D

REGRESSION TABLES

Table 1.1: Electoral Avoidance

	β	S.E.
Apathy	.081*	.021
Alienation	.040*	.014
Efficacy	–.027	.036
Trust	–.015*	.007
Political Knowledge	–.207*	.035
Age	–.169*	.038
Race	–.011	.023
Female	–.522*	.093
Education	.009	.032
Employment	.066*	.022
Income	–.080*	.032
Party Affiliation	–.040	.024
Political Ideology	–.054*	.027
Constant	2.062*	.589
N	1,646	
R^2	.326	

Regression model estimated using Stata 17.0's svy: regress command. Alternative model specifications using a Poisson estimation returned substantively similar results. Data from *Democracy InAction* Survey; see appendix for survey methodology and question wording. Dependent variable is Electoral Avoidance, an additive index variable that includes whether the respondent is not registered to vote, has not updated their voter registration after moving, has not voted in the past five years, has intentionally skipped an election in the past five years, or has accidentally missed an election in the past five years. Partisan affiliation runs from strongly Republican (1) to strongly Democratic (7). Political ideology runs from very liberal (1) to very conservative (7). Unit of analysis is the individual. Two–tailed significance tests. * *Statistically significant p£ 0.05.*

Table 1.2: Personal Responsibility to Register to Vote

	β	S.E.
Apathy	–.065*	.016
Alienation	.007	.009
Efficacy	.018	.027
Trust	.042*	.005
Political Knowledge	.138*	.023
Age	.104*	.022
Race	–.001	.015
Female	.271*	.06
Education	.017	.019
Employment	–.026*	.013
Income	–.008	.020
Party Affiliation	.020	.015
Political Ideology	.013	.017
Constant	1.979*	.446
N	1,904	
R^2	.373	

Regression model estimated using Stata 17.0's svy: regress command. Alternative model specifications using a Poisson estimation returned substantively similar results. Data from *Democracy InAction* Survey; see appendix for survey methodology and question wording. Dependent variable is Registration Responsibility, indicating the extent to which the respondent agrees that (s)he feels a personal responsibility to register to vote; higher values indicate agreement. Partisan affiliation runs from strongly Republican (1) to strongly Democratic (7). Political ideology runs from very liberal (1) to very conservative (7). Unit of analysis is the individual. Two–tailed significance tests. * *Statistically significant p£ 0.05.*

Table 1.3: Personal Responsibility to Vote

	β	S.E.
Apathy	–.051*	.016
Alienation	.004	.009
Efficacy	.039	.022
Trust	.047*	.005
Political Knowledge	.136*	.021
Age	.083*	.024
Race	.017	.015
Female	.330*	.059
Education	.015	.019
Employment	–.022	.013
Income	.021	.02
Party Affiliation	.034*	.016
Political Ideology	.010	.017
Constant	1.422*	.423
N	1,904	
R^2	.399	

Regression model estimated using Stata 17.0's svy: regress command. Alternative model specifications using a Poisson estimation returned substantively similar results. Data from *Democracy InAction* Survey; see appendix for survey methodology and question wording. Dependent variable is Voting Responsibility, indicating the extent to which the respondent agrees that (s)he feels a personal responsibility to vote; higher values indicate agreement. Partisan affiliation runs from strongly Republican (1) to strongly Democratic (7). Political ideology runs from very liberal (1) to very conservative (7). Unit of analysis is the individual. Two–tailed significance tests. * *Statistically significant p£ 0.05.*

Table 2.1: Campaign Avoidance		
	β	S.E.
Apathy	.060*	.016
Alienation	–.033*	.011
Efficacy	–.042	.030
Trust	–.041*	.006
Political Knowledge	.038	.030
Age	.051	.031
Race	.005	.020
Female	.123	.078
Education	–.056*	.024
Employment	.005	.019
Income	–.069*	.028
Party Affiliation	.016	.021
Political Ideology	.069*	.025
Constant	2.932*	.560
N	1,771	
R^2	.278	

Regression model estimated using Stata 17.0's svy: regress command. Alternative model specifications using a Poisson estimation returned substantively similar results. Data from *Democracy InAction* Survey; see appendix for survey methodology and question wording. Dependent variable is Campaign Avoidance, an additive index variable that includes whether the respondent has volunteered for a campaign, displayed a yard sign for a campaign, or donated money to a campaign. Partisan affiliation runs from strongly Republican (1) to strongly Democratic (7). Political ideology runs from very liberal (1) to very conservative (7). Unit of analysis is the individual. Two–tailed significance tests. * *Statistically significant p£ 0.05.*

Table 2.2: Personal Responsibility to Volunteer for a Campaign

	β	S.E.
Apathy	–.107*	.015
Alienation	.024*	.009
Efficacy	.032	.024
Trust	.050*	.004
Political Knowledge	–.105*	.024
Age	–.079*	.023
Race	–.034*	.015
Female	.017	.064
Education	.007	.018
Employment	–.059*	.013
Income	.014	.021
Party Affiliation	–.008	.015
Political Ideology	–.016	.019
Constant	2.806*	.406
N	1,904	
R^2	.434	

Regression model estimated using Stata 17.0's svy: regress command. Alternative model specifications using a Poisson estimation returned substantively similar results. Data from *Democracy InAction* Survey; see appendix for survey methodology and question wording. Dependent variable is Campaign Responsibility, indicating the extent to which the respondent agrees that (s)he feels a personal responsibility to volunteer for a campaign; higher values indicate agreement. Partisan affiliation runs from strongly Republican (1) to strongly Democratic (7). Political ideology runs from very liberal (1) to very conservative (7). Unit of analysis is the individual. Two–tailed significance tests. * *Statistically significant p£ 0.05.*

Table 3.1: Polling Avoidance

	β	S.E.
Apathy	.012	.015
Alienation	.040*	.009
Efficacy	.011	.024
Trust	.019*	.005
Political Knowledge	–.027	.026
Age	–.018	.023
Race	.030*	.014
Female	–.123	.066
Education	.041*	.019
Employment	.010	.015
Income	.036	.023
Party Affiliation	–.015	.016
Political Ideology	–.021	.020
Constant	–.870*	.495
N	1,625	
R^2	.119	

Regression model estimated using Stata 17.0's svy: regress command. Alternative model specifications using a Poisson estimation returned substantively similar results. Data from *Democracy InAction* Survey; see appendix for survey methodology and question wording. Dependent variable is Polling Avoidance, an additive index variable that includes whether the respondent has refused to take a poll or hung up on a pollster. Partisan affiliation runs from strongly Republican (1) to strongly Democratic (7). Political ideology runs from very liberal (1) to very conservative (7). Unit of analysis is the individual. Two–tailed significance tests. * *Statistically significant p£ 0.05.*

Table 3.2: Personal Responsibility to Take Polls

	β	S.E.
Apathy	–.09*	.019
Alienation	.021*	.010
Efficacy	.046	.028
Trust	.051*	.006
Political Knowledge	–.056*	.024
Age	–.009	.025
Race	–.025	.015
Female	.045	.069
Education	–.028	.020
Employment	–.039*	.016
Income	–.002	.022
Party Affiliation	.012	.018
Political Ideology	.006	.019
Constant	2.37*	.473
N	1,904	
R^2	.338	

Regression model estimated using Stata 17.0's svy: regress command. Alternative model specifications using a Poisson estimation returned substantively similar results. Data from *Democracy InAction* Survey; see appendix for survey methodology and question wording. Dependent variable is Polling Responsibility, indicating the extent to which the respondent agrees that (s)he feels a personal responsibility to take a poll; higher values indicate agreement. Partisan affiliation runs from strongly Republican (1) to strongly Democratic (7). Political ideology runs from very liberal (1) to very conservative (7). Unit of analysis is the individual. Two–tailed significance tests. * *Statistically significant p£ 0.05.*

Table 4.1: Avoidance of Contacting Elected Officials

	β	S.E.
Apathy	.056*	.012
Alienation	–.032*	.008
Efficacy	–.023	.023
Trust	–.022*	.004
Political Knowledge	–.005	.022
Age	.033	.02
Race	–.018	.014
Female	.056	.061
Education	–.084*	.018
Employment	.003	.015
Income	–.05*	.022
Party Affiliation	.011	.015
Political Ideology	.046*	.019
Constant	2.204*	.461
N	1,779	
R^2	.277	

Regression model estimated using Stata 17.0's svy: regress command. Alternative model specifications using a Poisson estimation returned substantively similar results. Data from *Democracy InAction* Survey; see appendix for survey methodology and question wording. Dependent variable is Elected Official Contact Avoidance, an additive index variable that includes whether the respondent has ever called or written to an elected official and/or attended a meeting with an elected official. Partisan affiliation runs from strongly Republican (1) to strongly Democratic (7). Political ideology runs from very liberal (1) to very conservative (7). Unit of analysis is the individual. Two–tailed significance tests. * *Statistically significant p£ 0.05.*

Table 4.2: Personal Responsibility to Contact Elected Officials

	β	S.E.
Apathy	–.112*	.016
Alienation	.032*	.009
Efficacy	.055*	.025
Trust	.045*	.004
Political Knowledge	–.021	.026
Age	–.029	.025
Race	.009	.015
Female	.064	.067
Education	.035	.019
Employment	–.015	.014
Income	–.01	.021
Party Affiliation	.019	.015
Political Ideology	.013	.018
Constant	1.955*	.435
N	1,904	
R^2	.363	

Regression model estimated using Stata 17.0's reg command. Alternative model specifications using a Poisson estimation returned substantively similar results. Data from *Democracy InAction* Survey; see appendix for survey methodology and question wording. Dependent variable is Jury Responsibility, indicating the extent to which the respondent agrees that (s)he feels a personal responsibility to contact elected officials about an issue; higher values indicate agreement. Partisan affiliation runs from strongly Republican (1) to strongly Democratic (5). Political ideology runs from very liberal (1) to very conservative (7). Unit of analysis is the individual. Two–tailed significance tests. * *Statistically significant p£ 0.05.*

Table 5.1: Jury Avoidance

	β	S.E.
Apathy	.009	.016
Alienation	.031*	.013
Efficacy	.01	.029
Trust	.021*	.009
Political Knowledge	–.033	.038
Age	–.159*	.038
Race	–.003	.026
Female	–.192*	.093
Education	–.004	.030
Employment	.02	.015
Income	.017	.030
Party Affiliation	.066*	.029
Political Ideology	.028	.035
Constant	–.153	.689
N	769	
R^2	.196	

Regression model estimated using Stata 17.0's svy: regress command. Alternative model specifications using a Poisson estimation returned substantively similar results. Data from *Democracy InAction* Survey; see appendix for survey methodology and question wording. Dependent variable is Jury Avoidance, an additive index variable that includes whether the respondent has ignored a jury summons, has lied to get out of jury service, or has attempted to get out of jury service (apart from lying). Partisan affiliation runs from strongly Republican (1) to strongly Democratic (7). Political ideology runs from very liberal (1) to very conservative (7). Unit of analysis is the individual who (1) is jury eligible, as indicated by being registered to vote, possessing a valid state ID or driver's license, and is not a convicted felon, and (2) stated they had received a jury summons. Two–tailed significance tests. * *Statistically significant p£ 0.05.*

Table 5.2: Personal Responsibility to Serve on a Jury

	β	S.E.
Apathy	–.048*	.024
Alienation	–.014	.013
Efficacy	.014	.033
Trust	.049*	.008
Political Knowledge	.071	.038
Age	.062	.039
Race	–.008	.02
Female	.114	.106
Education	.023	.03
Employment	–.019	.021
Income	.046	.037
Party Affiliation	.009	.025
Political Ideology	.069*	.03
Constant	1.901*	.627
N	798	
R^2	.272	

Regression model estimated using Stata 17.0's reg command. Alternative model specifications using a Poisson estimation returned substantively similar results. Data from *Democracy InAction* Survey; see appendix for survey methodology and question wording. Dependent variable is Jury Responsibility, indicating the extent to which the respondent agrees that (s)he feels a personal responsibility to serve on a jury; higher values indicate agreement. Partisan affiliation runs from strongly Republican (1) to strongly Democratic (5). Political ideology runs from very liberal (1) to very conservative (7). Unit of analysis is the individual who (1) is jury eligible, as indicated by being registered to vote, possessing a valid state ID or driver's license, and is not a convicted felon, and (2) stated they had received a jury summons. Two–tailed significance tests. * *Statistically significant p£ 0.05.*

NOTES

Introduction

1 Pew Research Center. 2023. "Americans' Dismal Views of the Nation's Politics." Available online at https://www.pewresearch.org/politics/2023/09/19/americans-dismal-views-of-the-nations-politics/.

2 Giorno, Taylor. 2022. "Negative Outside Spending Accounts for 69% of the $2.1 Billion Spent in Federal 2022 Midterms," *Open Secrets*. Available online at https://www.opensecrets.org/news/2022/11/negative-outside-spending-accounts-for-69-of-the-2-1-billion-spent-on-federal-2022-midterms/.

3 Johansmeyer, Thomas. 2021. "How 2020 Protests Changed Insurance Forever," *World Economic Forum*. Available online at https://www.weforum.org/agenda/2021/02/2020-protests-changed-insurance-forever/.

4 Turley, Jonathan. 2024. *The Indispensable Right: Free Speech in an Age of Rage*. New York: Simon & Schuster.

5 Taheri, Mandy. 2025. "Significant Number of Democrats View Party Negatively: Poll," *Newsweek*. Available online at https://www.newsweek.com/significant-number-democrats-view-party-negatively-poll-2108290.

6 Oreskes, Benjamin. 2025. "Why Zohran Mamdani's Boss in the Legislature Refuses to Endorse Him," *New York Times*. Available online at https://www.nytimes.com/2025/09/05/nyregion/mamdani-heastie-endorsement-mayor.html.

7 As of September 10, 2025, Mamdani held a 15.6 percentage point advantage in the RealClearPolitics Polling average and had been trending upwards in the polling for more than two months. See: https://www.realclearpolling.com/polls/mayor/general/2025/new-york/mamdani-vs-cuomo-vs-adams-vs-sliwa-vs-walden

8 Norman, Erin. 2024. "Polling Spotlight: Politics is an Afterthought for Most Americans," *State Policy Network*. Available online at https://spn.org/articles/polling-spotlight-politics-is-an-afterthought/.

9 Jones, Jeffrey M. 2013. "In U.S., 64% Want their Child to Avoid Career in Politics," *Gallup*. Available online at https://news.gallup.com/poll/163373/child-avoid-career-politics.aspx

10 Collins, Lois M. 2020. "Parents Don't Want their Kids to Become Politicians, Upcoming American Family Survey Finds," *Deseret News*. Available online at https://www.deseret.com/indepth/2020/9/10/21431119/american-family-survey-parents-kids-politicians-brookings-institution-trump-biden-racial-unrest/.

11 Cormack, Lindsey. 2024. *How to Raise a Citizen (And Why It's Up to You to Do It)*. New York: Jossey-Bass.

12 Talisse, Robert B. 2019. *Overdoing Democracy: Why We Must Put Politics in its Place*. New York: Oxford University Press.

13 Ibid.

14 Dahl, Robert A. and David Froomkin. 2025. "Democracy," *Britannica*. Available online at https://www.britannica.com/topic/democracy.

15 Desjardins, Jeff. 2019. "Mapped: The World's Oldest Democracies," *World Economic Forum*. Available online at https://www.weforum.org/agenda/2019/08/countries-are-the-worlds-oldest-democracies/.

16 Ibid.

17 Crawford, Amy. 2013. "For the People, by the People: What I Saw when I Participated in One of the Truest Forms of Democracy," *Slate*. Available online at https://slate.com/news-and-politics/2013/05/new-england-town-halls-these-experiments-in-direct-democracy-do-a-far-better-job-than-congress.html.

18 Ballotpedia. Nd. "Ballot Initiative." Available online at https://ballotpedia.org/Ballot_initiative.

19 Ballotpedia. Nd. "Legislatively Referred State Statute." Available online at https://ballotpedia.org/Legislatively_referred_state_statute.

20 Ballotpedia. Nd. "Legislatively Referred Constitutional Amendment." Available online at https://ballotpedia.org/Legislatively_referred_constitutional_amendment.

21 Caughey, Devin, and Christopher Warshaw. 2022. *Dynamic Democracy: Public Opinion, Elections, and Policymaking in the American States*. Chicago: University of Chicago Press.

22 Fox, Justin, and Kenneth W. Shotts. 2009. "Delegates or Trustees? A Theory of Political Accountability," *The Journal of Politics* 71(4): 1225–37.

23 Cormack, 2024, 130.

24 Madison, James. "Federalist No. 39," *The Avalon Project.* Available online at https://avalon.law.yale.edu/18th_century/fed39.asp.

25 Lupia, Arthur. 2015. *Uninformed: Why People Know so Little about Politics and What We Can Do About It.* New York: Oxford University Press, 3.

26 Ibid, 5

27 Delli Carpini, Michael X., and Scott Keeter. 1997. *What Americans Know about Politics and Why it Matters.* New Haven: Yale University Press, 5.

28 Adams, Kimberly. 2019. "What Federal Funding for Civics Reveals About American Political Discourse." *Marketplace.* Available online at https://www.marketplace.org/2019/11/06/what-federal-funding-for-civics-reveals-about-american-political-discourse/.

29 McGraw, Phillip. 2024. *We've Got Issues: How You Can Stand Strong for America's Soul and Sanity.* New York: Simon & Schuster, e-book 45.

30 Merriam-Webster. Nd. "Aristocracy." Available online at https://www.merriam-webster.com/dictionary/aristocracy.

31 Dictionary.com. nd. "Theo." Available online at https://www.dictionary.com/browse/theo.

32 Howard, Philip K. 2023. *Not Accountable: Rethinking the Constitutionality of Public Employee Unions.* Garden City, NY: Rodin Books. 55

33 National Conference on Citizenship. 2012. "Civic Health and Unemployment II: The Case Builds." Report available online at https://ncoc.org/wp-content/uploads/2011/09/2012IssueBrief_CivicHealth_UnemploymentII.pdf.

34 National Conference on Citizenship. 2011. "Civic Health and Unemployment: Can Engagement Strengthen the Economy?" Report available at https://ncoc.org/wp-content/uploads/2015/04/2011UnemploymentCHI.pdf.

35 United States Courts. Nd. "The U.S. Constitution: Preamble." Available online at https://www.uscourts.gov/about-federal-courts/educational-resources/about-educational-outreach/activity-resources/us.

36 Reagan, Ronald. 1967. "January 5, 1967: Inaugural Address (Public Ceremony)," *Ronald Reagan Presidential Library & Museum.* Available at https://www.reaganlibrary.gov/archives/speech/january-5-1967-inaugural-address-public-ceremony.

37 "Jury Duty." 2024. International Movie Database. Available online at https://www.imdb.com/title/tt22074164/.

38 McEvoy, Jemima. 2022. "At Least 13 Cities are Defunding their Police Departments," *Forbes.* Available at https://www.forbes.com/sites/jemimamcevoy/2020/08/13/at-least-13-cities-are-defunding-their-police-departments/.

39 Helm, Burt. 2017. "Pizzagate Nearly Destroyed My Restaurant. Then My

Customers Helped Me Fight Back," *Inc. Magazine*. Available online at https://www.inc.com/magazine/201707/burt-helm/how-i-did-it-james-alefantis-comet-ping-pong.html.

40 Sage, Sami, and Emily Amick. 2024. *Democracy in Retrograde: How to Make Changes Big and Small in our Country and in our Lives*. New York: Gallery Books, 10–1.

41 Details of the survey, including the methodology, questionnaire, and topline results can be found in the appendices at the end of this book.

42 Most analysts, myself included, will almost never make a causal interpretation of a regression model because of the possibility of omitted variable bias—the very real risk of leaving out a variable (usually an unknown one) that has a relationship with the dependent variable. Unless a regression model includes every variable—known and unknown—that have or could have a relationship with the outcome of interest, any causal claim is dubious at best and an outright, knowing lie at worst. This is why I say regression "helps approach a causal understanding" rather than provides a causal understanding.

Chapter 1

1 US Const. art. I, § 4.

2 Campbell, Angus, Philip E. Converse, Warren E. Miller, and Donald E. Stokes. 1960. *The American Voter*. Chicago: University of Chicago Press. See also, Lewis-Beck, Michael S., William G. Jacoby, Helmut Norpoth, and Herbert F. Weisberg. 2008. *The American Voter Revisited*. Ann Arbor: University of Michigan Press.

3 US Department of Justice. N.d. "The National Voter Registration Act of 1993 (NVRA)." Available online at https://www.justice.gov/crt/national-voter-registration-act-1993-nvra.

4 Brown, Robert D., and Justin Wedeking. 2006. "People Who Have Their Tickets but Do Not Use Them: 'Motor Voter,' Registration, and Turnout Revisited," *American Politics Research* 34(4): 479–504.

5 National Conference of State Legislatures. 2024. "Automatic Voter Registration." Available online at https://www.ncsl.org/elections-and-campaigns/automatic-voter-registration.

6 Thaler, Richard H. and Cass R. Sunstein. 2021. *Nudge: The Final Edition*. New York: Penguin Books.

7 National Conference of State Legislatures. 2025. "Online Voter Registration." Available online at https://www.ncsl.org/elections-and-campaigns/online-voter-registration.

8 Dēmos. 2020. "Executive Action to Advance Democracy: What the Biden-Harris Administration and the Agencies Can Do to Build a more Inclusive Democracy." Available online at https://www.demos.org/policy-briefs/executive-action-advance-democracy-what-biden-harris-administration-and-agencies-can.

9 Bragdon, Tarren and Stewart Whitson. 2022. "Voter Registration Drive: What's Biden Hiding?" *The Wall Street Journal.* Available online at https://www.wsj.com/articles/voter-drive-whats-biden-hiding-justice-department-freedom-of-information-foia-transparency-corruption-lawsuit-foundation-for-government-accountability-11650403740.

10 Dublois, Hayden. 2025. "How Deep is the Swamp? Why Taming the Liberal Bureaucracy is Essential." *Foundation for Government Accountability.* Available online at https://www.thefga.org/research/why-taming-the-liberal-bureaucracy-is-essential/.

11 FRC Action. N.d. "Voter Resources." Available online at https://www.frcaction.org/#voter_resources.

12 Wuthnow, Debbie. N.d. "Voter Registration Tools." Available online at https://ivoterguide.com/insights/254.

13 Faith Wins. N.d. "The Church Must Have a Voice." Available online at https://faithwins.org/take-action/.

14 Alberta, Tim. 2023. *The Kingdom, the Power, and the Glory.* New York: HarperCollins. e-book p. 164

15 Yes, I know voter fraud is a rare occurrence, but so is voter suppression. Both hamper the ability of citizens to vote and should be equally condemned.

16 National Youth Rights Association. N.d. "Voting Age Status Report." Available online at https://www.youthrights.org/issues/voting-age/voting-age-status-report/.

17 Ibid.

18 National Conference of State Legislatures. 2024. "Restoration of Voting Rights for Felons." Available online at https://www.ncsl.org/elections-and-campaigns/felon-voting-rights.

19 Cormack, Lindsey. 2024. *How to Raise a Citizen (And Why It's Up to You to Do It).* New York: Jossey-Bass, 141.

20 US Census Bureau. N.d. "Historical Reported Voting Rates," Table A-1. Available online at https://www.census.gov/data/tables/time-series/demo/voting-and-registration/voting-historical-time-series.html, Table A-1.

21 Ibid.

22 Banaji, Mahzarin R, and Larisa Heiphetz. 2010. "Attitudes," in *Handbook of Social Psychology, 5th ed.*, eds. Susan T. Fiske, Daniel T. Gilbert, and Gardner Lindzey. New York: Wiley, 353–93.

23 McDonald, Michael. N.d. "National Turnout Rates 1789–Present," *US Elections Project.* Available online at https://www.electproject.org/national-1789-present.

24 National Conference of State Legislatures. 2024. "Restoration of Voting Rights for Felons." Available online at https://www.ncsl.org/elections-and-campaigns/felon-voting-rights.

25 Maciag, Mike. 2014. "Voter Turnout Plummeting in Local Elections," *Governing*. Available online at https://www.governing.com/archive/gov-voter-turnout-municipal-elections.html.

26 Brady, Henry E., Sidney Verba, and Kay Lehman Schlozman. 1995. "Beyond SES: A Resource Model of Political Participation," *American Political Science Review* 89(2): 271–94, 271.

27 Clifford, Catherine. 2020. "'I Don't Plan to Vote Ever Again': The Psychology of Why So Many People Don't Vote, Even in 2020," *CNBC*. Available online at https://www.cnbc.com/2020/10/30/why-people-choose-not-to-vote.html.

28 Delli Carpini, Michael X., and Scott Keeter. 1997. *What Americans Know about Politics and Why it Matters*. New Haven: Yale University Press, 5.

29 Campbell, Angus, Gerald Gurin, and Warren E. Miller. 1954. *The Voter Decides*. Evanston, IL: Row, Peterson

30 Vecchione, Michele, and Gian Vittorio Caprara. 2009. "Personality Determinants of Political Participation: The Contribution of Traits and Self-Efficacy Beliefs," *Personality and Individual Differences* 46(4): 487–92. Available online at https://www.sciencedirect.com/science/article/abs/pii/S0191886908004479.

31 State Policy Network. N.d. "State Voices Public Opinion Tracker." Available online at https://spn.org/state-voices/.

32 Pew Research Center. 2024. "Public Trust in Government: 1958–2024." Available online at https://www.pewresearch.org/politics/2024/06/24/public-trust-in-government-1958-2024/.

33 Hetherington, Marc J. 1999. "The Effect of Political Trust on the Presidential Vote, 1968–96." *American Political Science Review* 93(2): 311–26.

34 Grönlund, Kimmo, and Maija Setälä. 2007. "Political Trust, Satisfaction, and Voter Turnout," *Comparative European Politics* 5: 400–22.

35 See, e.g., Coppock, Alexander, and Donald P. Green. 2016. "Is Voting Habit Forming? New Evidence from Experiments and Regression Discontinuities," *American Journal of Political Science* 60(4): 1044–62.

Chapter 2

1 Shea, Daniel M., and Michael John Burton. 2006. *Campaign Craft: The Strategies, Tactics, and Art of Political Campaign Management*. Newport, CT: Praeger, 181–3.

2 Cohen, Michael D. 2025. *Modern Political Campaigns: How Professionalism, Technology, and Speed Have Revolutionized Elections*. New York: Rowman & Littlefield, 6.

3 See, e.g., Shaw, Catherine. 2010. *The Campaign Manager: Running and Winning Local Elections*. Boulder, CO: Westview Press, and Shea and Burton 2006.

4 Shea and Burton, 2006, 183.

5 See, e.g., Panagopoulos, Costas. 2017. *Political Campaigns: Concepts, Context, and Consequences*. New York: Oxford University Press.

6 Specifically, I argue that direct mail is a novelty to younger voters that serves as a reminder of upcoming elections, and while older voters may not need the reminder, it can be an important tool in reaching them nonetheless. See Taylor, Travis N. 2016. "Reconciling Conventional Wisdom and New Data on Direct Mail," *The Mud Bath* [blog]. Available at https://themudbath.wordpress.com/2016/05/02/reconciling-conventional-wisdom-new-data-direct-mail/.

7 Green, Donald P., and Alan S. Gerber. 2008. *Get Out the Vote: How to Increase Voter Turnout,* 3rd ed. Washington, DC: Brookings Institution Press.

8 Cohen, Michael D. 2025. *Modern Political Campaigns: How Professionalism, Technology, and Speed Have Revolutionized Elections*. New York: Rowman & Littlefield, 173.

9 Rosenstone, Steven J., and John Mark Hansen. 2003. *Mobilization, Participation, and Democracy in America*. New York: Longman.

10 Ballot harvesting is when campaign workers and activists pick up completed absentee ballots, promising the voter they will return the ballots. Many states have outlawed ballot harvesting out of a concern for election integrity and ballot security. Still, in other states, such as California, ballot harvesting is still permissible and takes place regularly.

11 Green, Donald P., and Alan S. Gerber. 2008. *Get Out the Vote: How to Increase Voter Turnout,* 3rd ed. Washington, DC: Brookings Institution Press, 31.

12 Green, Donald P., and Alan S. Gerber. 2008. *Get Out the Vote: How to Increase Voter Turnout,* 3rd ed. Washington, DC: Brookings Institution Press.

13 Gray, Lawrence. 2007. *How to Win a Local Election: A Complete Step-by-Step Guide*, 3rd ed. Lanham, MD: M. Evans, 109.

14 Ibid.

15 Kush, Christopher. 2004. *The One-Hour Activist: The 15 Most Powerful Actions You Can Take to Fight for the Issues and Candidates You Care About.* San Francisco: Jossey-Bass, 129–30.

16 Feltus, William J., Kenneth M. Goldstein, and Matthew Dallek. 2017. *Inside Campaigns: Elections through the Eyes of Political Professionals*. Thousand Oaks: CQ Press, 185.

17 Rosenstone, Steven J., and John Mark Hansen. 2003. *Mobilization, Participation, and Democracy in America*. New York: Longman, 224.

18 Ibid, 43.

19 American National Election Studies. N.d. "Worked for a Party or Candidate." Available online at https://electionstudies.org/data-tools/anes-guide/anes-guide.html?chart=worked_for_party

20 Civic. N.d. "About Us." Available online at https://www.civicllc.com/about-us.

21 Atwell, Matthew N., Bennett Stillerman, and John M. Bridgeland. 2021. *Civic Health Index 2021: Citizenship During Crisis*. Report by Civic. Available online at https://millercenter.org/sites/default/files/2021-09/civic_health_index_2021.pdf.

22 Downs, Anthony. 1957. *An Economic Theory of Democracy*. New York: Harper and Row.

23 Green, Donald P., and Alan S. Gerber. 2008. *Get Out the Vote: How to Increase Voter Turnout*, 3rd ed. Washington, DC: Brookings Institution Press, 37.

24 Shea, Daniel M., and Michael John Burton. 2006. *Campaign Craft: The Strategies, Tactics, and Art of Political Campaign Management*. Newport, CT: Praeger, 183.

25 National Conference on Citizenship. 2011. "Civic Health and Unemployment: Can Engagement Strengthen the Economy?" p 4. Report available at https://ncoc.org/wp-content/uploads/2015/04/2011UnemploymentCHI.pdf.

26 Atwell, Matthew N., John Bridgeland, and Peter Levine. 2017. "Civic Deserts: America's Civic Health Challenge." Report available online at https://ncoc.org/wp-content/uploads/2017/10/2017CHIUpdate-FINAL-small.pdf.

Chapter 3

1 Clinton, Josh, and John Lapinski. 2024. "Once Again, Polls Missed a Decisive Slice of Trump Voters in 2024," NBC News. Available online at https://www.nbcnews.com/politics/2024-election/-polls-missed-decisive-slice-trump-voters-2024-rcna182488.

2 Sherman, Natalie. 2024. "Did the US Election Polls Fail?" BBC. Available online at https://www.bbc.com/news/articles/cj4ve004llxo.

3 RealClear Polling. 2024. "2024 National: Trump vs. Harris." Available online at https://www.realclearpolling.com/polls/president/general/2024/trump-vs-harris.

4 Rasmussen, Scott. 2024. "2024 Was a Pretty Good Election for the Polling Industry," Napolitan News Service. Available online at https://napolitannews.org/posts/2024-was-a-good-election-for-the-polling-industry.

5 Jackson, Natalie. 2025. "Polling in the 2024 Election," in *Campaign of Chaos: Trump, Biden, Harris, and the 2024 American Election*, ed. Larry J. Sabato, Kyle Kondik, and J. Miles Coleman. New York: Bloomsbury Academic, 140.

6 Jackson, Natalie. 2025. "Polling in the 2024 Election," in *Campaign of Chaos: Trump, Biden, Harris, and the 2024 American Election*, ed. Larry J. Sabato, Kyle Kondik, and J. Miles Coleman. New York: Bloomsbury Academic, 147.

7 Pasek, Josh, et al. 2025. "Task Force on 2024 Pre-Election Polling: An Evaluation of the 2024 General Election Polls," American Association for Public Opinion Research.

8 Ibid, 5

9 Ibid, 16

10 Ibid, 13

11 An interesting development I learned from a former colleague and current Ph.D. student at the University of Utah, Andrew Welhouse, is that some polling call centers now have the ability for the recipient's cell phone screen to display a message along with the unknown number that it is a survey call, in the same way the phone warns you that other calls are "probable spam." So, if your phone shows that an incoming call is a survey, answer it! Please? For me!

12 Fox, Justin, and Kenneth W. Shotts. 2009. "Delegates or Trustees? A Theory of Political Accountability," *The Journal of Politics* 71(4): 1225–37.

13 Mayhew, David R. 1974. *Congress: The Electoral Connection*. New Haven: Yale University Press.

14 Lenz, Gabriel S. 2012. *Follow the Leader?: How Voters Respond to Politicians' Policies and Performance*. Chicago: University of Chicago Press.

15 When I use the term "valid" to describe polls, I mean it in two senses. First, good polls must be valid externally, meaning we must be able to apply the findings from the sample (those who took the poll) to the population (the larger group who took the poll). Second, a good poll must have construct validity, meaning it is actually measuring what it claims to measure, in this case, public sentiment.

16 Taylor, Travis N. 2024. "To Build Trust in Polling, We Must Consider Institutional Constraints," *AAPOR Newsletters*. Alexandria, VA: American Association for Public Opinion Research. Available at https://aapor.org/newsletters/to-build-trust-in-polling-we-must-consider-institutional-constraints/.

17 Technically, the margin of error, as we calculate it, is the margin of sampling error for probability samples, and polls today do not have probability samples, even if they have rigorous, justifiable sampling. Truth be told, public opinion polls have never had true probability sampling, despite our best efforts.

18 Kennedy, Courtney. 2024. "Building Trust Through More Realistic Expectations . . . And a More Accurate Margin of Error," *AAPOR Newsletters*. Alexandria, VA: American Association for Public Opinion Research. Available online at https://aapor.org/newsletters/building-trust-through-more-realistic-expectations-and-a-more-accurate-margin-of-error/.

19 Young, Clifford, and Kathryn Ziemer. 2024. *Polls, Pollsters, and Public Opinion: A Guide for Decision-Makers*. New York: Cambridge University Press.

20 Kennedy, Courtney. 2024. "Building Trust Through More Realistic Expectations … And a More Accurate Margin of Error," *AAPOR Newsletters*. Alexandria, VA: American Association for Public Opinion Research. Available online at https://aapor.org/newsletters/building-trust-through-more-realistic-expectations-and-a-more-accurate-margin-of-error/. Some scholars, based on a meta-analysis of pre-election polls, have even suggested that, to account for the total error, pollsters should double the reported margin of error. See, e.g., Shirani-Mehr, Houshmand, David Rothschild, Sharad Goel, and Andrew Gelman. 2018. "Disentangling Bias and Variance in Election Polls," *Journal of the American Statistical Association* 113(522): 607–14.

21 American Association for Public Opinion Research. n.d. "Transparency Initiative." Available online at https://aapor.org/standards-and-ethics/transparency-initiative/#1667827133156-cdb2284e-75a2.

22 Asher, Herbert. 2007. *Polling and the Public: What Every Citizen Should Know,* 7th ed. Washington, DC: CQ Press: 57.

23 Scheckner, Jesse. 2024. "Poll: 72% of Florida Voters Oppose Bill Loosening Child Labor Protections," *Florida Politics* [blog] January 5. Available online at https://floridapolitics.com/archives/651346-poll-72-of-florida-voters-oppose-bill-loosening-child-labor-protections/.

24 Hillygus, Sunshine, Natalie Jackson, and McKenzie Young. 2014. "Professional respondents in non-probability online panels," *Online Panel Research: A Data Quality Perspective,* First Edition. Edited by Mario Callegaro, et al. Hoboken, NJ: John Wiley and Sons, 226–7.

25 Durand, Claire. 2024. "Polls A Week After the Convention," *Ah! The Polls* [blog] August 30. Available online at https://ahlessondages.blogspot.com/2024/08/polls-week-after-convention.html.

26 For a deeper dive into all things related to election polling, see the AAPOR Election Polling Resources page at https://aapor.org/election-polling-resources/.

27 Pew Research Center. 2017. "Methods 101: Random Sampling." Available online at https://www.youtube.com/watch?v=sonXfzE1hvo.

28 Taylor, Travis N. 2024. "September 02 Election Integrity Poll Summary," *Center for Excellence in Polling*. Available online at https://excellenceinpolling.com/poll/september-2024-election-integrity-poll-summary/.

29 Tierney, Abigail. 2024. "U.S. Number of Registered Voters 1996–2022," Statista. Available online at https://www.statista.com/statistics/273743/number-of-registered-voters-in-the-united-states/.

30 Pew Research Center. 2014. "2014 Political Polarization Survey," Table 3.5 Family Member Marrying Republican, Democrat. Available online at https://www.pewresearch.org/politics/2014/06/12/family-member-marrying-republican-democrat/.

31 Pew Research Center. 2016. "Partisanship and Political Animosity in 2016." Available online at https://www.pewresearch.org/politics/2016/06/22/3-partisan-environments-views-of-political-conversations-and-disagreements/.

32 Sanders, Lindley. 2020. "Americans are Less Likely to Have Friends of Very Different Political Opinions Compared to 2016," YouGov. Available online at https://today.yougov.com/politics/articles/32313-friends-different-politics-poll.

33 Geraci, John. 2022. *Poll-arized: Why Americans Don't Trust the Polls and How to Fix Them Before It's Too Late.* Austin, TX: Houdstooth Press.

34 Coffey, Sarah. 2024. "Kentucky Mid-Session Issues Poll Summary," *Center for Excellence in Polling.* Available online at https://excellenceinpolling.com/poll/kentucky-mid-session-issues-poll-summary/; Taylor, Travis N. 2023. "2023 Pennsylvania Workforce Poll," *Center for Excellence in Polling.* Available online at https://excellenceinpolling.com/poll/pennsylvania-workforce-poll/.

35 Not every poll that includes negative information is a push poll. Legitimate message testing surveys are frequently used by candidates, campaigns, and organizations to identify strengths and weaknesses, good and bad messages, opportunities and threats.

36 American Association for Public Opinion Research. 2015. "AAPOR Statement on 'Push' Polls." Available online at https://aapor.org/wp-content/uploads/2022/12/Push-Poll-508.pdf.

37 American Association for Public Opinion Research. 2021. "AAPOR Code of Professional Ethics and Practices." Available online at https://aapor.org/standards-and-ethics/#1667926573628-032a3101-d9a1.

38 Asher, Herbert. 2007. *Polling and the Public: What Every Citizen Should Know,* 7th ed. Washington, DC: CQ Press: 213.

39 This is why we refer to samples drawn from these opt-in online panels as non-probability samples, meaning not everyone in the population has an exactly equal chance of being selected to participate. The good news is that research has shown that they produce results that are indistinguishable from other modes that approach probability sampling.

40 Rogers, Kaleigh. 2024. "What that Surprising Iowa Poll Might be Telling Us," *The New York Times.* Available online at https://www.nytimes.com/2024/11/04/us/elections/iowa-selzer-poll-trump-harris.html.

41 Smith, Brian. 2024. "How do past Iowa Poll results compare with presidential election results in Iowa?" *Des Moines Register.* Available online at https://www.desmoinesregister.com/story/news/politics/iowa-poll/2024/11/02/how-do-past-iowa-poll-results-compare-to-iowa-election-results/76018755007/.

42 Silver, Nate, and Eli McKown-Dawson. 2025. "Silver Bulleting Pollster Ratings, 2025 Update," *Silver Bulletin.* Available online at https://www.natesilver.net/p/pollster-ratings-silver-bulletin.

43 Selzer, J. Ann. 2024. "Pollster Ann Selzer Ending Election Polling, Moving 'to Other Ventures and Opportunities,'" *Des Moines Register.* Available online at https://www.desmoinesregister.com/story/opinion/columnists/2024/11/17/ann-selzer-conducts-iowa-poll-ending-election-polling-moving-to-other-opportunities/76334909007/.

44 Norrander, Barbara and Clyde Wilcox. 2002. *Understanding Public Opinion*, 2nd ed. Washington, DC: CQ Press: 343.

Chapter 4

1 This summary of MADD's history is adapted from information contained on their website at https://madd.org/our-history/.

2 The phone number to the Congressional switchboard is 202-224-3121, and the operators can connect you to your representative's office or to either of your senators' offices.

3 Schulz, Kathryn. 2017. "What Calling Congress Achieves." *The New Yorker*. Available online at https://www.newyorker.com/magazine/2017/03/06/what-calling-congress-achieves.

4 Glassman, Matt. 2012. "On Writing Your Congressman." MattGlassman.com [blog]. Available online at https://www.mattglassman.com/?p=3139.

5 Fitch, Bradford, and Kathy Goldschmidt. 2015. "#SocialCongress 2015." *Congressional Management Foundation*.

6 Rosenstone, Steven J., and John Mark Hansen. 2003. *Mobilization, Participation, and Democracy in America*. New York: Longman, 43.

7 The ANES changed its question wording on this topic multiple times between 1992 and 2020. The wording is as follows for each year. The parenthetical next to each year is the variable name for the question in that year's ANES, which can be accessed by searching key word "contacted" at https://electionstudies.org/data-tools/anes-question-search/. Question wording by year: 1992 (V925701) & 1994 (V940628): Have you (or anyone in your family living here) ever contacted Representative (NAME #33 or 34) or anyone in (his/her) office? 2004 (V045266): Over the past five years or so, have you done any of the following things to express your views about something the government should or should not be doing? . . . Contacted a politician or government official either in person, or in writing, or some other way? 2012 (dhsinvolv_contact1): During the past 4 years, have you contacted or tried to contact a member of the US Senate or US House of Representatives, or have you not done this in the past 4 years? 2016 (V162198) & 2020 (V202030): During the past 12 months, have you contacted or tried to contact a member of the US Senate or US House of Representatives, or have you not done this in the past 12 months?

8 What about an elected official on the state or local level, such as a governor, mayor, or a member of the state legislature or city council, or someone on the staff of such an elected official? Have you contacted such a person in the past twelve months?

9 American National Election Studies. N.d. Variable V162202 Available online at https://electionstudies.org/data-tools/anes-question-search/.

10 American National Election Studies. N.d. Variable V202038 Available online at https://electionstudies.org/data-tools/anes-question-search/.

11 American National Election Studies. N.d. "Attended Meeting about Issue in Community or Schools." Available online at https://electionstudies.org/data-tools/anes-guide/anes-guide.html?chart=attend_meeting_about_community_issues.

12 Kush, Christopher. 2004. *The One-Hour Activist: The 15 Most Powerful Actions You Can Take to Fight for the Issues and Candidates You Care About.* San Francisco: Jossey-Bass, 97.

Chapter 5

1 *Batson v. Kentucky*, 476 US 79 (1986).

2 *Powers v. Ohio*, 499 US 400 (1991).

3 This is according to data from the National Center for State Courts, a nonprofit research organization that serves as a research and educational resource to state judges and court administrators around the country. Available online at https://www.ncsc-jurystudies.org/state-of-the-states/jury-data-viz.

4 In California, the grand jury can also serve as a government oversight body, investigating government agencies and policies. Thanks to Adam Probolsky for this insight.

5 Usually, it's a human person (or group of people), but sometimes a criminal defendant can be a business, organization, or other legal entity.

6 *Ramos v. Louisiana*, 590 US __ (2020).

7 Civil cases are not always between two people; parties can also include businesses or other legal entities.

8 Abramson, Jeffrey. 1999. *We the Jury: The Jury System and the Ideal of Democracy*. Cambridge, MA: Harvard University Press.

9 Gastil, John, E. Pierre Deess, Philip J. Weisner, and Cindy Simmons. 2010. *The Jury and Democracy: How Jury Deliberation Promotes Civic Engagement and Political Participation*. New York: Oxford University Press.

10 Ferguson, Andrew Guthrie. 2012. *Why Jury Duty Matters: A Citizen's Guide to Constitutional Action*. New York: New York University Press.

11 Taylor v. Louisiana, 419 US 522 (1975), at 522.

12 No relation to the author, as far as I know.

13 *Taylor v. Louisiana*, 419 US 522 (1975).

14 *J. E. B. v. Alabama ex rel. T. B.*, 511 US 127 (1994).

15 *Batson v. Kentucky*, 476 US 79 (1986).

16 *Batson v. Kentucky*, 476 US 79 (1986), at 94; internal citations omitted.

17 *Powers v. Ohio*, 499 US 400 (1991).

18 *Georgia v. McCollum*, 505 US 42 (1992).

19 *Edmonson v. Leesville Concrete Co.*, 500 US 614 (1991).

20 *United States v. Martinez-Salazar*, 528 US 304 (2000).

21 Pfautz, Michael W. 2015. "What Would A Reasonable Jury Do? Jury Verdicts Following Summary Judgment Reversals," *Columbia Law Review* (115): 1001.

22 Kalven, Harry, Jr., and Hans Zeisel. 1966. *The American Jury*. Boston: Little, Brown & Company.

23 Heuer, Larry and Steven Penrod. 1994. "Trial Complexity: A Field Investigation of Its Meaning and Its Effects," *Law and Human Behavior* 18(1): 29–51.; Eisenberg, Theodore, et al. 2005. "Judge-Jury Agreement in Criinal Cases: A Partial Replication of Kalven and Zeisel's 'The American Jury,'" *Journal of Empirical Legal Studies* 2(1): 171–207.

24 Gastil, John. 2008. *Political Communication and Deliberation*. Thousand Oaks, CA: Sage.

25 Gastil, John, et al. 2010. *The Jury and Democracy: How Jury Deliberation Promotes Civic Engagement and Political Participation*. New York: Oxford University Press, 10.

26 Hamilton, Alexander. 1788. "Federalist No. 78." Available online at https://constitutioncenter.org/the-constitution/historic-document-library/detail/alexander-hamilton-federalist-no-78-1788.

27 Easton, David. 1965. *A Systems Analysis of Political Life*. New York: John Wiley.

28 Caldeira, Gregory A., and John R. Wright. 1988. "Organized Interests and Agenda Setting in the US Supreme Court." *American Political Science Review* 82(4):1109–27.

29 Gastil, John, et al. 2010. *The Jury and Democracy: How Jury Deliberation Promotes Civic Engagement and Political Participation*. New York: Oxford University Press.

30 Green, Donald P. and Alan S. Gerber. 2004. *Get Out the Vote: How to Increase Voter Turnout*. Washington, DC: Brookings Institution Press.

31 Gastil, John, et al. 2010. *The Jury and Democracy: How Jury Deliberation Promotes Civic Engagement and Political Participation*. New York: Oxford University Press.

32 Consolini, Paula. 1993. *Learning by Doing Justice: Private Jury Service and Political Attitudes*. Doctoral dissertation: University of California–Berkeley.

33 US National Archives. "Declaration of Independence." Available online at https://www.archives.gov/founding-docs/declaration-transcript.

34 Ibid.

35 US Const. art. III, § 2.

36 For an overview of the Anti-Federalists' case against Article III broadly and the right to trial by jury specifically, see Moore, Tyler S. 2020. "Trimming the Least Dangerous Branch: The Anti-Federalists and the Implementation of Article III," *Tulsa Law Review* (56)1.

37 Fun fact: The $20 threshold in the Seventh Amendment has remained unchanged. Adjusting for inflation from 1791, when that amendment was ratified to 2025, the amount would be $671.26. https://www.officialdata.org/us/inflation/1791?amount=20.

38 Thomas, Suja A. 2016. *The Missing American Jury: Restoring the Fundamental Constitutional Role of the Criminal, Civil, and Grand Juries*. New York: Cambridge University Press.

39 *Powers v. Ohio*, 499 US 400 (1991).

40 *Batson v. Kentucky*, 476 US 79 (1986), at 79.

41 *Powers v. Ohio*, 499 US 400 (1991), at 409.

42 YouGov. 2018. "Jury Duty." Available online at https://d3nkl3psvxxpe9.cloudfront.net/documents/Results_for_YouGov_NY_Jury_Duty_167_20.7.2018.pdf.

43 Attanasio, John B. 2001. "Foreword: Juries Rule," *SMU Law Review* 54(5): 1684.

44 National Center for Health Statistics. 2024. "Assault or Homicide," Center for Disease Control. Available online at https://www.cdc.gov/nchs/fastats/homicide.htm.

45 Uniform Crime Report. 2019. "Burglary." Federal Bureau of Investigation. Available online at https://ucr.fbi.gov/crime-in-the-u.s/2019/crime-in-the-u.s.-2019/topic-pages/burglary.

46 Bruner, Aaron. N.d. "Interesting Traffic Ticket Facts," OK Traffic Ticket Defense. Available online at https://oktrafficticket.com/post/interesting-traffic-ticket-facts.

47 Australian Electoral Commission. N.d. "Voter Turnout – Previous Events." Available online at https://www.aec.gov.au/Elections/Federal_Elections/voter-turnout.htm.

48 It is also important to note that not all countries with compulsory voting enforce that mandate through punishment. Some do, though, and those countries are the ones with the highest turnout.

49 Cohen, Ed. 2023. "Poll Finds Judges are Concerned about Increasing Numbers of People Ignoring Summonses for Jury Duty," The National Judicial College. Available online at https://www.judges.org/news-and-info/poll-finds-judges-are-concerned-about-increasing-numbers-of-people-ignoring-summonses-for-jury-duty.

50 Thompson, Buster. 2018. "As Many as 1 in 5 People Here are Ignoring Jury Summonses, and Courts are Cracking Down," *Citrus County Chronicle*. Available online at https://www.chronicleonline.com/news/crime_and_courts/as-many-as-1-in-5-people-here-ignore-jury-summonses-and-courts-are-cracking/article_90dbd9de-dd40-11e8-bd90-177a5d37c477.html.

51 Ketterer, Samantha. 2020. "Battling the Jury Duty Problem, where Fewer than 1 in 4 Show Up," *Houston Chronicle*. Available online at https://www.houstonchronicle.com/news/houston-texas/houston/article/Battling-the-jury-duty-problem-where-fewer-than-15010187.php.

52 First Judicial District of Pennsylvania. 2018. "Juror Participation Initiative." Available online at https://www.courts.phila.gov/pdf/report/FJD_JPIC_Final.pdf.

53 McAdam, Jeff. 2020. "Court Comes to 'Screeching Hald' as People Skip Jury Duty," Fox 5 News. Available online at https://fox5sandiego.com/news/coronavirus/court-comes-to-screeching-halt-as-people-skip-jury-duty/.

54 Collins, Dave. 2020. "Jury Duty? No Thanks, Say Many, Forcing Trials to Be Delayed," FOX 5 News. Available online at https://fox5sandiego.com/news/national-news/jury-duty-no-thanks-say-many-forcing-trials-to-be-delayed/.

55 Richardson, Rachel. 2025. "Lack of Jurors across South Carolina Counties Delay Trials," WBTV3 News. Available online at https://www.wbtv.com/2025/04/15/lack-jurors-across-south-carolina-counties-delay-trials.

56 Chalabi, Mona. 2015. "What are the Chances of Serving on a Jury?" FiveThirtyEight. Available online https://fivethirtyeight.com/features/what-are-the-chances-of-serving-on-a-jury/.

57 Mize, Gregory E., Paula Hannaford-Agor, and Nicole L. Waters. 2007. *The State-of-the-States Survey of Jury Improvement Efforts: A Compendium Report.* National Center for State Courts, 24.

58 Ballard, Jamie. 2018. "How Many Americans Have Lied to Get Out of Jury Duty?" YouGov. Available online at https://today.yougov.com/politics/articles/21273-americans-jury-duty; Zakhareuski, Andrei. 2024. "Confession of a Juror: How Mandatory Jury Duty Impacts Americans," Bar Prep Hero. Available online at https://barprephero.com/confessions-of-a-juror/.

59 Jury eligible means they are either registered to vote and/or have a valid state identification card or driver's license and have never been convicted of a felony.

60 Wilson, Melanie D. 2020. "The Pandemic Juror," *Washington and Lee Law Review* 77(1): 65–96.

61 Gastil, John, et al. 2010. *The Jury and Democracy: How Jury Deliberation Promotes Civic Engagement and Political Participation.* New York: Oxford University Press.

Conclusion

1 Gorsuch, Neil. 2024. *Over Ruled: The Human Toll of Too Much Law.* New York: HarperCollins, 62.

2 Haidt, Jonathan. 2024. *The Anxious Generation.* New York: Penguin Press.

3 Journalist Christopher Fox Graham makes the case well: https://www.redrocknews.com/2025/04/04/political-civility-lost-in-era-of-memes-and-sound-bytes/.

4 See, e.g., Cho, Jaeho, et al. 2020. "Do Search Algorithms Endanger Democracy? An Experimental Investigation of Algorithm Effects on Political Polariza-

tion," *Journal of Broadcast & Electronic Media* 64(2): 150–72.

5 Putnam, Robert, and Lewis Feldstein. 2003. *Better Together: Restoring the American Community*. New York: Simon & Schuster.

6 Twenge, Jean M. 2023. *Generations: The Real Differences Between Gen Z, Millennials, Gen X, Boomers, and Silents—and What They Mean for America's Future*. New York: Simon & Schuster. See also, Haidt, Jonathan. 2024. *The Anxious Generation: How the Great Rewiring of Childhood is Causing an Epidemic of Mental Illness*. New York: Penguin Random House.

7 Adams, Kimberly. 2019. "What Federal Funding for Civics Reveals About American Political Discourse." *Marketplace*. Available online at https://www.marketplace.org/2019/11/06/what-federal-funding-for-civics-reveals-about-american-political-discourse/.

8 Taylor, Travis N. 2024. "How to Raise a Citizen," *The Politics Guys* [blog] August 14. Available online at https://politicsguys.com/how-to-raise-a-citizen/.

9 *Whitney v. California*, 274 US 357 (1927), at 377.

10 Oldenburg, Ray. 1989. *The Great Good Place: Cafés, Coffee Shops, Community Centers, General Stores, Bars, Hangouts, and How They Get You through the Day*. Boston: Da Capo Press.

11 Rauch, Jonathan. 2025. *Cross Purposes: Christianity's Broken Bargain with Democracy*. New Haven: Yale University Press.

12 Brooks, Arthur. 2007. *Who Really Cares*. New York: Basic Books.

13 Putnam, Robert D. 2000. *Bowling Alone: The Collapse and Revival of American Community*. New York: Simon & Schuster.

14 Putnam, Robert D. and Lewis M. Feldstein. 2003. *Better Together: Restoring the American Community*. New York: Simon & Schuster.

15 Cohen, Michael D. 2025. *Modern Political Campaigns: How Professionalism, Technology, and Speed Have Revolutionized Elections*. New York: Rowman & Littlefield, 221.

16 Dionne, E.J., Jr., and Miles Rapoport. 2022. *100% Democracy: The Case for Universal Voting*. New York: The New Press.

17 See, recently, Kostelka, Filip, Shane P. Singh, and André Blais. 2024. "Is Compulsory Voting a Solution to Low and Declining Turnout? Cross-National Evidence Since 1945," *Political Science Research and Methods* 12(1): 76–93.

18 See, e.g., Dionne, E.J., Jr., and Miles Rapoport. 2022. *100% Democracy: The Case for Universal Voting*. New York: The New Press, chapter 4.

19 Panagopoulos, Costas. 2008. "The Calculus of Voting in Compulsory Voting Systems," *Political Behavior* 30(4): 463.

20 Dionne, E.J., Jr., and Miles Rapoport. 2022. *100% Democracy: The Case for Universal Voting*. New York: The New Press, 128.

21 Ibid., 129.

22 Tallise, Robert B. 2019. *Civic Solitude: Why Democracy Needs Distance*. New York: Oxford University Press.

23 Reagan, Ronald. 1967. "January 5, 1967: Inaugural Address (Public Ceremony)," *Ronald Reagan Presidential Library & Museum*. Available at https://www.reaganlibrary.gov/archives/speech/january-5-1967-inaugural-address-public-ceremony.

24 United States Courts. Nd. "The U.S. Constitution: Preamble." Available online at https://www.uscourts.gov/about-federal-courts/educational-resources/about-educational-outreach/activity-resources/us-constitution-preamble

INDEX

B

C

D

E

R

S

T

W

Y

Z

ABOUT THE AUTHOR

Travis N. Taylor, Ph.D., is the senior market research manager at the Center for Excellence in Polling, a project of the nonpartisan think tank, the Foundation for Government Accountability. He is also the president and chief research officer at Strategic Insights Research, LLC, a professional research group that works in polling, trial consulting, and market research for faith-based organizations and businesses. He has previously worked as a campaign manager, campaign consultant, state legislative aide, congressional legislative correspondent, and university instructor. He has managed or consulted for more than eighty political campaigns and dozens of trials in both state and federal courts and has conducted more than 300 public opinion research projects.

Dr. Taylor has published academic research in *Journal of Law and Courts*, *Judicature*, *The Jury Expert*, *Critique*, and the *Oxford Handbook of Political Representation in Liberal Democracies*. He has also contributed numerous op-eds and media commentary, including in *RealClearPolitics*, *The Hill*, *Congressional Quarterly Roll Call Guide*, *CQ*

Connectivity, *The Washington Times*, *The Free Press*, *The Blaze*, *Daily Caller*, *The Daily Beast*, *Wisconsin State Journal*, KJRH 2News (Tulsa, OK, NBC affiliate), *Cincinnati Enquirer* (Ohio), *Louisville Courier-Journal* (Kentucky), WRFL Radio (Kentucky), and *LaCrosse Tribune* (Wisconsin). *Democracy InAction* is his first book.

He has also testified in the Ohio Senate, the Ohio House of Representatives, and the Indiana House of Representatives.

Dr. Taylor earned his Ph.D. in political science with an emphasis on public opinion, state judicial selection, and public policy from the University of Kentucky. He also holds a master's degree in political science from the University of Kentucky, a master's degree in political management from The George Washington University's Graduate School of Political Management, and a bachelor's degree in political science from the University of Louisiana.

When he is not asking voters or jurors for their opinions, he enjoys spending time with his family, reading, tae kwon do, and cycling. He lives with his wife and their two sons outside Tulsa, Oklahoma. He is active in both his church and community.

Democracy In Action

How Citizen Apathy Threatens America And What We can Do About It

Travis N. Taylor Ph.D

Alternative cover design by Teten Taylor, age 9.